THE PERFECT AQUARIUM

THE PERFECT AQUARIUM

The Complete Guide to Setting Up and Maintaining an Aquarium

Jeremy Gay

Reader's Digest

The Reader's Digest Association, Inc.
Pleasantville, New York

A READER'S DIGEST BOOK

This edition published by The Reader's Digest Association, Inc., by arrangement with Hamlyn Books, a division of Octopus Publishing Group Ltd, 2-4 Heron Quays, London, E14 4JP.

FOR HAMLYN BOOKS
Executive Editor: Trevor Davies
Project Editor: Kate Tuckett
Executive Art Editor: Leigh Jones
Design: One2six Creative Limited
Illustrators: Brindeau Mexter
Special photography: Neil Hepworth
Production Manager: Ian Paton
Picture Researcher: Aruna Mathur

FOR READER'S DIGEST
U.S. Project Editor: Marilyn J. Knowlton
Copy Editors: Barbara Booth, Andrea Chesman
Senior Project Designer: George McKeon
Executive Editor, Trade Publishing: Dolores York
President & Publisher, Trade Books: Harold Clarke

Address any comments about *The Perfect Aquarium: The Complete Guide to Setting Up and Maintaining an Aquarium* to:
 The Reader's Digest Association, Inc.
 Adult Trade Publishing
 Reader's Digest Road
 Pleasantville, NY 10570-7000

For more Reader's Digest products and information, visit our website:
 www.rd.com (in the United States)

Printed and bound in China

1 3 5 7 9 10 8 6 4 2

NOTE TO OUR READERS
All do-it-yourself activities involve a degree of risk. Skills, materials, tools, and site conditions vary widely. Although the editors have made every effort to ensure accuracy, the reader remains responsible for the selection and use of tools, materials, and methods. Always obey local codes and laws, follow manufacturer's operating instructions, and observe safety precautions.

Library of Congress Cataloging-in-Publication Data:

Gay, Jeremy.
 The perfect aquarium : the complete guide to setting up and maintaining an aquarium / Jeremy Gay
  p. cm
 Includes index
 ISBN 0-7621-0670-0
  1. Aquariums. 2. Aquarium fishes. I. Title

SF457.3.G39 2007
639.34--dc22

2005054103

CONTENTS

INTRODUCTION

Keeping fish is often a part of people's lives beginning in childhood. Many children are introduced to the world of pet care when they first get a goldfish or two and a bowl to keep them in. The idea of having to maintain and care for fish in an aquarium may at first seem like a chore, but a few trips to an aquatic store will soon make keeping an aquarium an appealing prospect and tempt many people to delve further into fishkeeping and all the delights associated with it.

No other type of pet care offers such variety and opportunities for the owner to express his or her own personality, with aquarium design and species choice becoming real art forms in themselves. Creatively designed aquariums offer us a window into a tiny underwater world that would normally be ignored, and the life that is contained within that world is totally fascinating.

The aim of this book is to give clear, practical instructions about the day-to-day running of an aquarium and the care of its inhabitants, as well as to inspire and educate the fishkeeper. It will be of interest to fishkeepers at all levels of experience, from the complete novice through to the accomplished aquarist.

Coldwater, tropical, and marine fish are described in detail, along with important information about their size, feeding habits, compatibility, and the type of aquarium in which they should be kept. The profiles include species information and advice on the proper care of live aquatic plants and marine invertebrates. In addition to describing how to choose, purchase, and site a tank, there are equipment tips and advice on maintenance regimes. Your responsibilities as fishkeeper are explained clearly in the sections on basic fish care and healthcare.

Fishkeeping is a tremendously absorbing and relaxing hobby. The calming effect that an aquarium has on a space and the people around it has long been proven. It is no coincidence that in potentially stressful situations, such as a dentist's waiting room, there is often an aquarium. Scientific investigations have shown how simply watching fish can help lower blood pressure and provide an antidote to the stresses of modern life. This book encapsulates what all discerning fishkeepers aspire to create and demonstrates exactly how that can be achieved. A thriving aquarium is within everyone's reach. Happy fishkeeping!

Above This red ranchu is simple to keep, relaxing to watch, and should be within the grasp of anyone wishing to keep fish.

Right Neon tetras are deservedly popular tropical fish and are stocked by all aquatic stores. They remain small and can be kept in small tanks.

Below The Picasso triggerfish is beautifully marked and is also an intelligent pet, but it's not for beginners.

WHAT TYPE OF AQUARIUM?
Coldwater, tropical, or marine?

The inspiration to set up your own aquarium will probably have come from effective display tanks in aquatic shops, offices, or restaurants, from books or magazines, or even through television, where aquariums are regularly used as backdrops on studio sets. But once you have decided to begin fishkeeping, you will immediately be confronted by a number of choices, the first and most fundamental one being which type of fish you would like to keep.

Types of fishkeeping and water

Even as an absolute fishkeeping beginner, you may already be familiar with the names of some fish species, such as the common goldfish (*Carassius auratus*), clownfish (*Amphiprion ocellaris*), and Siamese fighting fish (*Betta splendens*) (see pages 127–32, 233, and 135), but you may not be aware that these three species demand three different types of water and that to keep the three together would be impossible.

There are three different types of water, and between them they can accommodate almost every aquarium fish that is available to the aquarist. They are coldwater, tropical, and tropical marine (usually referred to as only marine).

Fishkeeping ancient and modern

The art of keeping coldwater fish is the oldest form of fishkeeping and started in China about a thousand years ago. Marine fishkeeping is the youngest form of fishkeeping but is growing in popularity. It began in the 1950s and was aided by improvements in air travel and also by the invention of the plastic bag, which made the transportation of fish possible. But the technology and knowledge were still not sufficient to keep many marine fishes and invertebrates healthy in captivity, and prices were prohibitive. It was not until the 1980s that marine aquariums could be widely kept with success. Marine fish continue to be the most demanding of aquarium fish, and it has taken much understanding and resources to enable them to thrive in man-made environments.

Fishkeeping FAQs

Q What is the difference between coldwater, tropical, and marine fish?

A The difference is that coldwater and tropical fish come from freshwater environments, such as rivers and lakes, whereas marine fish come from the sea, which is always salty.

Q Why can't freshwater and saltwater fish be kept together?

A Fish have evolved over millions of years to suit their particular environment, either saltwater or freshwater. This has resulted in the body of a saltwater fish functioning differently from that of a freshwater fish, which means that neither is able to survive in the other's environment.

Q Why can't coldwater and tropical freshwater fish be kept together?

A The answer again is because over time species of fish have evolved physically to suit their particular environment, and they may not be able to function in water that is the wrong temperature for them. Goldfish (see pages 127–32) can tolerate water temperatures as low as 39°F (4°C), but a Siamese fighting fish (see page 135) will start to decline in health if it is kept at temperatures lower than 68°F (20°C).

Q Are there any coldwater marine fish?

A Yes, there are thousands of species living in cooler seas all over the world, but they are not commonly kept in aquariums. These fish require more oxygen than tropical fish, which means that their water environment has to be cooled by artificial means. This is more expensive than heating aquarium water, so this is one reason coldwater marine fish are not as popular as tropical fish. In addition, there is a wider choice of colorful small fish from tropical seas, so more suitable species are available for the home aquarium.

Q What type of fish should I start with?

A If you have never kept aquarium fish before, then start with coldwater or tropical fish until you have learned a bit more about the hobby. Both types contain some hardier fish species that will tolerate a couple of mistakes here and there. In addition, hardy tropical and coldwater fish can be kept in conditioned tap water, whereas marine fish really need purified water, which will then need to be made more salty. So, tempting though marine fish are, leave them in the store for the time being.

Far left The goldfish is the most commonly kept pet in the world and is often the first choice for beginners.

Middle left A clownfish is a tempting purchase but needs to be kept in the right kind of aquarium.

Left The Siamese fighting fish loves tropical temperatures and must be housed in a tropical tank.

Levels of difficulty

Although some species of fish come from the same environment in nature, when it comes to transferring them to an aquarium environment, some are easier to keep than others. That is, once they are in the home aquarium, some settle in better, take food more readily, and may even breed, whereas others may sulk, refuse to eat certain foods, and may not live happily with their tank mates.

Species variation

The term "level of difficulty" can be applied to all aquarium fish that have been kept by aquarists. Traditionally, species like goldfish and guppies (*Poecilia reticulata*) (see pages 127–32 and 158) have been kept by generations of fishkeepers across the world with marked success, and as a result they have gained a reputation for being easy to keep. These fish species are therefore categorized as hardy.

Although other species, such as the discus (*Symphysodon* spp.) (see page 147), have been kept many times for many years by a number of aquarists, their keepers have noted that if the species' exacting requirements are not met, the fish will quickly fall into a physical decline. This acts as a spur to some dedicated aquarists to invest their resources above and beyond the normal fishkeeping regime and budget in order to develop specialized aquariums in which they can keep these fish in good condition. Any fish species that requires extra care, knowledge, and experience to be kept alive and well in an aquarium is known as sensitive.

Hardy fish

Within coldwater, tropical, and marine fish species there are both sensitive and hardy fish, but generally speaking, coldwater fish are hardier than marine fish, since they have adapted to the differing seasonal changes of their environment. Tropical marine fish, which naturally inhabit coral reefs, experience little alteration in their environment from year to year and so are not used to dealing with or adapting to change.

The tropical freshwater species of the world inhabit so many different environments that there is a huge selection of hardy and sensitive species to choose from. These fish are therefore a good halfway choice in terms of level of

Below This oscar is easy to keep but grows very large and will eat smaller fish. It is not a community fish.

Bottom The guppy is a natural prey fish in the wild and is at the bottom of the fish food chain.

difficulty between coldwater and marine. If you want to keep some of the more difficult marine species, it is advisable to try other, easier forms of fishkeeping first. Many practices and techniques, including water changing, water testing, and maintenance, are common to all types of aquarium fishkeeping. So, familiarizing yourself with a basic understanding of fish healthcare and behavior will equip you with the knowledge, experience, and confidence to move on to more challenging fish.

Community and noncommunity

The underwater environment, like the terrestrial one, is inhabited by predators and prey. Very small fish tend to be low down in the food chain, whereas other, larger fish, using tactics like camouflage or brute force, eat their way up the food chain to become "apex predators."

In the context of the aquarium, predator fish are known as "noncommunity" fish, and the

Above The dwarf fuzzy lionfish is specially adapted to eat fish, but it carries venomous spines to avoid being eaten itself.

group includes species that are territorial or very specialized in their care requirements and so need a specially designed aquarium to cater for them. A mixture of aquarium fish that do not grow too large, eat each other, or cause any other kind of trouble are known as "community" fish.

Because of the aforementioned factors, noncommunity species should not, in any circumstances, be kept with community species, and it is mostly the community species that are featured in this book. Community fish also make up the bulk of any aquatic store's stock, and a community tank will appeal to more people because it will contain a diverse mixture of fish with a wide range of different colors and shapes. A well-maintained tank full of color and movement makes for the perfect aquarium.

Range of choice

One of the wonderful things about aquarium fishkeeping is the degree of choice that is available to the aquarist. In fact, fishkeeping offers a far greater choice than in any other sphere of pet keeping, and there are thousands of fish species to choose from. This level of choice means that there is a fish that will appeal to everyone, whether it is colorful, odd-looking, beautiful, or downright ugly.

Species availability

Out of the three main types of fish—coldwater, tropical, and marine—tropical fish are the largest represented group, with hundreds of species available at any one time, even from smaller pet and aquatic retailers. Many species of tropical marine fish are also available, but they are represented in much smaller numbers by the aquatic trade, with no more than fifty species being regularly for sale, even from specialty retailers. Coldwater fish have the least number of species to choose from—most are linebred forms of the common goldfish (*Carassius auratus*) (see page 127)—with only about twenty species currently being available. See the chart below for an at-a-glance comparison of the characteristics and stocking requirements of the three main types of aquarium fish.

Coldwater fish

Do not be put off by the comparatively limited choice in coldwater fish, because what they lack in variety, they certainly make up for in volume, being available in the millions all over the world. There is a great deal of enjoyment to be had from keeping goldfish, because they are rewarding when correctly kept and will repay the owner with many years of absorbing and relaxing viewing.

Tropical marine fish

As we have seen, tropical fish are widely available in a large range of species, including fish for all fishkeeping skill levels, while coldwater fish are always available and are easy to keep. So what do the marines have to offer? The answer is just about everything else. Coral reefs are among the wonders of the natural world. As a marine fishkeeper, you can wake one morning and decide you would like a fish that is bright pink, or orange with white stripes or oddly shaped, and you would be able to find a species that fits the bill.

The range in color and shape of many of the reef fish, sometimes verging on the bizarre, remains something of a mystery to science, but it presents the aquarist with a unique opportunity to keep fish that look as if they were hand-painted. Be aware, though, that marine fishkeeping is challenging as well as rewarding, and some species will make your inexperience or ignorance tragically apparent by their untimely deaths.

The solution is to research the species that appeal to you most and, as a responsible fishkeeper, to leave them in the store if you cannot provide for them. Like all areas of fishkeeping, there are some species that adapt better to aquariums and there is plenty of variety to be had.

Livestock comparison of the three fish types

TYPE OF FISH	VARIETY OF SPECIES	AVAILABILITY	FISH-STOCKING DENSITY	COST OF SETUP
Coldwater	Low	High	Low	Low
Tropical	High	High	High	Low
Marine	High	Low	Low	High

Top A tropical community tank will offer the greatest livestock choice for the hobbyist, and the fish are widely available.

Middle Coldwater tanks are limited as to species choice, but there are interesting forms of goldfish in several color variations.

Right A marine reef tank provides an environment for a wide range of fish and invertebrates, but they are less commonly available and can be expensive.

Aquarium styles

There are many different ways in which an aquarium can be decorated, including traditional styles, ranging from planted underwater gardens and streambeds to elaborate fantasy kingdoms, with castles, model divers, and bridges. All have their place in aquarium fishkeeping, with some styles being more functional than others. All the various themes and design approaches can be divided into two main categories, ornamental and natural.

Ornamental

Ornamental aquariums are those that have been arranged in such a way as to provide a pleasing picture, with fish added to complement the design. An ornamental design can replicate a natural environment, such as a coral reef, but will not necessarily use live corals or even reef fish, but may instead use replica corals and rocks or perhaps incorporate ornaments, like shipwrecks, which are not in realistic scale with the miniaturized scene.

Benefits of ornamental aquariums

False decor can be easily removed and cleaned and will never affect water quality in the way that a dying plant or coral would. It also enables owners to put their fish in the context of what would normally make up their natural diet in the wild, but with no risk of the replicas being eaten. The main criticism that can be made of an ornamental tank is that it does not realistically represent the natural environment from which the fish originate. However, fish such as fancy goldfish have been commercially bred and have no natural environment. Indeed, if they were released into a natural pond, they probably would not survive.

Inspiration

The best place to gain inspiration for an ornamental-themed tank is an aquatic retailer, since your design will be governed by the ornaments and decor ranges that are available. These include sunken wrecks, Greek and Roman ruins, and fluorescent decorations.

Natural

Natural-themed home aquariums are designed to imitate the beauty of nature. The decor, from the substrate to the rockwork and finishing decoration, will be the aquarist's representation of a natural scene, using either natural materials or cleverly made replicas. Popular subjects for natural-themed aquariums include fast-flowing mountain streams, sandy riverbeds, rocky lakes, and planted tropical ponds, as well as vibrant coral reefs, which incorporate the whole range of reef wildlife.

Appropriate layouts

To reflect the natural world accurately, the layout of this style of aquarium should be anything but symmetrical, and decoration should be arranged haphazardly or to scale, so that it represents an actual piece of nature. The layout of the decor can range from an arrangement of a few simple rocks and roots to a complex group planting or specially constructed as a biotope (see below).

Biotopes

A biotope tank is where all the fish, and sometimes the plants, come from the same area in the world and represent a mini-ecosystem. A popular biotope used in tropical freshwater aquariums is that of the Amazon, where species that live together in the wild are kept together in the aquarium. Biotopes are popular because fish with similar requirements can be kept alongside

Tip

Public aquariums can be invaluable sources of inspiration for biotope or other themed aquariums.

Above The aquarium pictured would be classed as natural, with wild-type fish and plants coexisting in harmony with each other.

Above This aquarium is bordering on the ornamental with linebred forms of fish and plants in a careful arrangement.

Above This marine aquarium is based on a natural reef, with live rocks and corals and reef fish decorating the tank.

each other as nature intended, and the contented aquarist can view a slice of river system that is far removed from his or her living room.

However, biotopes have their limitations in that predator fish cannot be kept with prey fish. Also, what the aquarist may believe is an authentic biotope could include fish that in the real environment live far away from each other and would therefore never swim together in the wild. Indeed, the Amazon basin takes up much of the huge continent of South America, and in

the wild, a particular South American fish species may live thousands of miles from the tank mates you have chosen for it.

Inspiration

Nature, unsurprisingly, is the best source of inspiration for naturally themed aquariums. Study stream- and riverbanks, lake sides, and beaches. Here you will observe how aquatic plants and animals naturally colonize the hard landscape, providing a balanced picture of natural beauty.

Cost implications

Your first aquarium need not be an elaborate affair or expensive. All fish require clean, well-oxygenated, well-filtered water of the appropriate temperature. They should also be kept in an aquarium that is suitable for their size and level of activity. The aquarium will need a cover (or hood), and that cover may also need to accommodate a light for viewing fish and for aiding plant or coral growth.

Start-up equipment

Whether you will be keeping coldwater, tropical, or marine fish, if you are starting from scratch, you will need the following hardware:
• aquarium
• hood
• filter
• substrate
• water conditioners
• test kit
• thermometer
• heater/thermostat (for tropical fish)
• decoration
• polystyrene tiles (for cushioning the tank base)
• stand

Tank costs

Smaller tanks, as you would expect, are generally much cheaper to buy and equip than larger ones. This is because:

1. The glass is thinner because there is less water pressure.
2. Filters and air pumps do not need to be as powerful because there is a smaller volume of water.
3. You simply need less of everything—less substrate, fewer water conditioners, a smaller light, and a less powerful heater.

Bear in mind, however, that although larger aquariums cost more to set up than smaller ones, they do have the advantage of holding more fish. If larger tanks are beyond your budget, do not even consider buying larger fish.

Top An air-powered box filter is cheap and will adequately filter a small tropical or coldwater tank.

Middle This air-powered foam filter is used by those on a budget and those who breed fish and have tanks containing small fry.

Bottom A top-of-the-range external power filter provides excellent filtration for all forms of fish but is expensive.

Fish costs

Coldwater and tropical fish, such as mass-cultured, easy-to-keep fish like goldfish and danios (see pages 127–32 and 151–52), are among the least expensive fish. Marine and tropical fish include some of the most expensive fish, but on average marine fish cost more than tropical species. However, as more marine fish are being bred in captivity, prices are falling, but tropical or coldwater aquariums can be set up and run for a fraction of marine aquariums.

Running costs

Running costs are incurred in the maintenance of the aquarium and also in the cost of electricity. An average system will have at least three electrical devices plugged in at any one time—the light, heater, and filter. However, a specialized system or reef tank might have up to eight electrical devices working at once. Water pumps, such as power filters and powerheads, use very little power. However, multiple lighting systems for large planted or reef aquariums can use several hundred watts of energy over the required duration of 12 hours a day, resulting in a marked increase in your electricity bill.

Below A test kit is one of the most important items on the shopping list and should not be overlooked.

The following is a breakdown of the items necessary for everyday maintenance, including how often they need to be replenished or replaced where appropriate:

- filter—replace foam every six months (see page 38)
- lighting—replace tube every twelve months
- condensation tray—replace every twelve months
- fish food
- medications
- test kits
- water conditioners
- pump impellers
- algae magnets/pads
- plant fertilizers
- marine salt (for marine tanks only)

Tip

When considering what size tank to choose, ask the retailer what a setup including decoration and fish would cost. That way you can find out whether it is within your budget.

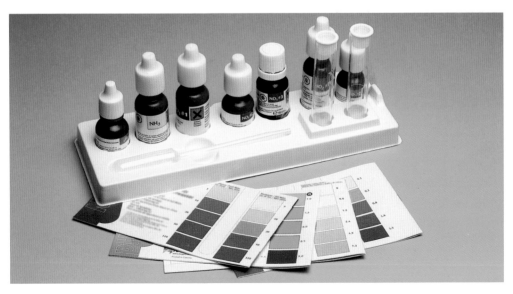

The demands on your time

When you are deciding on which type of fish you would like to keep and what sort of aquarium you want, also give some thought to how much time you can devote to fishkeeping. All types of livestock make constant demands on the owner, and essential maintenance means just that—it simply has to be done! Fish will always need feeding and their water will always need to be changed, so bear this in mind when you are choosing a particular system. For example, a larger tank, with a proportionately greater number of fish, will mean larger water changes, which will take more time and energy to carry them out.

Routine tasks

To give a better idea of what is involved in aquarium fishkeeping, the lists below detail the daily, weekly, and monthly tasks. Some of these are optional and will depend on the particular type of fish you are keeping, but most of them will have to be built into your routine to ensure responsible and rewarding fishkeeping.

Daily tasks
• Check water temperature
• Feed the fish
• Turn lights on and off
• Check all fish are present
• Check fish health

Weekly tasks
• Test aquarium water
• Wipe algae from the front glass
• Change some of the tank water (twice weekly is fine)
• Add plant food/coral additives
• Replace water lost through evaporation

Monthly tasks
• Replace carbon in filter
• Vacuum gravel
• Prune plants
• Maintain filter
• Clean covering glass and light tubes

Time-saving strategies

Now that you can see at a glance the range of routine tasks you will need to undertake, you should have a better understanding of how much work is involved in keeping fish. However, don't let this put you off! Some of these tasks take only a matter of minutes to carry out and do not cost anything at all, and even though others are more time-consuming, they can often be combined into one weekly or monthly task—combining gravel vacuuming with algae wiping, for example, or filter maintenance with water changing. If they are carried out properly and efficiently, even these combined tasks should take no longer than an hour to complete (see page 103).

Time-consuming setups

Some styles of aquarium and species of fish will take longer to maintain than others. The more dedicated fishkeeper may decide to specialize in one area of the hobby and make more time to accommodate it. Bear in mind that you can never fully judge from the outset the demands the hobby will make on you—many aquarists, for instance, find themselves unexpectedly in a situation where they have to invest in more aquariums and equipment as a result of their fish breeding.

The discus (*Symphysodon* spp.) (see page 147) is a prime example of a relatively more demanding and less forgiving species of fish. To keep this species in top condition, more water changes and more feeding will need to be carried out than might be expected for a more average tropical community fish.

Tanks containing more livestock than others will also ultimately take up more of your time. A heavily planted aquarium, for instance, will require more time for maintenance of the plants as well as the fish. Reef aquariums can contain many more invertebrates than fish, and all marine life is inevitably more delicate than their freshwater equivalents.

Above Regular vacuuming of the gravel doesn't take long and keeps the aquarium healthy.

Right Discus are demanding of time and care, and if they are neglected, their health will quickly decline.

Assessing your available time

After considering all these factors, you need to assess realistically how much time you can devote to your fishkeeping and then tailor your choices accordingly. If you frequently go away on vacation, hardy coldwater or tropical species are probably the best choice for you. If you have time and space for only one aquarium, do not buy fish that breed readily or grow large, and if you move frequently, avoid setting up complex aquariums, because the process of dismantling, transporting, and reinstallation will be very stressful not only for you but also for the livestock.

Caring for your fish

It is absolutely essential that you understand the responsibilities involved in having live animals in your care and that you treat your pet fish properly. Any animal in human care must be provided with appropriate food, water, and living space, as well as quality of life. Because fish have a limited capacity for communicating with humans and expressing emotion, signs of their unhappiness and distress can be all too easily and frequently missed.

Above In nature fish have not evolved to deal with ammonia, and they can be harmed or even killed by it in captivity.

How to prevent suffering

Many types of fish have, unfortunately, suffered maltreatment over the years at the hands of inexperienced aquarists, and it is up to each individual fishkeeper to ensure that his or her fish do not suffer a similar fate. All fish should be kept in filtered aquariums, including species that often are not, such as goldfish and Siamese fighting fish (*Betta splendens*) (see pages 127–32 and 135)—and do not let anyone convince you otherwise. It is hard to draw parallels between fish being kept in ammonia-filled water, which is what results from a lack of filtering (see below), and any equivalent situation in human life, but suffice to say that ammonia is toxic and even tiny amounts, as little as one part per million, can kill most fish.

Why water filtering is essential

Fish produce toxic ammonia when they breathe, urinate, and defecate. In nature, this ammonia is simply washed away by the vastness of the body of water that fish inhabit, causing them no harm, but when fish are kept in a confined body of water, they will be exposed to the damaging ammonia, and their bodies are not designed to cope with it.

All aquariums or bowls should be fitted with a filter, which provides an area in which special bacteria live and consume the ammonia (see pages 38–39). These bacteria are the fishkeeper's friends and help to keep our fish alive. They should not be exposed to untreated tap water because this contains chlorine or chloramines, which kill all types of bacteria, including the beneficial ones. An aquarium that does not contain such a filter is dangerous to fish and may cause their death.

Thriving and surviving

Provided with the right conditions, fish will not just survive but thrive in an aquarium. Goldfish, for instance, can grow up to 12 inches (30 cm) long, will enjoy the company of their fellow fish, and will spawn when sexually mature. The responsible fishkeeper should ask many

Left An internal power filter can be the life-support system for the fish in your aquarium.

questions and research as thoroughly as possible what each species needs to thrive. Read all manner of aquatic literature, join a fish club, seek advice from experienced friends or neighbors, and make regular visits to your aquatic retailer. A complete beginner can gain much experience in as little as one year and could be considered an expert in five. With experience and knowledge under your belt, you can become your own expert and start to answer your own questions and solve your own aquatic-related problems, all the time gaining more and more knowledge of this fascinating hobby.

Knowing your own limitations

If your spare time is limited, your schedule is very busy, and your budget is not very elastic, then fishkeeping may not be the hobby for you. The emphasis is on "keeping," and the tasks involved in maintaining fish for the long term go hand in hand with the pleasure of watching them. So take a little time to think about what the fish would prefer, and if you cannot provide what is best for them, then they are better left in the store.

Fish care dos and don'ts

Do
- ✔ Change the water regularly
- ✔ Stock the tank slowly
- ✔ Remove uneaten food
- ✔ Use adequate filtration
- ✔ Test the water regularly
- ✔ Provide spacious accommodation

Don't
- ✗ Wash filter media, the material used to purify the water (see pages 38–39), under the tap
- ✗ Stock the tank too quickly
- ✗ Overfeed the fish
- ✗ Flush fish down the toilet
- ✗ Keep incompatible fish
- ✗ Keep fish in small bowls

Left This heavily stocked cichlid aquarium would not be possible without regular maintenance and the right filtration.

CHOOSING AND LOCATING THE TANK

Which tank?

When you are choosing your first tank, make sure you are buying the right tank for you and your fish. There is a wide range of tank designs available—from columns and hexagons to globes and corner tanks—but none is more suitable than the standard rectangle. This is because rectangular tanks, being two or three times as long as they are wide, have a large surface area for the exchange of gases and the uptake of oxygen by the water. Also, fish have adapted to swim horizontally and not up and down, so a rectangle is better for them in terms of the swimming space it provides.

Size matters

Bigger is better for any aquarium, because even a large aquarium is very small when compared to the natural range that any fish has been used to in the wild. The larger the tank, the more water it will hold and the more fish it will be able to sustain and support. It will also provide more stable water conditions than a small tank. Also consider the body shape of the fish that you wish

Below This built-in power filter houses the pump, the filter medium, and the heater thermostat within it.

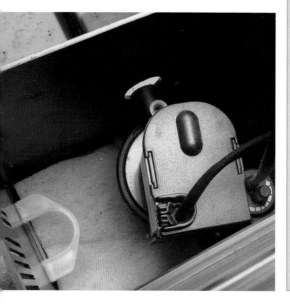

Choosing the right tank

- Ask the retailer what the tank is made from, because plastic tanks scratch very easily.

- Ask if the tank comes with a guarantee against leaking.

- Find out if the tank needs to be cushioned on polystyrene tiles (see page 27), as some do not.

- Calculate the tank volume (see pages 24–25). Some ornate tanks hold far less water than standard rectangles.

- See how easily additional equipment, such as automatic feeders, can be fitted.

- If it is a large tank, will it fit through the front door?

- Is your floor/stand strong enough or will it need additional support (see page 31)?

to keep. Tall-bodied fish tend to come from deep water, so they should be kept in correspondingly deep tanks. Shoaling fish need to be kept in groups, so the tank should be of a suitable and adequate size to accommodate a small shoal.

Design considerations

Some unconventional tank designs are more aesthetically pleasing than the standard rectangle, but they can be difficult to clean and distort the image of the fish. Circular aquariums not only distort the fish image, but as you walk closer to the tank, your image is distorted to the fish, causing them to take flight and possibly injure themselves. Some circular aquariums and bowls have only a small opening at the top, making it difficult to add decorations to the tank.

Systemized tanks

A systemized tank is an aquarium that has built-in filtration. Some systemized aquariums also come with heating and lighting, leaving only decoration to be chosen before filling the tank with water. A systemized tank may also be cheaper than its individual components.

Setups

Aquarium setups are an easy way of buying a tank and the extra equipment you need because, like a systemized tank, the manufacturer has chosen the appropriate equipment for you. The

> **Tip**
>
> Explain to your aquatic retailer which fish you wish to keep because the tank you have in mind may not be suitable. For instance, open-topped aquariums are appealing and popular but are unsuitable for fish that frequently jump, such as the marbled hatchetfish (*Carnegiella strigata*) (see page 139) from South America.

setup goes one stage further than the systemized tank, however, as it will also include water conditioners and other essentials, such as a thermometer, together with an instruction guide. Aquarium setups represent genuine value for the beginner, because the cost of the individual parts far exceeds that of the setup.

The safe choice

There are many factors involved in making your choice of tank, so choose a tank that is within your budget, is of an average size, and was manufactured by a reputable firm. Name-brand tanks are popular because they are the right price and have a good reputation for not leaking.

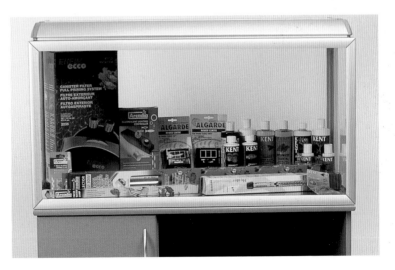

Right This aquarium setup comes with everything you need to get started, and will probably not be expensive.

Aquarium volume

Knowing the volume of your aquarium is vital if you are to choose the appropriately sized equipment to go with it or to judge the correct measures or dosages of treatments and medications. Aquarium dimensions will be listed in metric or imperial measurements, but calculating the volume is easy in both. Once calculated, write the tank volume down in metric and imperial for future reference.

Making realistic calculations

When the volume of an aquarium is calculated by using its outer dimensions, the result will be the gross volume. This means that the figure does not take account of any decoration that might be used, which would displace water, and assumes that the tank would be filled right up to the top edge. In reality, most tanks are filled to within about 2 inches (5 cm) of the top edge and lose volume through displacement by gravel and rocks. Short of filling your aquarium with a measuring cup, take 10 percent off the total gross volume for a more realistic figure.

Calculating surface area

You need to know the surface area of an aquarium to determine how many fish it will hold, as well as being part of the equation for calculating volume. This is simple to do by following this example.

An aquarium 24 x 15 x 12 inches (60 x 38 x 30 cm) is 24 inches (60 cm) long, 15 inches (38 cm) high and 12 inches (30 cm) wide.

Simply multiply the length by the width to obtain the area in square centimeters or inches: 24 x 12 inch (60 x 30 cm) = 288 square inches (1,800 sq cm).

Calculating gross volume

To calculate the volume of the tank, take the area and multiply it by the height or the middle dimension (in imperial, convert the inches into feet, so the area calculation is 2 x 1 foot = 2 square feet), to reach the figure in cubic feet or cubic centimeters:

2 x 1. 25 square feet (1,800 x 38 sq cm) = 2.5 cubic feet (68,400 cu cm)

Calculating surface area
The surface area of the aquarium is calculated by multiplying the length by the width.

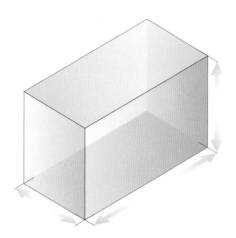

Calculating volume
The volume of the aquarium is calculated by multiplying the surface area by the height.

Imperial volumes are measured in gallons, and metric volumes in liters and milliliters. To convert the volume in cubic feet to gallons, multiply by 6.23; to convert the volume in cubic centimeters into liters, divide by 1,000: 2.5 x 6.23 (68,400 ÷ 1,000) = 15.58 gallons (68.4 liters) gross volume.

Stocking levels

Nearly all aquariums are overstocked in the sense that if there was a power failure, there would be insufficient bacteria in the water to break down the waste or not enough water volume to dilute it. There would also be insufficient area for the exchange of gases, including oxygen, to take place.

When we stock our aquariums, the amount of fish that it will safely hold will be governed by the size of the filter and the subsequent bacteria colony it houses, the amount of dissolved oxygen in the water, and the regularity of the water changes (see page 170). Experts and experienced aquarists have collated information on stocking levels, but due to the many influencing factors, including those detailed above, opinions continue to vary. It is important to remember that stocking levels are guidelines only, and modern technology, along with a better understanding of water quality, is enabling heavier yet safer stocking of fish in aquariums. Due to the high turnover of water in marine tanks in relation to their volume, stocking levels are specified as fish length per volume rather than surface area as for tropical and coldwater aquariums.

Stocking FAQ

Q **Why do aquatic retailers keep so many fish in each tank, yet they won't let us do the same at home?**

A Many aquatic stores have a high turnover of fish, and their tanks are for holding purposes only and are not permanent homes for the fish. Overstocking in tanks is compensated for by more regular feeding, more regular water changes (up to twice a day), systemized aquariums, where stock tanks are joined to other tanks for increased water volume, and a dedicated team of staff who cares for the fish on a permanent basis. This level of professional care simply cannot be provided by the aquarist at home.

Calculating cubic volume
A 24 x 15 x 12 inch (60 x 38 x 30 cm) aquarium showing a cube (12 x 12 x 12 inch/30 x 30 x 30 cm) within it.

A guide to stocking levels

TYPE OF FISH	STOCKING LEVEL
Coldwater	1 inch (2.5 cm) of fish per 24 square inches (60 sq cm) of tank water surface area
Tropical	1 inch (2.5 cm) of fish per 12 square inches (30 sq cm) of tank water surface area
Marine	1 inch (2.5 cm) of fish per 2 gallons (9 liters) of tank water volume, in a fish-only aquarium; 1 inch (2.5 cm) of fish per 4 gallons (18 liters) of tank water volume for reef aquariums

Tank construction

The use of glass in aquarium construction is as old as the hobby itself, but there is more to tank construction than you might think. Glass is brittle and water is heavy, so combining one to hold the other is no mean feat. The aquarium construction industry has brought the hobby to the state it is in today, with a range of types and styles of tank that will suit everyone's needs.

The role of silicone

Modern glass tanks are held together with silicone, but it was not always the case. In the early days of tank construction, glass panes were held in an angled iron frame with putty. The tanks were extremely heavy, and over time the frames would rust and the putty would become flaky and consequently need replacing. With the invention of strong silicone, glass could be safely bonded and withstand the tremendous pressure from the water inside it. Tanks became lighter and leaks were less frequent. Silicone is still used today to build all forms of glass aquarium, with both clear and black silicone being universally popular.

Glass thickness

Water is very heavy, and a tank full of water must be built to withstand the considerable pressure exerted by the water inside it. The taller the tank, the greater the pressure will be, so thicker glass is used, and the cost of the tank will increase proportionally. Tanks up to 18 inches (45 cm) high with ¼-inch (6 mm)-thick glass are sturdy enough to withstand the pressure and are generally in a considerably cheaper price range than taller tanks, regardless of their length. Tall tanks of 24 inches (60 cm) and over will be built with ⅜-inch (1 cm), ½-inch (1.2 cm), and even as much as ⅝-inch (1.5 cm) glass. This, of course, will cause the price to rise accordingly.

For extra safety, many tall tanks will come with a double base. On such tanks another, identical piece of glass is attached to the base of the tank with aquarium-grade silicone adhesive, giving extra rigidity and strength. If you buy a large glass tank, make sure that you remember to ask whether it will come with a double base.

Tip

Unfortunately, glass tanks do scratch, so be careful when decorating and maintaining the tank. Avoid direct contact between the glass and rockwork and gravel, and check that algae pads are free of grit when you wipe surfaces (see pages 168–69).

Floating-base tanks

A popular method of tank construction is to incorporate a floating base. The bottom pane of glass is raised and glued inside the four walls of the tank. The bottom of the tank is then placed inside a plastic base frame, eliminating the need for a cushioning layer of polystyrene tiles (see opposite). The effect is a neater tank base and bottom trim, with no visible polystyrene. When purchasing a tank, check which type it is with your retailer so that you can be absolutely sure that you can safely dispense with the polystyrene tiles otherwise you could possibly be dealing with an unwelcome flood.

Acrylic tanks

Acrylic is stronger, lighter, and clearer than glass and is becoming popular with many aquarists and for public aquariums. Tanks can be made as a single piece, resulting in incredible strength, and scratches can be buffed out. Acrylic, however, does remain more expensive than glass and must be cleaned with softer pads, which are specially designed for use on acrylic tanks.

Do-it-yourself tanks

Building your own tank is an inexpensive alternative to buying one ready-made, but much care must be taken in the construction process. The glass must be cut using a diamond cutter, which will produce a sharp edge. Wear gloves when handling the glass and always ventilate the area when using silicone. Use G-clamps to hold the panes together and allow one day per $\frac{1}{32}$ inch (1 mm) of glass thickness for the silicone to cure before filling it with water. For your first tank, start small, because it will be cheaper and easier to build.

Cushioning your tank

Glass is extremely brittle, and the base of the tank should always be properly cushioned to even out any regularities from the surface below. An all-glass tank will therefore need to be placed on polystyrene tiles when it is lifted into place and before it is filled with water. Failure to do so may result in the tank cracking and the loss of the guarantee.

Below The black trim on the base of this aquarium hides a floating base, so it does not need to be placed on polystyrene tiles.

Aquarium furniture

The top and bottom of your aquarium are not only there to frame the living picture within it but they must also be functional to allow ease of maintenance. Stands and cabinets must also be strong and level. But our tastes are not all the same, so cabinets, like tanks, come in all shapes and sizes to suit different people's budgets and also to suit people's different tastes in furniture and home decoration.

Stands

A stand is a basic requirement for an aquarium, because without one it would be sitting on the floor. Stands must be made by professionals or purchased from an aquarium retailer because aquariums are heavy enough to buckle living room furniture, potentially causing disaster.

Stands are made from metal and are usually coated in a layer of plastic. They are traditionally produced in black, but silver is also a popular color. They come flat-packed (known as a knock-down) or ready-assembled in several styles. Double stands can be ordered to take two aquariums, one above the other. Polystyrene tiles will need to be used for cushioning all glass aquariums (see page 27).

Cabinets

Cabinets offer the aquarist more features than a stand, in that cupboards are provided for external filters, equipment, and storage, as well as a shelf for displaying or storing any ornaments or aquatic literature. They are produced in all wood finishes to match existing furniture and are also available in contemporary designs.

When you are choosing a cabinet, make sure that it is specifically for aquatic use, because household furniture is unsuitable. Some cabinets may need cushioning on the surface with polystyrene tiles, so check with your retailer before buying. Cabinets can be bought separately as the bottom half or with a matching hood. They are also available as part of a complete unit consisting of hood, aquarium, and base.

Hoods

The hood has the dual function of housing any lighting and preventing fish from jumping out of the aquarium. The choice is huge, ranging from simple plastic and metal hoods to customized polished wood canopies. Most aquarists prefer matching hoods and cabinets, because the effect is more aesthetically pleasing. Note that some plastic hoods will not have proper provision for installing lights, and one-piece hoods, which need to be removed for maintenance, are not as easy to use as those with hinges. Modern hoods need to be versatile: a marine tank hood may need to accommodate lighting, filter pipework, and a protein skimmer.

Stand or cabinet?

TYPE OF FURNITURE	PROS	CONS
Knock-down stand	Available off the shelf flat-packed or ready-assembled	Limited choice of designs and colors; nowhere to hide/store equipment and wiring
Wooden cabinet	Available in any size, color and design; provision to hide/store equipment and wiring	May have to be specially ordered; must be placed on a level surface to avoid warping; must be kept dry

Right This cabinet provides storage for an external filter and any accessories. Cabinets come in a variety of different colors, too.

Cover glasses

The primary functions of cover glasses are to prevent evaporation and to stop fish from jumping out of the tank. They can be made from glass, when the usual approach is to place two sheets as runners that can be slid past each other, providing access to both ends of the tank. Plastic cover glasses (or condensation trays) are also available, and are cheaper, but the glass ones are preferable.

Tip

Clean your cover glass regularly to remove algae buildup and precipitation from filter outlets, both of which will impede light penetration. Wooden cabinet setups usually come complete with cover glasses.

Which hood?

TYPE OF HOOD	PROS	CONS
Plastic	Cheap and widely available; lightweight	Unsuitable for large tanks because they are flimsy; some styles will accommodate little or no lighting; poor access
Metal	Cheap and widely available; lightweight and will accommodate a light ballast at the rear; reasonable access	Dated in design and can dent; limited capacity for accommodating multiple lighting
Wooden	Can be made to any size and will accommodate multiple lighting; available in any color or finish; provides the best access	May warp if exposed to water for prolonged periods; some sizes may have to be specially ordered

Positioning the aquarium

The appropriate positioning of the aquarium is crucial both for the safety of the tank and for the long-term health of its inhabitants, so take time to consider all the external environmental factors involved before making a final decision on where it should be positioned. In the average living room there are a number of sites that can be chosen or avoided.

Choosing the site

In deciding where to site your tank, bear in mind that you can never have enough power outlets on hand, as the necessary electrically powered equipment will take up many sockets. Place the tank next to, but not directly over, electrical outlets so that they are out of the way of dangerous water drips. Make sure that the plugs can be removed without the cabinet being in the way, because once filled, it will be impossible to move.

Fish can suffer from stress if the tank is wrongly sited, and the success of the aquarium as a whole can be compromised. The diagram below illustrates a possible arrangement that may be suitable for the tank.

Heat exposure

Warmth from indoor heating can affect the tank and may cause stress on the glass if it is extreme enough. Never place an aquarium next to a fire, or radiators, or portable heaters.

Drafts can chill fish, which can cause them to suffer from whitespot (see page 180). They will also trigger tank heater/thermostats more often, shortening their life.

Natural light

Sunlight catching the tank can cause more problems than benefits for an aquarium. Exposure to direct sunlight can cause algal blooms and the temperature of the tank to rise.

Suitable living room layout

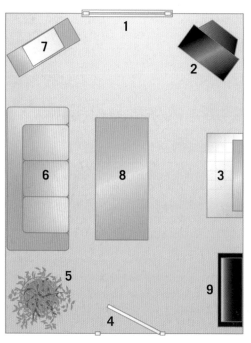

1 Window
2 TV
3 Fireplace
4 Door
5 Plant
6 Sofa
7 Stereo
8 Coffee table
9 Aquarium

Avoid sunlight exposure

Avoid heat exposure

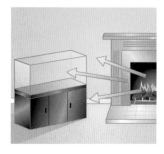

Vibration

Vibration in the form of noise from audio equipment and televisions should be avoided, because sound travels quickly through water and will stress the fish. Doors slamming and thudding floorboards will also transfer straight to the tank, causing nervous fish and erratic behavior.

Flooring

Heavy tanks should not only be placed on appropriate stands and cabinets (see page 28) but also on a floor that can take the additional weight. With the average tank weighing some 220 pounds (100 kg) when full, wooden floorboards should be examined to check their suitability. The footprint of a tank is larger when it is on a cabinet than when it is on a stand with four legs, which is an advantage. More pressure is exerted from each leg of a stand, causing possible warping of wooden floorboards and an uneven tank. If a stand is used with wooden floorboards, spread the weight by placing the feet of the stand on a large piece of plywood.

Tip

If you want to install a very large tank, check that it is going to fit through the door before you buy. If it looks as if it will not fit, windows may have to be removed or the tank may have to be built on site.

Tip

Before siting the tank, check which way the floor joists run and place the length of the tank across as many joists as possible, thus spreading the load. Floorboards normally run the opposite way to floor joists, so this should give a quick indication.

Lifting

Even empty tanks are heavy, so get help when you lift the aquarium into position. Use proper lifting techniques, and if you are moving a large tank, run through with everybody beforehand where the tank will be placed in case somebody needs to put it down in a hurry. Clear the area of any objects that may cause hazards when lifting and make sure that the floor is dry and not slippery.

Placement

Check that the surface is level before and after the final positioning of the tank. An uneven tank will cause pressure to be exerted on the tank and cabinet, and if a tank is even slightly leaning, it will be inherently unstable.

Below Use a level to make sure that both the aquarium and the cabinet surfaces are level before filling the tank with water.

EQUIPMENT
Filtration

Filtration is the life-support system for any aquarium and is vitally important for the well-being of the fish that live within it. Without exception, all aquarium fish need filtered water that is free from pollutants. Unfiltered aquariums are not safe for live fish, since, unless the water is changed several times a day, fish become poisoned by their own waste products and may die as a result.

Mechanical filtration

This is carried out by passing water through media that are designed to trap particles and remove them from the water column (the area of water between the surface and the bottom). Mechanical filter media can be in the form of a sponge or fine wool, and are cheap and readily available (see pages 38–39). Most filters work mechanically, and the effectiveness of the process is indicated by the way the tank water clears.

Biological filtration

This method harnesses the power of nature by providing areas within the filter where microscopic bacteria can live and multiply (see page 20). The media should have a high surface area in relation to their volume, so that more bacteria can live within the space. Examples of this media include porous ceramic materials, lava chips, plastic hoops, and fine sponges (see page 39). This is the most valuable form of filtration for the fish, and every aquarium should have a biological filter.

Chemical filtration

This process is where chemical pollutants and metals are removed from the water by special absorbant resins and granules (see pages 40–41). Once saturated, the media are normally spent, so are then discarded and replaced. The most common form of chemical medium available is aquarium-grade carbon, which can remove dyes, odors, and medications from tank water, as well as chlorine from tap water.

Which filtration method is best?

A combination of all three forms of filtration is recommended to ensure that all aspects of water purification will be effectively carried out, leaving fresh, clear water for the fish to inhabit. Be aware, though, that as good as any filtration system is, it is not a substitute for regular water changes (see pages 170–71) and will also need maintaining in its own right. Mechanical media will need to be rinsed or replaced about every month to prevent blockages, and biological media should be rinsed about every two months in tank water (not tap water; see page 38) to remove any detritus.

Chemical media are rarely used on their own, except for purifying water at the source (such as filtering tap water or rainwater). Zeolite is sometimes used in bags when water is transported over long distances, but neither carbon nor Zeolite would make effective long-term media for keeping fish if they were used exclusively.

While you cannot overfilter aquarium water, you can underfilter it without noticing immediately. Water tests that indicated that ammonia or nitrite were present in the water for more than a few weeks would suggest inadequate biological media compared to the number of fish. The solution to this would be to opt for a larger filter or to double up and add another identical filter to the tank, perhaps at the opposite end.

A good filter both clears and breaks down water, but before you buy, consider factors such as ease of maintenance and service. The advantage of mass-produced, name-brand filters is that lots of stores will stock spare filter media and all the other parts, such as impellers, that are also needed.

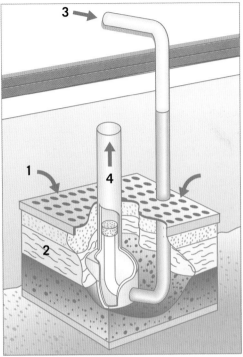

Internal box filter
1 Lid of filter perforated to provide inlet
2 Water drawn down through layers in filter
3 Attachment to air pump
4 Vertical return pipe

Left An external filter combines mechanical, biological, and chemical filtration, making it an excellent choice for any tank.

When deciding which type of media is the best all around, the prize must go to the humble sponge. Although the sponge is the cheapest option, its mechanical and biological filtering properties make it the only medium that can be used as an effective method of filtration in the aquarium. When maintained properly, it can be very effective, even when used on very sensitive fish like the discus. So if budget has to come into the equation, an air-powered sponge filter or internal power filter will always be the best option.

Tip

As good as any biological filter medium may be, when you purchase it, it will be dry and sterile and must be matured for several weeks before becoming fully colonized with bacteria and therefore effective.

Internal filters

Internal filters are the simplest form of filtration available and are suitable for beginners and professional breeders alike. Because they are contained within the aquarium, there is no risk of flooding and they are largely easy to operate.

Air-powered filters

These include foam filters, undergravel filters, and box filters. They are a gentle form of filtration, making them suitable for use with young fry. A variety of media can be used with a box filter. Power comes in the form of an air pump, which is connected via an air line to the filter. Air pumps sit outside the tank and blow air through the filter. As the air rises up through the filter, water is also drawn through and particles are trapped in the filter medium

(see pages 38–39). All three forms of filter use beneficial bacteria to break down the fish waste and make the water safe for the fish.

Upgraded undergravel filters

As mentioned above, these are usually air-powered but can be upgraded by fitting a powerhead—a universal underwater pump—to the riser stem. Undergravel filters have been enormously successful in the past, because the gravel is used as the filter bed and consequently the filter is largely invisible. They are, however, prone to clogging if not properly maintained, leading to loss of bacteria and related potential problems. They are also detrimental to plant growth because the roots are exposed to an unnatural flow of water over them.

Sponge filter
1 Attachment to air pump
2 Sponge acts as filter
3 Central plastic core to the filter
4 Water leaves with higher oxygen content

Undergravel filter
1 Perforated undergravel plate
2 Gravel layer covering plate
3 Uplift riser stem
4 Airstone and air line
5 From air pump

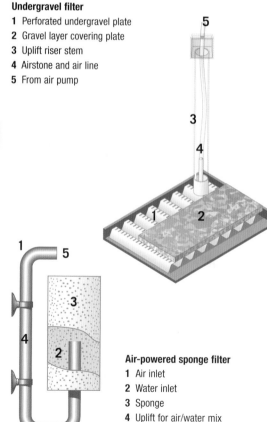

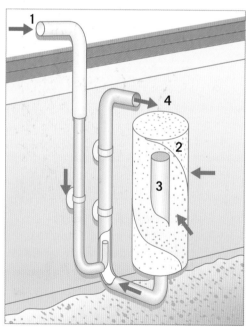

Air-powered sponge filter
1 Air inlet
2 Water inlet
3 Sponge
4 Uplift for air/water mix
5 Air/water outlet

Powerheads attached to underground riser stems
1 Perforated filter plate **2** Gravel layer **3** Uplift **4** Powerhead

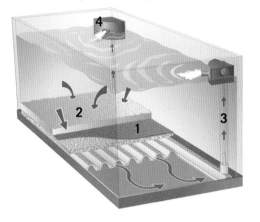

Internal power filter
1 Water inlets
2 Sponge
3 Powerhead
4 Water outlet

Internal power filters

These filters are powered by a powerhead (see above), which sits inside or on top of the main body of the filter. Water is drawn through the media by the pump, again trapping particles as it goes, but powerheads can move much more water an hour than air pumps, resulting in the water being filtered more times an hour. The advantages of this are that more waste can be drawn in, clearing the water faster, and a current is provided in the water by the powerhead as water is returned to the tank.

Internal power filters vary in size and power consumption and are suitable for all sizes of aquarium. Many come with built-in flow adjusters and multidirectional outlets. The media volume will vary depending on the model, but as a general rule, choose a model with a large media area as well as a good turnover of water. Venturi devices (see pages 42–43) add extra aeration for no extra power and are an advantage in most aquariums.

Multistage internal filters

Multistage internals are the best type of internal power filter available. They combine all the advantages of internal power filters, including Venturi devices and a high turnover, but also contain a larger area for media and a

Multistage internal power filter

1 Filter inlet	**5** Fine sponge
2 Heater	**6** Ceramic medium
3 Carbon medium	**7** Powerhead
4 Coarse sponge	**8** Filter outlet

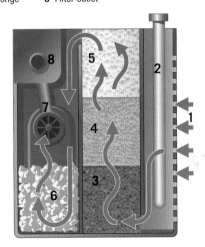

range of filter media for total filtration. Mechanical, biological, and chemical filtration can all be taken care of inside the unit and most have an area in which to place a heater/thermostat.

The only disadvantage of such models is that they are physically larger than all other internal filters and will be clearly visible in the tank.

External filters

External filters are the best off-the-shelf form of filtration available to the aquarist because they combine large solids-handling capability with high turnover, large media capacity, and several forms of filtration. They are more expensive than internal filters, but the benefits outweigh the initial cost. They can also be hidden in cabinets under aquariums, making them inconspicuous.

Size

The larger size of external filters makes them suitable for larger aquariums, and they are a popular choice when keeping large, messy fish, such as oscars (*Astronotus ocellatus*). Their larger media capacity also means that the filter can physically support more fish than a smaller model by having more media surface area available for bacteria (see pages 38–39). When it comes to filtration, you cannot overfilter—you can only have too much turnover. Therefore, an external filter has a larger media capacity in relation to its turnover compared to most internal filters.

Priming

This is a term used for getting the filter working, because when it is first placed under the aquarium, the tank water must be drawn through the pipework and into the unit. The aquarium should be filled with water before priming the filter. Models and manufacturers differ in their chosen method of priming, but look for a model that uses a lever or plunger to start water trickling down the pipework and into the filter body. Once the unit is full of water, the filter can be switched on, and after a few minutes of blowing air bubbles out that were trapped in the medium, it should be working normally.

The old way of priming a filter was to fill the body of the filter with tank water, then suck the water down the pipework by mouth with the filter switched on. This method always causes a small flood, and self-priming filters were warmly welcomed by aquarists when they arrived on the market.

Leaking

Leaking external filters are much less frequent than they were when they were originally introduced. The usual suspects were metal clips

External power filter
1 Inlet with shut-off tap
2 Perforated plate
3 Coarse sponge
4 Ceramic medium
5 Fine sponge
6 Priming device
7 Outlet with shut-off tap

and O-rings, but developments in design have led to improved clips, easier installation, and fewer problems. Faulty installation by the aquarist can lead to leaks, and novices should seek advice from retailers before installing an external filter for the first time.

Hoses should be tightly connected and given a tug to check that they will not come off while the filter is running.

Accessories

The external filter has the advantage of having many accessories available for fitting to different types of tank and returning the water in different ways. The spraybar is a worthwhile attachment for returning water to the tank, because it breaks up the strong jet of water and provides a more gentle current. It can also provide extra aeration when it is placed under the surface of the water, because it can cause significant surface agitation.

Disadvantages

The high turnover of external filters can be a little too powerful for plants, so choose a smaller model and stock your aquarium with fewer fish if you are planning a heavily planted tank. The slots in the intake pipe are also large enough to pull in young fry, so cover the pipe with a sponge sleeve if necessary.

Tip

It is a good idea to be present for several hours after an external filter is fitted, just to make sure that there are no leaks.

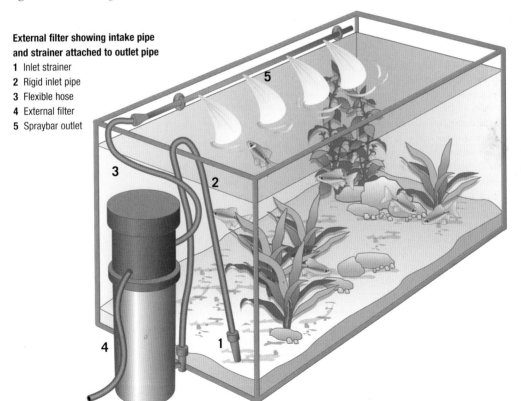

External filter showing intake pipe and strainer attached to outlet pipe

1 Inlet strainer
2 Rigid inlet pipe
3 Flexible hose
4 External filter
5 Spraybar outlet

Filter media

The medium in any filter is the material used to clear the water in the aquarium, to break down the waste, and to absorb any chemicals in the water. The three types of media are known as mechanical, biological, and chemical and have been specially designed to aid those three types of filtration (see pages 32–33). They can all play a vital role in helping to produce clear tank water that is free from pollutants and therefore a healthy environment in which fish can thrive.

Above Wool is the simplest and cheapest form of mechanical filtration medium.

Mechanical media

The purpose of this type of medium is to trap particles that are in free suspension in the water column. Evidence of good mechanical filtration will be water that is free of debris and particulate matter. Almost anything can be used to get in the way of the dirt when running through water in this simple form of filtration, but the following are the most commonly used media.

Wool

Synthetic polymer wool is an effective form of mechanical filtration, and it is both cheap and simple to use. It can be employed as a prefilter that is, the first medium that comes into contact with the dirty water. It is quite fine and will quickly stop much of the dirt in suspension but will need to be replaced or washed almost weekly in most situations. Place in the area of the filter that has first contact with the water. Wool is rarely used as a biological media, so it can be washed in untreated tap water (see below).

Sponge

Sponge is an effective mechanical medium, which is available in a range of forms, from fine to coarse. Its irregular internal make up causes water to slow down when flowing through it and dirt particles to be trapped within it. It can be washed out more easily than wool, so needs less frequent replacement.

Sponge can become dual purpose once it has been colonized with beneficial bacteria, thus assuming the additional role of a biological

filter. To do this, it must be kept clean but washed only in old tank water to maintain the bacteria. Washing a sponge under the tap would kill off its bacteria and reduce it to its mechanical-filtration function only. A simple sponge is the only form of filtration for air-powered foam filters and most internal filters (see pages 34–35), so its intended purpose is dual, as a mechanical and biological filter.

Biological media

This is the most important form of media available to the aquarists, as its high surface area will encourage a large colony of beneficial bacteria to inhabit it (see page 20). The turnover from the pump will provide the bacteria with food in the form of waste and oxygen, which is vital for the bacteria's survival. For this reason, make sure that the mechanical filters placed before it are effectively trapping detritus and not letting too much get through, which might otherwise block surfaces and lessen oxygen flow.

Again, no biological media should be washed under tap water, which contains chlorine or chloramines, because the bacteria will be killed, leaving a sterile environment.

Ceramics

This popular form of biological filtration is highly porous, containing lots of tiny holes, which offer a large surface area for bacteria in

Above Sponge is a very versatile medium because it works both mechanically and biologically.

Above Ceramic biological media have a high surface area to provide lots of space in which bacteria can live.

that they can cling to areas inside the medium as well as outside. If kept clean, the medium should not need replacing. It comes in the form of ceramic rings or blocks and is intended largely for use with external power filters (see page 36) and multistage internal filters (see page 35). A large capacity of ceramic medium should ensure plenty of bacteria living within it once it is mature and therefore a healthy aquarium.

Other biological media

Anything that has a large surface area in relation to its volume can be used as a biological medium, as long as the material is safe to use with fish. Items suitable for making home-made filters include children's plastic building bricks and even hair curlers. Gravel can also be used in quantity to provide a large overall surface area.

Gravel is the only material used in undergravel filtration and each stone will be coated with a layer of beneficial bacteria. When placed at depth, undergravel filter beds are quite large compared to the tank volume and so are generally quite effective.

Other biological media include plastic media (similar to hair curlers), called bio-balls, which have a large surface area in relation to their mass. Bio-balls and other plastic media are quite large and so are usually only used as media in

> **Tip**
>
> **Sponge should be replaced when it has lost its original shape and does not spring back into shape when squeezed.**

pond filters or large commercial filters on sizable tanks.

They are also commonly used in something called a trickle filter. This is a large plastic tube filled with bio-balls, which act as a biological filter. Water is dispersed at the top of the tube and falls down through the medium, wetting the surfaces as it goes. The advantage of having a thin coating of water over the balls instead of their being completely submerged is that the medium is exposed to more oxygen from the air and so can support lots of aerobic bacteria. However, the disadvantages of trickle filtration are that the water must fall with gravity back into the tanks, which means that the filter must be placed above it and also that you will need some form of mechanical filtration available to remove the particles and to keep the bio-balls clean.

Above Carbon is the most widely used form of chemical filtration and removes dyes and odors.

Above This pouch containing Zeolite is used in filters to remove ammonia and nitrite from water.

Chemical media

To filter water chemically involves using man-made products that have been designed to remove certain substances from the water, such as dyes, odors, proteins, medications, nitrates, and phosphates. Most will absorb to the point of saturation and need to be removed and replaced. Some can be recharged, but check the manufacturer's recommendations.

Carbon

This is the most common form of chemical filter media and is widely used throughout the aquatic hobby. Its main benefit is that it successfully removes dyes and odors from the water, leaving it crystal clear. Its main drawback is that it can also soak up medications and plant foods, so use it for its advantage but remove when treating sick fish. Activated carbon has been formed at an even higher temperature than normal carbon, so it does its job more effectively, since it has a larger surface area.

In normal usage, carbon should be regarded as saturated and removed from the filter every four to six weeks.

Zeolite

Zeolite removes ammonia from aquarium water and is a good product for use in emergencies but can cause problems if used long term. Filter bacteria consume harmful substances, such as ammonia and nitrate, and convert them into less harmful nitrate (see page 110). So, these beneficial bacteria depend on the ammonia produced by fish for their survival. When the ammonia is removed chemically by Zeolite, the friendly bacteria are destroyed, which is not a problem in itself. However, when the Zeolite becomes saturated and cannot absorb any more ammonia, the friendly bacteria are no longer present to deal with the continual production of ammonia from the fish. The result is a tank that has neither chemical filtration nor functioning biological filtration, which can trigger a sharp rise in toxic ammonia to levels that can kill fish. Zeolite is available ready mixed with carbon or on its own.

Peat

Peat is not used for what it removes but for what it adds to aquarium water. It has been widely used in aquariums in the past for the humic acids that it leaches into the water, which help to lower carbonate hardness and slightly acidify the water. It also turns the water the color of tea. The advantages to the aquarist are that acidic water with low carbonate hardness is what natural water is like in tropical areas such as the Amazon, so providing these conditions aids conditioning and breeding of the species originating in those areas.

Peat plates are sometimes seen in stores, and they are designed to aid plant growth. They have drawbacks in that as the peat decomposes, it may foul the water and make vacuuming difficult.

Above Peat will stain water the color of tea and can be used to stimulate black water habitats.

Above Phosphate-removal resins are becoming more widely used because they help to prevent algae growth.

It has been found that peat has very little effect on softening water, that it is very hard, and with the advent of more effective water softeners, such as reverse osmosis (or RO) units (see page 84), peat is now largely redundant.

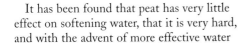

Comparison of filter media

TYPE OF FILTER	PROS	CONS
Wool	Cheap and widely available	Poor biological medium; liable to clogging and reducing water flow; needs frequent replacement
Sponge	Cheap; works both mechanically and biologically; tried and tested filter medium	Reduced biological capacity when clogged; needs regular cleaning
Ceramics	Huge surface area for bacteria	Expensive; must be used in conjunction with mechanical medium
Carbon	Cheap; polishes water; removes chemical pollutants	Needs replacing to avoid saturated medium leaching; removes plant food
Zeolite	Removes ammonia; good for emergencies and transporting fish over distances	Disturbs biological filters by removing the food source of the bacteria
Peat	Provides tannin-stained black water; lowers hardness in water	Not an ideal water softener, because capabilities are limited; stained water can make a tank look dirty

Aeration

Fish, just like other animals, need oxygen, and in nature oxygen in the water is provided by plants and from the movement of water. A large body of water such as a lake can provide oxygen for fish just from having a huge surface area, which provides lots of room for carbon dioxide (CO_2) to escape and for oxygen to dissolve.

Different oxygen requirements

In the aquarium fish are kept at a much higher volume than in the wild and consequently need additional aeration to survive. Indeed, the beneficial filter bacteria that we want to colonize the filter (see page 20) and the surfaces are aerobic, meaning that they too use oxygen and actually compete with the fish for available oxygen. A well-oxygenated aquarium will therefore sustain more bacteria and more fish.

The amount of oxygen that a body of water can hold will depend on its temperature. Cold water holds masses of oxygen, whereas warmer water has significantly less. Fish have evolved to suit the amount of oxygen that is available to them depending on where they live. A salmon, for example, needs lots of well-oxygenated, cool water, whereas a tetra (see pages 139–44), coming from a warmer environment, needs less.

Some species have taken oxygen intake one stage further by being able to breathe atmospheric air. The warmer ranges of the world have waters that would not normally sustain live fish because they are hot and stagnant and therefore hold very little dissolved oxygen. Popular aquarium fish such as Siamese fighting fish (*Betta splendens*) and gouramis (see pages 135 and 135–37) have developed an organ called the labyrinth organ, which enables them to use oxygen from the atmosphere and to survive in oxygen-poor waters.

Tip

Choose an air pump that has a high output but low noise. Place it near the tank to keep pressure in the tubing high.

How to provide oxygen

Oxygen can be provided for the aquarium by using an air pump or a Venturi device connected to a filter. Tablets can also be used but are not to be relied on and are mainly aimed at small bowls. Growing plants are not an adequate option, because although they produce carbon dioxide, they use oxygen at night as part of the process of photosynthesis.

Air pumps

An air pump works by pumping air from the atmosphere through a tube and into the aquarium. The air is pumped by way of a vibrating rubber diaphragm, which pushes air up the tube. There are varying sizes of air pump available to suit all sizes of aquarium, from very tiny to multiple banks of tanks and commercial applications. Typically, air pumps come as a single or double outlet, but large pumps can run several air lines at once. They can be noisy and are prone to "walk," meaning that the vibration they produce causes them to move.

Air pumps are not waterproof. Do not allow them to be splashed, and never place them in the water. In the event of a power failure, water may back-siphon down the air line and into the pump, causing unit failure. To prevent this from happening, always fit a nonreturn valve. The moving parts inside the pump are breakable and should be serviced or replaced periodically.

Venturi devices

A Venturi device fits onto the outlet of a power filter and uses the force of the water to draw in air, causing bubbles to be created like those of an air pump. Venturis are cheap and come as standard with some types of power filter. They do not use any electricity. Venturis need to fit onto the outlet of a power filter to work, and the more powerful the pump, the more bubbles you will get. Some come fitted with a small air filter and silencer, which will need replacing or cleaning. They do not pump air at pressure as an air pump does, so cannot be used to run an air-operated feature. A heavily stocked aquarium will certainly benefit from the addition of a Venturi because it will help to keep aerobic bacteria levels high. If you are overstocked with fish, the additional bacteria may be the only thing keeping your fish alive.

If the pump fails, so does the Venturi, meaning no aeration or filtration for the fish. They can also block sometimes and need to be near the surface of the water to work. The action of the device is just as noisy as an air pump.

Right An airstone in operation. Bubbles rise to the surface, causing agitation and gaseous exchange.

Piston air pump
1 Power cord
2 Piston-squeezed air
3 First air outlet
4 Second air outlet
5 Flywheel pushes piston

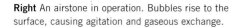

Heating and temperature control

The temperature of the world's oceans and waterways differs considerably, and the fish that inhabit each ecosystem have evolved to thrive in a certain temperature range. Fish that we consider to be tropical live in a water temperature of 75–86°F (24–30°C) all year round, with tropical marine fish living in a more stable environment of an almost constant temperature of 75°F (24°C). Heating the water in an aquarium to the temperature required for tropical species is both simple and inexpensive.

Heating equipment

There are several types of heating elements available, including special mats and cables, but the essential item you need to heat and regulate the temperature in your aquarium is a heater/thermostat. When a heating element at the bottom of the heater heats up, the water in contact with the outside of the heater warms. A thermostat reads the temperature of the water and turns the heater on and off to maintain the desired temperature. The heater and thermostat are housed in a glass tube with a sealed top. This piece of equipment is placed fully submerged in the tank, the temperature adjusted and then plugged in for 24 hours a day.

Above The top of this heater thermostat has a dial for easy temperature adjustment and can be completely submerged.

Choosing a heater/thermostat

There are several sizes of heater/thermostat available, varying in power from 25 to 300 watts. The wattage required depends on the volume of water to be warmed—the 25-watt size will heat an aquarium 12 inches (30 cm) long, while the largest size will heat a tank of 48 inches (120 cm) long. For tanks larger than this, two heater thermostats can be used to take the strain. If you have an odd-sized tank or are unsure about the appropriate size heater for your tank, consult the table opposite.

Manufacturer's recommendations for heater/thermostat size are based on the assumption that the exterior environment will already be at "room temperature"—that is, around 68°F (20°C). For aquariums kept in rooms or outhouses that have lower temperatures, more powerful heaters should be used, as they will have to work harder in doing more heating. For example, a tank of 24 inches (60 cm) long routinely kept below 68°F (20°C) will need a heater normally rated for an aquarium 36 inches (90 cm) long.

Installing the heater

The heater should be placed at the back of the aquarium in an area where it will receive flow from the filter and thus disperse heat more evenly around the tank. Heaters are quite unsightly and can detract from the beauty of an aquarium if they are in full view. To overcome this problem, position it in a rear corner and add some decoration in front to conceal it. To work effectively, the heater must also be placed away from any objects that could come into contact with it, including the substrate, because this can affect heat dispersion.

Safety precautions

The fact that the heater is housed in a glass tube makes it a fragile piece of equipment that should be handled with care. Avoid touching

Heating FAQs

Q What happens if I choose a heater that is too small for my tank?

A It will take longer to heat the tank in the first place, and the heater will consequently come on more often. This extra use may cause the heater to fail in a short space of time.

Q What happens if I choose a heater that is too large for my aquarium?

A It will simply turn on and off less. However, more powerful heaters tend to be longer in size, so they will look more prominent in a small tank.

Q If a heater fails, will it boil my fish?

A This happens less and less these days, since heaters are more reliable than ever. Some heaters have been specifically designed to turn off if they fail, so check for this safety feature when you buy one.

Q How many types of heater are available?

A There are many brands of heater that are all quite similar. Some have toughened glass, which guards against the risk of shattering. Some also regulate temperature differently. The conventional type of thermostat uses a bimetallic strip, which expands and contracts, turning the heater on and off (this could fail in the on position). The other type uses a microchip to control the thermostat, which can be more accurate.

Q Are there any new technological developments in aquarium heating?

A Heaters have now been developed that can be connected to the filter pipework and external filters, thus removing them from the tank altogether. Heat core technology has now also produced heaters that heat more gently, and this type can be handled and moved when still hot.

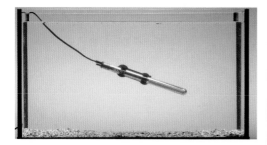

Above A heater thermostat in operation. Note that it is placed at an angle and above the gravel.

What size heater/ thermostat do you need?

TANK SIZE	HEATER/THERMOSTAT SIZE
12 inches (30 cm)	25 watts
24 inches (60 cm)	50 watts
30 inches (75 cm)	100 watts
36 inches (90 cm)	150 watts
39 inches (100 cm)	200 watts
48 inches (120 cm)	300 watts

the end containing the element, which will be very hot. When moving or removing the heater from the water, turn it off for some time beforehand, because if it is removed from the water while still hot, the glass may shatter, requiring immediate replacement. Also, if the heater is positioned near to rockwork or used in tanks housing catfish (see pages 154–55) or other large, boisterous fish, it is a good idea to fit a heater guard. This is a simple, inexpensive device, consisting of a tough, plastic sleeve with perforations to allow the flow of heat, and it slides around the heater body and protects it from impact, as well as protecting fish from being burned by its heat.

Lighting

Lighting can turn a dull tank into a vibrant picture full of color and life. Many fish are adapted to use their coloration during signaling and courtship, and plants simply cannot survive without light. Aquarium lighting comes in the form of artificial light provided by fluorescent tubes or by high-powered pendent lighting.

Fluorescent light

Fluorescent tubes are the most common form of aquarium lighting. They are a variation on the lighting used in many retail outlets and industry, but have been specially developed for the aquarium market. Fluorescent tubes have a long life (several thousand hours) and are bright relative to their energy consumption. They run at a cooler temperature than bulbs, making them suitable to be placed inside a hood.

They are powered by a light starter unit, which consists of a box plugged into the outlet and two cables, each with a cap that fits onto either end of the tube. The power of the light starter unit should be matched to the wattage of the tube, because a starter unit that is too small may not succeed in lighting the tube.

Fluorescent lighting is available in different spectrums, which are designed to replicate types of lighting experienced under water. Very white light tubes are referred to as daylight tubes and are designed to replicate the midday sun. Blue tubes are known as moonlight tubes and replicate exactly that, but special actinic blue tubes are aimed at marine corals that grow at depth under the sea. Light tubes that appear quite pink when lit are color-enhancing and will highlight fish colors. They may also aid plant and coral growth.

Light fittings

Starter units are normally supplied with clips and plastic screws to be fitted inside a hood. Once secure, the end caps can be fitted to the tube and the tube pushed into the clips. The starter unit should be placed in a well-ventilated, dry place behind the aquarium.

Most end caps are splashproof and provide a degree of protection to the electrical ends of the tube. They should fit the tube tightly and not allow any condensation to penetrate the tube.

Waterproof lighting is available and will survive accidental submerging of the lights for up to 30 minutes. The end caps on these units should be tightened when fitted, and the rubber O-rings should be replaced annually.

Different lighting requirements

The strength of the lighting and the length of time that the light should stay on during the day will depend on the livestock that you intend to keep. Low lighting is preferred by species that are naturally active at dawn and dusk, and especially those that would normally only be active at night. Loaches, including the coldwater weather loach (*Misgurnus anguillicaudatus*) and the tropical clown loach (*Botia macracantha*) (see pages 133 and 147), will be much happier if kept in low lighting, as will most catfish, such as the zebra plec (*Hypancistrus zebra*) (see page 155).

At the opposite end of the scale, there are those fish that are exposed to bright light in the wild and would prefer those conditions

Boosting the light

Light output from a single tube can be increased by up to 100 percent by using a reflector. Polished metal reflectors bounce down into the aquarium light that would otherwise be lost or absorbed by the roof of the hood. They can be used in conjunction with standard light tube clips, and several will fit inside a hood. They have the added advantage of blocking out bright light when you lift the hood for maintenance.

replicated in the aquarium. Gouramis (see pages 135–37) and livebearers such as guppies (*Poecilia reticulata*) (see page 158) are well used to the full glare of the tropical sun. However, for many fish, ambient room lighting can be sufficient for much of the day.

Live plants and corals are dependent on light for their energy and survival, so the lighting should be connected to a timer and come on for 10–12 hours a day. Too little light can cause the slow death of plants and corals. All fish need a day-and-night light cycle to be replicated, so light should be on at some point during the day.

In aquariums not containing live plants, excess light can be a major cause of algae. High-specification lighting should not be used for viewing fish in these circumstances.

Right This hood has waterproof end caps for protection and a built-in reflector to maximize light penetration.

Below A modern "luminaire" lighting system, complete with multiple lighting and different spectrum bulbs.

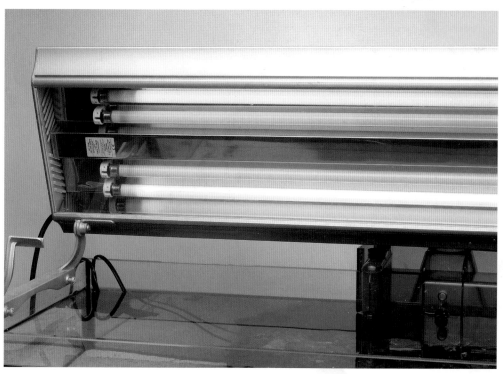

Light tubes

There is a wide selection of fluorescent tubes available, each designed for a different role when lighting the aquarium. A single type of tube can be used or they can be combined in setups using multiple tubes to meet the aquarist's exacting requirements. The color or spectrum of the tube can also play an important role, not only for fish color but also for plant and coral growth.

Color temperature

The color temperature of a light tube is not easy to recognize but does affect plant growth and fish coloration. How color temperature affects us is merely what effect it has on the appearance of the tank when it is lit by a different part of the spectrum. Color temperature is measured in units known as Kelvins, and this will be specified on the packaging of a light tube when purchased.

To simplify the quantifying of color temperature, aquatic light tubes are available with Kelvin ratings of between 2,000 and 20,000. Aquatic plants do best in lighting between 4,000 and 10,000 Kelvin, and they will not utilize ratings any higher than that. Light-loving fish (see pages 46–47) will be fine in any rating, but their coloration will look different.

Right Tubes come in different lengths to fit different-sized hoods. They should span right across the aquarium.

Daylight tubes

Daylight tubes have a Kelvin rating of around 10,000. They are the brightest of the fluorescent tubes and are designed to mimic full tropical sunshine. They can be used with coldwater and tropical setups to provide a bright, clean atmosphere. Plants benefit from their addition, and the green leaves are highlighted by the spectrum. Fish colors look brighter but not richer, and some species may find it too bright (see pages 46–47). Algae growth will also increase, so add algae-eating fish and keep the duration of the light strictly timed.

Color-enhancing tubes

Tubes that enhance the colors of fish are very popular for obvious reasons. Red and blue fish coloration will be highlighted, and species such as goldfish and cardinal tetras (*Paracheirodon axelrodi*) (see page 142) look especially colorful. Color enhancers can be used on their own or combined with daylight tubes to provide high-spectrum lighting. Plants can grow under color-enhancing tubes, but so will algae. They are still the best choice for single-tube systems, as they are good all-around tubes with a long life. Color-enhancing tubes differ in rating but go up to 18,000 Kelvin.

Plant-growth tubes

Plants need lighting that is high in the red end of the spectrum if they are to grow to their full potential. They also benefit from inhibited algae growth, so plant tubes have been specifically designed not to encourage algal growth. Fish coloration is not brilliant when exclusively using these tubes, but the effect can be considered

"natural," as it does not make the fish look too gaudy. Plant-growth tubes are available in ratings under 10,000 Kelvin.

Above To provide lighting similar to this deep-water coral reef, use marine light tubes with a rating of 20,000 Kelvin.

How many light tubes?

Any mixture of light tubes with different spectrums can be used for aquariums containing only fish, and how many you use will depend on whether the species kept prefer low or bright lighting (see pages 46–47). However, in aquariums with live plants, available light is important for plant growth. Tanks 12 inches (30 cm) long or less will be fine with one light tube, but consult the chart (right) for how many tubes are needed for larger tanks. For larger planted aquariums over 24 inches (60 cm) deep, you could use metal halide lighting with bulbs designed for freshwater (see page 209). Light from all fluorescent tubes can be greatly enhanced by using a reflector (see page 46).

Light tube requirements for planted aquariums

TANK DEPTH	NUMBER OF LIGHT TUBES
12 inches (30 cm)	1
15 inches (38 cm)	2
18 inches (45 cm)	3
24 inches (60 cm) and over	4–6

AQUARIUM DECORATION

Substrates

The substrate of any aquarium is the material placed on the bottom of the tank for decoration. Traditional substrates include sands and gravels, found naturally in any body of water. In most freshwater aquariums the substrate should be inert, which means that it will not dissolve or leach elements into the water, thus affecting the pH of the tank water (see pages 104–5).

Pea gravel

This material is an excellent choice for coldwater and tropical aquariums and is safe to use with all types of fish. It is available in sizes from ⅛ inch (4 mm) up to ¾ inch (2 cm), and its round particles make it good for fish that like to dig. It will not readily compact and it can also be easily cleaned. Pea gravel should be used in a layer about 2 inches (5 cm) deep. It offers good anchoring for plants.

Top Pea gravel is suitable for all types of aquarium.
Middle Silica sand is a useful planting substrate.
Bottom Silver sand is made up of tiny grains.

Which substrate?

TYPE OF SUBSTRATE	PROS	CONS
Pea gravel	Easy to clean; inert; safe for all fish	Too coarse for some plants to grow in
Silica sand	Cheap; natural looking; good for plant growth	Needs thorough washing when purchased to remove dust
Silver sand	Very natural looking; suitable for all aquariums	Prone to clogging; particles can end up in filter chambers and powerheads
Colored gravel	Brightens up aquariums; popular with children	Colors fade over time; bright colors attract algal growth
Grit	Small enough to anchor plants	Can be dirty when first purchased

Top Coral sand is only suitable for marine aquariums.
Middle Colored gravels are decorative and bright.
Bottom Grit provides a good anchoring for plants.

How to wash substrates

1. Half fill a clean bucket with the dry substrate.

2. Place the bucket under a tap or hose, turned on to full power, and fill the bucket with water.

3. Use your hand to agitate the substrate vigorously, which will cause the water to become dirty.

4. Pour away the water and repeat the process until the tap water remains clear in the bucket.

Silica sand

Silica is available as a sand and a grit and can be used in all freshwater aquariums. It is very dirty when first purchased and will take a lot of rinsing before the water runs clear. Its color is similar to that of soil, and it creates a nice effect for natural-style aquariums. Its small particle size is useful for plant growth and it should be used at a depth of between 1 inch (2.5 cm), where there are no natural plants, and 4 inches (10 cm) for heavily planted aquariums.

Silver sand

This is the original universal aquarium substrate, given that it is found naturally all over the world in streams, rivers, lakes, and oceans. Its name is a little inaccurate, since its overall color is golden. It needs to be washed thoroughly when first purchased, and it can be messy. Some plant species are better suited to it than others. For a heavily planted tank, mix silver sand with substrate fertilizer and use a heating cable to prevent stagnation.

Colored gravels

There is a huge market for colored gravels, and every imaginable color is available, from black to shocking pink. Light colors will attract algal growth and must be regularly cleaned to prevent it. Black gravel can look attractive in natural-style aquariums and highlights fish and plant coloration. Wash all colored gravels thoroughly before introducing them to the tank, since much of the gravel will have lost its paint covering in the bag.

Grit

Grit is a term used for substrates with a particle size between fine sand and fine gravel—that is, $1/16$–$1/8$ inch (2–3 mm)—and is fine enough to encourage plant root growth within it.

Rocks

The use of rock in the aquarium is as old as the hobby itself, and there are now many types available. Rockwork can provide a backdrop, hiding places for fish and potential spawning sites, and not many aquariums are without it in some form.

Lava rock

Lava looks really good in aquariums and has the advantage of being light in relation to its mass, meaning that it does not displace as much water as other rocks. However, it can be sharp and should not be used as the only form of rock in aquariums housing grazing fish, such as sucker-mouthed catfish. It is available in both carved and solid forms and can be cut with a saw. Some pieces of lava are so porous that they float when they are placed in water, so check that this is not the case when purchasing.

Slate

Slate can be used for many purposes in the aquarium and can be built into caves, stacked, used to hold gravel back and as spawning sites for egg-depositing fish. It is safe for all types of freshwater aquariums and is easily cleaned. It comes in silver, blue, purple, and rustic forms, but they are all variations on gray. It can be split using a hammer, and any remaining sharp edges should be removed by breaking them off with pliers to expose a thicker edge.

Cobbles

These represent rounded stones found in rivers and streams, and their smooth edges make them a good choice for aquariums. They are heavy, so should be placed with care, and are not very stable when stacked. Most are inert (see page 50), but it is difficult to tell by looking, since a cobble can be a rounded form of any rock.

Granite

Granite is a decorative rock that is inert (see page 50) and therefore safe for all freshwater aquariums. It looks like marble when wet and is

Top Lava rock stacks easily and is light but can be too abrasive for some fish.

Middle Slate can be used to make caves in the aquarium, and some fish choose it to deposit their eggs on.

Bottom Cobbles are smooth and heavy and are used to create riverine environments in aquariums.

a much cheaper alternative. It is heavy, so handle with care, and use flatter pieces when stacking. It looks quite natural when employed exclusively and is smooth enough to be used as spawning surfaces by egg-depositing fish (see page 190).

Sandstone
This rock is suitable for all freshwater aquariums and looks especially good when used with plants. It can be a little dusty, so wash thoroughly before placing it in the tank. It stacks well but may be too coarse for egg layers (see pages 188–91), so provide slate or flowerpots alongside it.

Limestone
Limestone is not easily identified by the novice, so it should be tested for the presence of lime (see chart below). It will raise pH and hardness

Tip

Rocks can be heavy enough to break glass aquariums, so use extreme caution when adding them to the tank.

when placed in water (see page 104). It should, therefore, be used only with fish that prefer hard water, such as livebearers and East African lake cichlids (see pages 144–46). Its major disadvantage is that it is very heavy, but it can look extremely natural and effective when it is used as boulders in some natural-style aquariums.

Which rocks are best for which aquarium?

TYPE OF ROCK	BEST USES AND LIMITATIONS
Lava rock	All types of freshwater aquariums, including soft water setups, such as Amazonian (see page 40), and marine-fish-only and reef tanks (see pages 216–17 and 222–23)
Slate	Suitable for all types of freshwater aquariums, including soft water setups, such as Amazonian; unsuitable for marine aquariums, since it does not naturally occur as part of the reef environment
Cobbles	Suitable for all types of freshwater aquariums, including soft water setups, such as Amazonian; unsuitable for marine aquariums, since they do not naturally occur as part of the reef environment
Granite	Suitable for all types of freshwater aquariums, including soft water; unsuitable for marine aquariums, since it is not aesthetically appropriate
Sandstone	All types of freshwater aquariums, including soft water; unsuitable for marine aquariums, since it is not aesthetically appropriate and because calcium-rich rocks are preferable
Limestone	Some freshwater aquariums that contain fish that naturally occur in and prefer water with a pH of around 8 (see pages 104–5); can be used in marine aquariums because of its pH-buffering capacity, but will not look as authentic as other marine-suitable rocks

Wood

Wood can be used very effectively as a design feature in aquariums and helps to provide a natural setting. Not all wood is safe to be used in aquariums, so obtain wood only from aquatic retailers. Fish use wood for camouflage and hiding places, and it can also be used to highlight planting.

Driftwood

This is a generic term for wood available from aquatic retailers. Not all of it is actually driftwood, but the important factors are that it is safe for use in aquariums and that it sinks. Other types of wood include "curio" wood, which is quite contorted and gnarled, and Mopani wood, which has a two-tone effect.

Wood water-staining effects

No driftwood is totally fossilized, and it will continue a slow rate of decomposition in water. This will involve a leaching of tannins into the water. Tannins acidify the water and turn the water the color of tea. Stained water is in keeping with many natural tropical habitats, such as the Amazon, and it can help to give a scene more authenticity. Overstaining of the water, however, can cut down light levels and may make the water look dirty. To remove discoloration, add carbon to the filter (see page 40).

Planting on wood

Both ferns and mosses can be grown on driftwood to produce a very pleasing effect. The plants should be tied to the wood using thin fishing line and then left for several weeks in the aquarium to establish. The plants should root onto the wood within that period of time, and the fishing line can be removed, leaving a highly natural-looking feature. Suitable plant species include Java moss (*Vesicular dubyana*) (see page 75), Java fern (*Microsorium pteropus*) (see page 73), anubias (*Anubias* spp.) (see page 69), and African fern (*Bolbitis heudilotti*).

The advantages of plants growing from wood are that the whole feature can be lifted and vacuumed beneath; fish that like to dig can be kept with these plants with no risk of uprooting them, and no specialized substrate is necessary. They are all also tolerant of low lighting levels and a wide range of water conditions.

Decorating with leaves

If you wish to take the natural approach one step further, you could consider adding some leaves to your setup. First of all, you must find the right kind of leaves. Beech and oak leaves are the only type considered absolutely safe for use in aquariums because they do not leach anything other than tannins into the water. Leaves from other tree species may be added by accident and are largely innocuous, but the leaves of the ash tree are poisonous to fish. The best advice is to play safe. Fallen oak and beech leaves are easily found lying around in parks—the leaves must already be brown and withered, so are best collected in winter. The leaves then have to be boiled to make them sink.

The effect of using leaves is one of a flooded forest and is entirely authentic, with many South American, African, and Asian species of catfish being very grateful for the extra cover (see page 138). The leaves do not last forever, however.

Using wood for food

Some species of South American catfish of the genus *Loricariidae* actually eat wood as part of their natural diet. They use their specialized mouths to rasp away pieces of the wood, from which they extract lignin. If you keep this group of fish, collectively known as plecs, it is recommended that at least one piece of driftwood is provided for this purpose.

Tip

Driftwood can be presoaked or boiled to remove most of its tannins. This will result in less staining of the water.

Above Driftwood can make very good decorative features in aquariums and will be welcomed by fish that prefer cover.

Below This anubias plant is growing on the wood and is not attached to the substrate.

Ornaments

For the discerning fishkeeper, ornaments may have no place in the aquarium, but some do not know what they are missing. Fish are not fussy about what their home looks like, and species that like to hide may just as happily reside under a bridge made from resin as one made from piled stones. For those of you that like a colorful underwater wonderland, they are a must-have.

What can you use as an ornament?

If an ornament is safe to use in an aquarium—which means only buying specially designed ornaments from aquatic retailers—then there is no reason why you should not use it. Ornaments can be added to freshwater and marine aquariums, and because they are usually made in molds, they are lightweight and do not displace much water. To aid the creative process, series of designs based on the same theme are available (see chart) and can be used to surprisingly good effect.

Ornaments for dual purposes

Ornaments need not be purely decorative objects. Their secondary function can be to hide equipment or to offer a place for fish to hide inside. Again, being molded, they are often hollow and some provide caves with that specific function in mind. Ornaments are often used by catfish and cave-dwelling catfish (see pages 154–55) to reside and breed in, and the owner benefits from an aquascape that is unspoiled by either flowerpots or bits of pipe.

Replicas

Apart from miniature castles and sunken shipwrecks, replicas of natural products are also available, ranging in scale from miniatures to actual size. Replicas can be used in place of real items in an aquarium where the latter would be unsuitable, since they do not leach any noxious

Creating themes with ornaments

THEME	WHAT TO USE
Greek and Roman ruins	Use replica urns, statues, and colosseums to create atmospheric underwater landscapes
Skeletons	Very common in tanks containing piranha (*Serrasalmus* and *Pygocentrus* spp.); use replica skulls and scaled-down human skeletons to create a scary underwater scene
Fluorescent	Combine fluorescent gravels with fluorescent castles and bridges to brighten up a dull tank
Animated	Use several air-operated features to bring movement and entertainment to the tank
Natural	Combine plastic plants with imitation rocks and roots to create a replica riverbed
Coral Reef	Use replica corals, shipwrecks, and treasure chests for a Treasure Island-type effect

Above This replica bridge ornament may look just like a bit of fun, but it can be used by fish to hide under.

Right Fake corals can be used to decorate aquariums housing fish that would destroy the real thing.

substances into the water. Replicas of sunken logs, for example, will not stain the water and break down over time, unlike driftwood (see page 54). Fake corals may look a little gaudy when they are newly purchased, but once a covering of coralline algae has taken hold, they look much more natural and can be kept with fish that would destroy real coral.

Air-operated ornaments

Some ornaments can be automated by connecting them to an air pump so that the buoyancy provided by the bubbles moves them. The typical air-operated ornaments are eternally popular with children and also have the advantage of adding oxygen to the water. They are available in many different shapes, including divers, clamshells, revolving wheels, and magic carpets. Most will need to be used in conjunction with a control valve on the air line to regulate how much air is sent to them; otherwise they will float to the surface.

Cleaning

To clean an ornament, rinse it under the tap and use an old toothbrush or impeller cleaning brush to remove any unsightly algae growth and the buildup of detritus. If the ornament has been painted, don't attempt to brush it too hard because you may remove the paint and expose the molded plastic. However, some fading and deterioration of ornaments is normal and to be expected. Some aquatic stores also sell special cleaning solution for soaking ornaments and dissolving the dirt.

Artificial plants

Artificial plants have come a long way since they were first introduced and now look more realistic than ever. Their durability also makes them suitable to be kept with fish that would destroy live plants and those that would eat the real thing. They are useful for hiding equipment and making areas feel more secure for nervous fish, and, of course, they will tolerate any type of water.

Why use artificial plants?

Many species of fish are found in the vicinity of live plants in the natural world, but they are there to eat them as well as use them for cover. Using artificial plants in place of live plants provides an effective solution to this problem, since they can provide cover without being on the menu.

In any case, growing live plants is not always straightforward and can turn a functional aquarium into something resembling a nursery, involving the use of high-specification lighting and fertilization (see pages 64–67). For those who want an easy life, artificial plants are a good idea, because all they will need is occasional cleaning.

Plastic plants

There is a huge range of plastic plants, and they replicate most species of aquatic plant and some terrestrial plants, too. They come in different sizes for planting in the foreground, midground, and background of the tank, and specimen plants are also available. You will discover that most types of plastic plant are modular in design, so that pieces

can be pulled off one stem and added to another. They are impervious to all medications and water conditions and, because of this, will last almost forever.

Silk plants

Silk is an alternative material for replica aquarium plants, and because it is a finer material than plastic, the plants move in the water more naturally and have realistic leaf shapes. They are cheap and can be mixed with live plants and not stand out as being fakes. Many types are available and they are easily anchored in the gravel.

Plant mats

Plastic plants are also available on square mats designed to be placed in the substrate. Each mat contains a number of the same plants, mimicking the complete planting schemes used in display aquariums, and the effect can be quite dramatic. Each plant can be removed to introduce irregularity into the design or to accommodate other decor, such as rocks or wood.

Below Plastic plants come in all shapes and sizes to replicate live plants and are tough and durable.

Cleaning artificial plants

A plastic plant-cleaning solution especially for use with aquariums is available, but plastic plants can also simply be washed under the tap. Use an old toothbrush to reach the stubborn areas. Alternatively, add a little household bleach to tap water to make a mild solution. Make sure the solution is deep enough to cover the plants completely, put them in the solution, and they should soon be clean and looking new again. Make up a separate solution of tap water in which to plunge the plants and remove the residue from the bleach. To make extra sure that all traces of the bleach are removed, give them a lengthy rinse under the tap, and they will then be ready to place back in the aquarium. Always wear gloves to protect your hands when cleaning in this way.

Silk plants are quite durable and can be cleaned with an abrasive pad or a plastic plant-cleaning solution formulated for aquatic use.

Tip

There are many species of algae-eating fish, including the bristle-nose catfish (*Ancistrus temminckii*) (see page 154) and the red-tailed black shark (*Epalzeorhynchus bicolor*) (see page 152), which are well adapted to consume the algae that form on the leaves of artificial plants. By adding some of these fish to your tank, they may well do the job of cleaning for you and acquire a source of food at the same time.

Backgrounds

An appropriate background is important if you want to imitate an underwater scene in your aquarium. They can give the effect of increased depth and can also hide any trailing cables. Internal and external backgrounds can be purchased, or you can make one yourself. Three-dimensional backgrounds are popular and provide an instant aquascape.

The benefits of backgrounds

Fish can benefit greatly from a background. First, it can help them to feel more secure by being able to swim up against it and know that nothing will approach them from that side. Second, dark backgrounds show the coloration of fish to best effect, giving them a more natural appearance, which in turn gives you greater viewing pleasure.

Paper backgrounds

These come in many styles but are usually a laminated print of an underwater scene. Plain versions are also available, in blue and black, and they have the advantage of not detracting from

the natural beauty of the fish. They can be attached to the outside glass with tape or applied inside the aquarium, where the picture will become much more visible. If fixing to the outside of the tank, make sure that no water gets between the paper and the glass, otherwise wet patches will be highlighted.

Structured backgrounds

These add rather more realism to the aquascape because they are actual three-dimensional backgrounds that are fitted to the inside of the

Below A paper background showing a print of a real, decorated aquarium containing live plants.

Tip

Always buy a little more than you need of a paper background, then trim it to length after partly fastening it in place.

aquarium. Some are realistic models of rock faces and tree stumps, and they protrude far into the tank, creating real depth. Others are relatively flat impressions of tree bark. All are made synthetically and can be cut to size and glued in place permanently to the back glass using aquarium-grade silicone adhesive. However, this process can be impeded by the design of the bracing bars across the top of the tank, so investigate their suitability before purchasing, as they can be quite expensive and will be a waste if they will not fit into the tank.

Do-it-yourself backgrounds

Making your own background allows you to put your individual imagination and creativity to use. A homemade background can be as simple as applying a coat of gloss paint to the outside glass to provide permanent color, or as elaborate as designing a three-dimensional image. Styrofoam blocks can be carved or melted into shapes resembling rock faces, and they can then be painted or covered in sand to give a realistic finish. Cork floor tiles have also been used with success, and ferns and mosses can be tied to them with fine fishing line so that they grow up the vertical sides. Alternatively, you can thread a needle with the fishing line and actually stitch the roots to the cork tiles.

Rocks can be stacked along the back glass to provide a real rock face, which will be appreciated by many species of fish. Choose flat rocks, like slate, to form vertical heaps or stack carved lava rock to provide lots of nooks and crannies (see page 52). Rock fragments can also be used to great effect by gluing the pieces to the glass using aquarium-grade silicone adhesive.

Before you fit a homemade background, it is wise to make a mock-up by fitting a background in a cardboard box that is the same size as your aquarium. If you change your mind halfway through, your tank will still be intact.

Tip

Whatever material you decide to use for your homemade background, make sure that it is completely safe for aquarium use, and check that once it is permanently fastened, no fish can get stuck behind it or use it to stay out of the way of the net.

The benefits of live plants

Aquatic plants can look stunning when they are properly displayed, but they offer many additional benefits to the aquarium and its inhabitants, as you will see. However, if they are to provide any of the following benefits, you will have to meet their needs, which includes providing appropriate lighting, fertilization, and substrates.

Filters

Because they are part of the nitrogen cycle (see page 110), growing plants can aid water quality in the aquarium. Nitrates and phosphates are used by plants as natural fertilizers, and heavily planted tanks will contain very little of these chemicals, as the plants will have used them up. This low-nitrate environment will help to keep the fish in good health, as their natural habitats are low in nitrate, and fish have evolved to suit those conditions.

Establishing an ecosystem

Planted aquariums can take over the main role of biological filtration in the tank, and tiny ecosystems can be formed. Carefully designed planted tanks with live fish can be established without the use of filters, and they act in the same way as planted pools do in nature, with the plants using up all the nutrients. To avoid problems, fish numbers have to be very low and feeding very closely monitored. Also, if ammonia were to become present at any point—for example, from a dying fish—then the plants would not be able to remove the ammonia as quickly as a colony of

Tip

Plants can also utilize toxic ammonia from the fishes' waste products, which is a huge benefit to aquariums. New tanks with a lot of growing plants will not experience such erratic increases in ammonia levels as those without, and the whole system will be much more stable (see pages 112–13).

Aquatic plants in the aquarium
1. Submerged plants take nutrients from the substrate and the water
2. Floating plants can use abundant CO_2 from the air
3. Immersed plants can take nutrients from the substrate and water and CO_2 from the air

 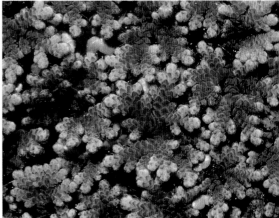

Above and above right Floating plants, such as *Pistia stratiotes* (above) and *Azolla* spp. (above right), soak up nitrates and phosphates and cut down available light, helping to kill off algae.

aerobic filter bacteria (see pages 38–39). This type of tank should be attempted only by the experienced aquarists.

Controlling algae

Nitrate and phosphate will encourage unsightly algal growth, but in planted aquariums, as we have seen above, these chemicals are largely used up by the plant life, making it much more difficult for algae to take hold. Planting can also cut down the available light reaching surfaces such as gravel, and less light can mean less algae. Heavily planted tanks that are properly maintained may well contain no algae whatsoever, which is very rare in freshwater and marine aquariums, and every other aquarium contains some unsightly algae in one form or another.

Providing aeration

As plants photosynthesize, they use carbon dioxide (CO_2) and produce oxygen. In the daytime, planted aquariums will be full of dissolved oxygen and fish will be healthy (see page 42). Systems using carbon dioxide fertilization (see page 65) should be stocked slowly with fish, and fish and aerobic filter bacteria will naturally adapt to changing oxygen levels throughout the day, making extra aeration unnecessary.

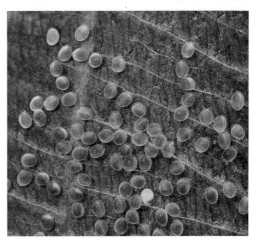

Above Large-leaved plants may be used as spawning sites by egg-depositing fish, like some cichlids.

Spawning

Plant leaves have many uses when it comes to aiding some fish species to spawn. Fine-leaved, feathery plants, such as *Myriophyllum aquaticum*, and *Cabomba caroliniana* (see pages 74 and 70), can be used to catch the eggs falling from egg-scattering fish that spawn overhead. Large-leaved plants are often picked by angelfish (*Pterophyllum scalare*) and harlequins (*Rasbora heteromorpha*) (see pages 146 and 153) as spawning sites. Surface vegetation is also used by bubble-nesters to anchor their nests (see pages 189–90).

Growing live plants

Growing plants underwater is not as simple as growing plants outdoors in a garden. The sterile substrate of most aquariums is there to anchor plants but offers no nutrient value, and lighting for too long with the wrong spectrum can cause nuisance algae, which will choke the already weakened plants. An aquarium specially set up to promote plant growth is the answer.

Lighting

All aquatic plants need light. Some need more than others, but on average, aquariums lit by two or more light tubes are preferable for plant growth (see page 49). Daylight and plant-growth tubes should be used in combination to provide a rich illumination that mimics tropical sunshine and promotes photosynthesis. Cover glasses (see page 29) should be cleaned regularly to let maximum light penetrate through to the plants.

Lights should be placed on a timer, set to come on for 10–12 hours a day—any longer will promote algae. Indeed, the leaves of *Hygrophila polysperma* appear to close if exposed to light for long. To maximize light penetration, fit reflectors to each tube (see page 46).

Substrates

For a substrate to be beneficial to plants it must be deep enough for the roots to grow and fine enough to hold nutrients but not let too much water flow through. For this reason, larger,

smoother substrates should be avoided and finer grained substrates, like silica sand, fine quartz, and silver sand, used instead (see pages 50–51). They can be mixed together, but bear in mind that smaller grains will eventually work their way to the bottom, so always place silver sand at the bottom if combining substrates.

Substrates should be added to a depth of 2–4 inches (5–10 cm) and can be sloped from back to front to give an illusion of depth. Wash all substrates thoroughly; once in the aquarium, dust can cover leaves and hinder growth.

Substrate heating

Heating the substrate by installing heating cables is of benefit to plants. This is because the convection currents created by heating cables are gentle and slow when compared to currents from pumps, so the gentle warming of the substrate replicates the warmth of the sun and slowly makes nutrients available to the plants' roots. The cables are of low wattage and do not need to

Below Laterite granules contain fertilizers that will promote root development in live plants.

Below A heating cable creates gentle convection currents within the substrate to encourage growth.

be connected to a thermostat. Heating cables should be fitted before a substrate is added.

Filters

The best filters for planted aquariums are those that have a large biological capacity and a turnover that is not too strong (see pages 32–35). Aim to turn the aquarium volume over not more than three times an hour and place the outlet of the filter 2 inches (5 cm) under the water to avoid oxidizing all the nutrients. Venturis and other aeration devices should not be used for this reason (see pages 42–43).

The filter should be set up before any fish are placed in the aquarium. Aerobic filter bacteria will be present in aquariums containing fish and will be in a quantity that relates to the amount of waste and oxygen present. Moving the outlet 2 inches (5 cm) under the water on an existing setup will cause less oxygen to be created, depriving filter bacteria and fish, which have been lost in this way. Therefore, set the filter up, put plants in the tank, then stock slowly with fish. In that way, the bacteria will grow to suit the conditions.

Carbon should be removed from filters in planted aquariums because it soaks up plant foods (see page 40).

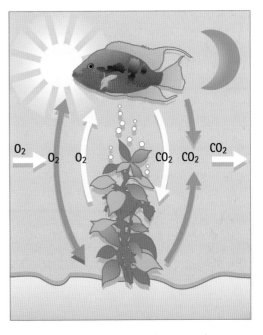

Above As live plants photosynthesize, oxygen is produced in the daytime and carbon dioxide is produced at night.

Plant fertilizers

Fertilizers come in three forms: liquid, tablet, and carbon dioxide (CO_2). An aquarium with proper lighting and substrate will still be lacking in plant foods, which growing plants need to develop their structures. Liquid plant food is the easiest to administer and should be added once a week. Calculate the dosage carefully, since overdosing may result in algae taking a hold. Some species that do not form large rootstocks, such as *Myriophyllum aquaticum*, *Cabomba caroliniana* (see pages 74 and 70), and *Elodea* spp., can grow quite well on liquid plant food alone.

Tablet fertilizers can be dropped into the tank or placed in the substrate and are of benefit to species that have large rootstocks, such as Amazon sword plants *Echinodorus bleheri* (see page 72). They are a more direct way of feeding plants and last longer than liquid foods, but many aquarists use a combination of both.

Tip

To obtain good plant growth, remember the following points. Plants need:
- good lighting
- the right substrate
- fertilization

Carbon dioxide

Using carbon dioxide (CO_2) in an aquarium may seem like a retrograde step to a new fishkeeper, because carbon dioxide is harmful to fish and, if it is present in too great a quantity, can kill fish and filter bacteria. So why would we want to add it to the tank? The answer is because plants absorb CO_2 and use it as part of the photosynthesizing process. Carbon (derived from carbon dioxide) is a building block, and plants cannot do without it. Photosynthesis creates oxygen, which is released into the water to the benefit of fish and filter bacteria.

The benefits of using carbon dioxide fertilization for aquatic plants are noticeable, and some species cannot be properly cultivated without it. To understand why plants benefit from carbon dioxide fertilization, we must look at how it occurs in nature.

Carbon dioxide in the natural environment

Most aquatic plants in the natural world do not grow in the main rivers, where, in a similar way to an aquarium, they are devoid of plant foods, such as iron, and there is little or no fertilizer in the substrate. Moreover, the water is well oxygenated and fast flowing. Instead, plants grow in abundance in shallow pools and muddy, nutrient-rich streams. Here, the flow of water is less strong, and particles of matter settle to the bottom, forming a rich loam through which the plants' roots take up their food.

In the shallows the light is intense and the water holds less oxygen than in the main river. The plants produce oxygen as they photosynthesize and take up CO_2 from the water, and when their stalks reach the surface, their leaf type changes to one that can take up even more CO_2 from the atmosphere.

The aquarium is just like the river and needs to be changed to conditions like that of a pond or stream if plants are to thrive, which includes slowing the water flow and adding fertilizers and bright light. However, we want to grow the plants that usually take their CO_2 from the surface when they become marginal plants as entirely submerged species so that we can view the intricate submerged form of the plant. So CO_2 is added to the water to feed the plants.

How to add CO_2

As we have seen, carbon dioxide can be harmful to animals and fish if too much is present, so it needs to be added slowly and in a controlled manner so that the plants use it up quickly and replace it with oxygen through photosynthesis. CO_2 units come in two main types: pressurized cylinder systems and basic systems that utilize CO_2 as the by-product from mixing yeast and sugar. Pressurized systems are better because dosing can be controlled with valves and the system can be shut off at night, when the plants themselves produce CO_2 and take up oxygen.

CO_2 is added to the water by both types of system through the use of plastic tubing and a diffuser. When the tube is placed under water, the gas escapes from the end. A diffuser is then connected to the tube with the intention of holding that bubble under the water for a prolonged period so that it dissolves. The bubble makes its way up through a series of baffles, which are designed to slow its passage through the water, thus increasing contact time and diffusion into the water. By the time the bubble gets to the surface, it will have almost disappeared.

Planting a bunch plant

1. Remove the weighted strip from the plant (see page 78).

2. Remove the foam collar.

3. If there is more than one individual plant, divide them into separate plants, and cut away old roots with scissors.

4. Push the plant about 2 inches (5 cm) into the substrate with your fingers.

5. Pile up the substrate around the base of the plant.

Planting a potted plant

1. Remove the plastic basket from around the rootball.

2. Tease away the rock wool to expose the bare roots (see page 78).

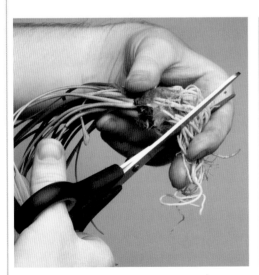

3. Separate into individual plants and trim any new, white roots with scissors.

4. Push the plant 2 inches (5 cm) into the substrate with your fingers. Pile up the substrate around the base of the plant.

Aquarium plant profiles

Planted aquariums are highly rated by aquarists and are regarded as among the most beautiful artistic creations to which one can aspire. A well-managed planted tank will not only be beneficial to the well-being of the fish within it, but the living picture that is created will also do a great deal to enhance the home environment that is around it.

What do the plant profiles tell you?

The most commonly available aquarium plant species are featured in the following plant profiles, which include information on their origins, size, and care requirements in the aquarium. The general comments are based on personal, hands-on experience, and there is also practical advice for those who wish to try growing the species.

Ease of keeping

A plant that is described as "easy" is one that many people have previously succeeded in growing, not always in perfect conditions, yet the plant has always shown signs of growth. An easy species may, therefore, be attempted by those of all skill levels in the hobby, including complete beginners. Do not forget, however, that the most basic requirement of all plants is light, and without light, and its correct duration, no plant will thrive.

Lighting conditions

Also listed in the profiles are each plant's lighting requirements. Dim lighting indicates an aquarium lit by only one fluorescent light tube without a reflector fitted; moderate lighting has one or two standard fluorescent tubes with reflectors fitted, and bright lighting means high-specification lighting consisting of three or more light tubes with reflectors, or pendant and metal halide lighting (see pages 46–49 and 208–9). Plants listed as requiring dim light will also grow well in bright light, but plants requiring bright light yet not receiving it will not grow well and may die.

Tip

Some fish species are notorious for being plant eaters, and goldfish (see pages 127–32) are among them. Fresh plant leaves and stems will prove too tempting to them, so opt for artificial plants instead (see pages 58–59) or no plants at all.

Water parameters

The profiles also cover the type of water needed by the species and any relevant comments about its habits and care. You will note that most species are happy in hard or soft water with a high or low pH. This is a testament to the hardiness of most species if their key requirements (light and fertilization) are met. Remember, however, that for the perfect planted aquarium RO (reverse osmosis) water (soft water) is used because of its low nitrate and phosphate values and the fact that soft water with a low pH can hold more CO_2 than hard water. RO water that has been remineralized and fertilized is always the best choice for all plant species.

Dragon Flame *Alternanthera reineckii*

Origin South America

Size 18 inches (45 cm)

Temperature 68–82°F (20–28°C)

Water parameters Soft and acidic, pH 6–7

Ease of keeping Moderate

Light conditions Bright

Comments This plant adds lovely red coloration to a planted tank that may otherwise be entirely green. For best results, use bright lighting and CO_2 injection (see page 66), because without it the leaves will turn green and the plant may start to struggle. Plant dragon flame towards the back because it quickly reaches the surface.

Anubias *Anubias barteri*

Origin Africa

Size 6 inches (15 cm)

Temperature 68–82°F (20–28°C)

Water parameters Soft to hard, pH 6–8

Ease of keeping Easy

Light conditions Dim to bright

Comments Anubias should be grown on wood or rocks and not in the substrate. This slow-growing plant has an appeal all of its own, and can be placed in all types of freshwater aquariums. There are several varieties of the species, including *Anubias barteri* 'Nana,' which has smaller leaves.

Giant Red Bacopa *Bacopa caroliniana*

Origin USA

Size 15 inches (38 cm)

Temperature 68-82°F (20–28°C)

Water parameters Soft to hard, pH 6–8

Ease of keeping Moderate

Light conditions Bright

Comments The leaves of this species turn quite red in bright light and given CO_2 fertilization (see page 66). It should be planted in the midground or background and is often used in aquariums featuring a relatively dense display of plants because it does not grow out of control like some other species.

Green Cabomba *Cabomba caroliniana*

Origin USA

Size 36 inches (90 cm)

Temperature 64–82°F (18–28°C)

Water parameters Soft to hard, pH 6–8

Ease of keeping Moderate

Light conditions Bright

Comments Cabomba is an excellent space filler and can be used to capture the eggs of egg-scattering fish (see page 188). It appreciates good lighting, and bunches should be separated into strands (see page 78). There is a red species, but it requires more light and CO_2.

Indian Fern *Ceratopteris thalictroides*

Origin Worldwide

Size 24 inches (60 cm)

Temperature 68–82°F (20–28°C)

Water parameters Soft to hard, pH 6–8

Ease of keeping Easy

Light conditions Bright

Comments Indian fern can also be grown as a floating plant, and it produces a different leaf shape when it is exposed to the atmosphere. It is easy to grow and suitable for many types of tropical aquarium. It is always more successful in bright light.

Crypt *Cryptocoryne wendtii*

Origin Sri Lanka

Size 6 inches (15 cm)

Temperature 68–82°F (20–28°C)

Water parameters Soft to hard, pH 6–8

Ease of keeping Easy

Light conditions Dim to bright

Comments Crypts are suitable for aquariums with low lighting, and they stay short, so can be grown in small tanks or placed at the front of larger tanks. The red tints in the dark green leaves of many crypts are attractive, and they are an undemanding species in general.

Amazon Sword Plant *Echinodorus bleheri*

Origin South America

Size 18 inches (45 cm)

Temperature 68–86°F (20–30°C)

Water parameters Soft to hard, pH 6–8

Ease of keeping Easy

Light conditions Moderate

Comments Amazon sword plants are readily available and make great midground specimen plants. They send out large root systems and appreciate the addition of substrate fertilizers (see page 65). Their large leaves may fall victim to overgrazing by algae-eating catfish (see pages 154–55), so make sure that the two are not combined.

Pygmy Chain Sword *Echinodorus tenellus*

Origin USA

Size 4 inches (10 cm)

Temperature 68–82°F (20–28°C)

Water parameters Soft, pH 6–7

Ease of keeping Moderate

Light conditions Bright

Comments This species should be planted in the foreground where it will spread rapidly by runners and form a thick carpet that will look effective. If given insufficient light, the plant will send out vertical runners and reach over other plants to gain more light. Do not combine with algae-eating catfish (see pages 154–55).

Water Wisteria *Hygrophila difformis*

Origin Southeast Asia

Size 18 inches (45 cm)

Temperature 72–82°F (22–28°C)

Water parameters Soft to hard, pH 6–8

Ease of keeping Easy

Light conditions Bright

Comments This plant is a good space filler and provides an interesting texture in any planting scheme. Bunches should be separated into individual plants (see page 78) and grown in a small space so that the lower leaves are not shed. Plant either in the midground or background of the aquarium.

Java Fern *Microsorium pteropus*

Origin Southeast Asia

Size 12 inches (30 cm)

Temperature 64–82°F (18–28°C)

Water parameters Soft to hard, pH 6–8

Ease of keeping Easy

Light conditions Dim to bright

Comments Java fern is a hardy plant that should be tied to a rock or piece of wood and not grown in the substrate (see pages 64–66). Its leaves are tough enough to withstand some plant-eating fish species. It propagates by producing plants at the ends of its leaves, which can be removed and replanted.

Brazilian Milfoil *Myriophyllum aquaticum*

Origin Worldwide

Size 24 inches (60 cm)

Temperature 64–82°F (18–28°C)

Water parameters Soft to hard, pH 6–8

Ease of keeping Moderate

Light conditions Bright

Comments This species is a good space filler and can act as a spawning mop for egg-scattering fish species (see page 188). It often arrives bunched, and stems should be removed before planting (see page 78). Use bright lighting and CO_2 fertilization to get the best from the plant (see pages 48 and 66).

Crystalwort *Riccia fluitans*

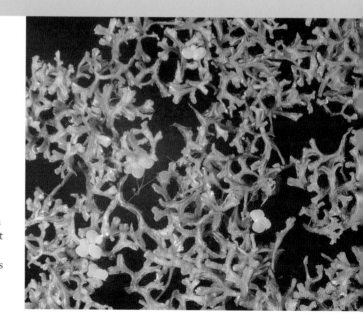

Origin Worldwide

Size ½ inches (1.25 cm)

Temperature 64–82°F (18–28°C)

Water parameters Soft to hard, pH 6–8

Ease of keeping Moderate

Light conditions Bright

Comments This beautiful bright green floating plant is always purchased in portions, as the tiny strands mat together. If it is grown on the surface as a floating plant, it grows well, since it receives bright light and abundant CO_2 (see pages 48 and 66).

Vallisneria *Vallisneria americana*

Origin Asia

Size 36 inches (90 cm)

Temperature 68–82°F (20–28°C)

Water parameters Soft to hard, pH 6–8

Ease of keeping Easy

Light conditions Moderate

Comments Vallisneria, a popular background plant, is typical of aquatic plants that have long leaves that sway in the flow of water. It is hardy and will grow in nearly all water conditions, making it suitable for any freshwater setup. It spreads very rapidly by sending out runners.

Java Moss *Vesicularia dubyana*

Origin Southeast Asia

Size 2 inches (5 cm)

Temperature 64–82°F (18–28°C)

Water parameters Soft to hard, pH 6–8

Ease of keeping Easy

Light conditions Dim to bright

Comments Java moss is an excellent addition to any tropical tank; it is easy to grow and provides valuable cover and spawning sites for fish. It does well in all conditions, but bright light and CO_2 make the moss grow thick, like a carpet (see pages 48 and 66).

Arranging the decorative elements

How you arrange the decoration in your aquarium can have a dramatic impact on the effect it will create on the viewer. Compositions can range from a formal planting scheme to a mountain stream with boulders placed haphazardly or a pristine coral reef with life covering every available surface. There are also some tricks that you can employ to make your tank appear to be a different shape.

Substrates

The first factor that can have a significant effect on the look of the tank is the color of the substrate (see pages 50–51). Light-colored substrates, such as coral sand, silver sand, and quartz, can brighten up the tank and when illuminated will always make the tank look light and sunny. Dark substrates, on the other hand, will absorb light and produce a more moody impression of shady backwaters and forest streams. Dark colors can also really enhance the rich coloration of the plants and fish in the aquarium and make the tank look more atmospheric and mysterious.

If you create a sloping layer of substrate, it can bring an increased sense of depth to the tank as a whole.

Tall tank
1 Substrate at average depth
2 Tall driftwood used vertically
3 Tall plants break the surface

Making a tank appear taller

○ Use a thin layer of substrate.

○ If there are rocks, stack them up right to the surface of the water.

○ If you use driftwood (see page 54), obtain root look-alikes with vertical branches that will break the surface of the water.

○ If planting, use tall plants and plant them at one end of the aquarium, leaving an off-center space clear of plants. Also, bank the substrate more on one side than the other.

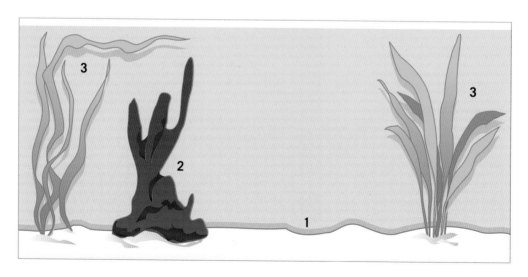

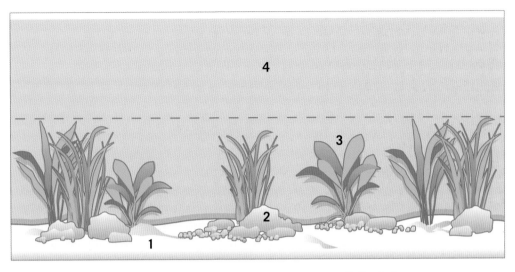

Shallow tank
1 Deep, even substrate
2 Rounded pebbles placed flat
3 Short plants planted across tank length
4 Area above halfway line left clear

Making a tank appear longer

○ Use around 4 inches (10 cm) substrate at an even depth across the tank base.

○ Aquascape with rocks or wood (see pages 52 and 54), placing them flat so that they do not reach more than halfway up the tank.

○ If using plants, choose short species that will not reach the surface of the water, and plant along the whole length of the tank. The end result when compared to the tall-tank approach above will be quite different.

Rocks

Rocks can be used singly to break up planting and complement plants or can be stacked to form a solid backdrop (see pages 52–53). For biotope setups (see pages 14–15), use authentic-looking rocks and match up the striations to give the illusion of an exposed escarpment. Place rocks in a way that they would naturally fall and not upright on their narrowest end. Avoid mixing too many types of rock, as this is not how they would be found in nature, and, in addition, do not combine smooth rocks with rough rocks.

If stacking rocks, clear the base and build the structure from it, so that if any fish dig around the structure at a later stage, they will not be able to undermine it by removing substrate and cause a fall. Use aquarium-grade silicone adhesive to anchor heavy rocks securely in place to make the rock stack much more stable, thus eliminating the risk of a rock fall.

Aquascaping effects

It is important to avoid symmetrical arrangements in your decorating scheme. Instead, plan your decoration to the left or right of center and build your aquascape around that point. The scene will look less contrived and more convincing.

Fish can even add to the depth illusion. Use narrow-bodied fish, such as danios, in tanks that are made to look long, and tall-bodied fish, such as angelfish, in tanks that are made to look tall.

Planting schemes

Arranging plants in an aquarium can be similar to planting a garden. Tall species should be planted towards the back and large species given room to grow. Some species clash strongly in terms of color and foliage, and this needs to be taken into consideration in the planting scheme, as do the varying requirements for light of different species.

Preventing algae

To prevent algae building up in the early days of establishing your planted aquarium, introduce a lot of plants from the start. A total of 50–60 individual plant stems in a 24 inch (60 cm) square aquarium should not be considered excessive. Choose species that will rocket to the surface of the water within days of planting, as they will strip the water of excess nutrients and provide shaded areas once they are at the surface.

Bunch plants

Cuttings that have been wrapped in a weighted metal strip at their base are an inexpensive way of buying plants. Many plants do not suffer from being treated in this way, and new roots will quickly form. Push them into a deep substrate at least 1 inch (2.5 cm) apart (see page 67).

Below The planting in this aquarium is so dense that it even covers the substrate.

Potted plants

Specimen plants and plants with a large root stock, such as *Echinodorus* spp. (see page 72), are best purchased in pots. They have been grown out of the water in high humidity where their leaves can take full advantage of bright light and CO_2 in the atmosphere. Instead of soil, they are grown in rock wool, which should be teased away from the roots before planting (see page 67). Potted plants are whole plants complete with root stock, and they are strong and can be relied on to establish quickly and grow heartily.

Plants that have been grown out of the water are known as immerse and have rigid leaves that can hold their own weight. When placed under the water and grown submerse, the immerse leaves will be shed and new, more delicate leaves will emerge to cope with the new environment.

Planting design techniques

You may argue that a natural-looking tank should not be arranged at all. However, you would not photograph a beautiful landscape with a tree in front of you. Although plant heights differ in the aquarium, most tanks are viewed only from the front and tall planting hides what is behind it.

Planting the tank is best carried out when the tank is half-full, when plants can be arranged and are less buoyant than when the tank is filled. Start by placing tall plants at the back, then specimen plants in the middle and finally foreground plants at the front. Planting will always look more effective if plants are in groups.

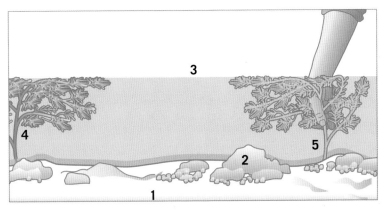

Planting a tank
1 Lay gravel first
2 Next add rocks
3 Half-fill the tank with water
4 Start at the rear corners
5 Push roots into substrate

Plant for pleasing effects
1 Plant in groups
2 Use different plants to complement each other
3 Short plants around rocks
4 Heavy planting prevents algae

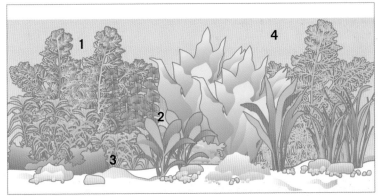

Ideal arrangement of plants
1 Slope substrate up towards the back of the tank
2 Place tall plants at the back
3 Place short plants at the front
4 Small, carpeting plants will cover some substrate as they grow

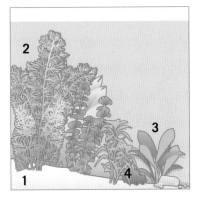

SETTING UP YOUR FIRST AQUARIUM

Safety precautions

Fishkeeping features the rare combination of water and electricity. If the two are improperly mixed, it will spell disaster. At best, the aquarist may receive a shock; at worst, an electrical shock can result in the death of the fish and, more importantly, the aquarist.

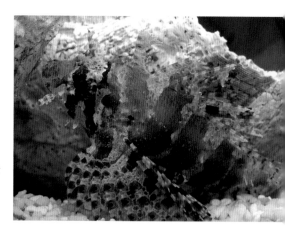

Above Lionfish have venomous spines so should never be handled and are an unwise choice for children.

Above right Moray eels can inflict real damage when they bite. Always feed them using aquarium tongs.

Above far right Never underestimate the power of a piranha's bite. They have evolved to eat flesh.

Electricity

Always use a qualified electrician for any electrical work and unplug equipment for maintenance. All equipment should be considered dangerous if the cables or plugs are damaged. All new equipment should come with a plug for the correct voltage.

Electricity dos and don'ts

Do
- ✔ Set up the aquarium a short distance away from the socket to avoid any water splashes from the tank
- ✔ Use a drip loop to collect any drips before using an electrical socket
- ✔ Plug equipment into an independent safety cut-off switch

Don't
- ✘ Stretch cables—have them extended by a professional
- ✘ Overload sockets
- ✘ Make your own junction boxes
- ✘ Do any electrical work over the surface of the water

Glass

Glass aquariums can be dangerous for obvious reasons, so do not place them where they will be in the way. New tanks may have sharp edges, so wear gloves when carrying them. Large tanks can be very heavy, so use proper lifting procedures (see page 31). Tanks full of water should never be lifted. This could cause injury or even a small flood.

Fish

Some fish can be dangerous and should be handled with care. Large predatory fish can cause serious wounds from biting, and huge "tankbusting" fish can cause injury through handling and aggression. There are also many venomous fish that should ideally not be handled at all. If they have to be handled, gloves must be worn and hands thoroughly washed afterwards.

Consult the chart opposite to see which fish must be treated with special care and caution, together with their relevant hazards.

Dangerous fish and their hazards

TYPE OF FISH	HAZARDS
Lionfish (*Dendrochirus* and *Pterois* spp.) (see page 239)	Venomous spines around the head; should not be handled
Pufferfish (*Arothron*, *Diodon* and *Tetraodon* spp.) (see page 237)	Poisonous skin and sharp spines when inflated; sharp teeth
Cichlids (see pages 144–147)	Larger cichlids invariably have teeth and a strong bite; some are also territorial
Piranha (*Serrasalmus* and *Pygocentrus* spp.)	Although mostly timid in captivity, they are capable of tearing flesh
Catfish (see pages 154–155)	Most carry erectable fin spines to avoid being swallowed by predators
Loaches (see pages 133 and 147–148)	Even clown loaches (*Botia macracantha*) (see page 147) carry spines by the eye that can become erect when stressed
Marine Angelfish (see pages 231–232)	Most have spines by the gill plate, used in fighting and in anti-predation
Tangs or Surgeonfish (see pages 229–230)	Tangs or surgeonfish have erectable spines near the base of the tail
Moray Eels (*Gymnothorax* spp.)	All have incredibly sharp, backward-pointing teeth that are not designed to let go, and the group have a bad attitude to match
Stingrays (*Potamotrygon* spp.)	All have a venomous spine at the end of the tail that can be raised and used to impale

Making tap water safe

Water from the tap is the chief source of water used in aquariums. A lot of time and money is used to sterilize tap water and make it safe for us to drink, but in the state that it reaches us, it can be harmful to fish and detrimental to an aquarium if it is not treated. For this reason, tap water must always be treated with a dechlorinating liquid before it is added to the tank. For a better understanding of exactly what chemicals are contained in your tap water, contact your local water supplier.

How tap water is harmful

Tap water comes to us in a sterilized state, fit to drink. Chlorine or chloramine is added to kill bacteria in the pipework along the way, but it will also kill beneficial bacteria in the aquarium and filter and may harm fish.

Dechlorinating tap water

Dechlorinators are good-value additives, and every aquarist should have enough to carry out several water changes (see pages 170–71). Dechlorinating solutions are available from all aquatic retailers. They are not expensive and can be bought in bulk to keep down the cost even further. They get to work right away when added to tap water, leaving no need for water to be preprepared. Overdosing causes no harm, and in hot weather double dosing is recommended because water authorities may increase levels of chlorine in the supply. As well as removing chlorine and chloramines, some dechlorinating solutions also neutralize heavy metals in the water supply.

Automated mixing

Alternatively, for automated mixing of the dechlorinating solution with tap water, you could also use a powerhead (a universal underwater pump) or airstone (see below), powered by an air pump. You can treat the whole volume of water before filling the aquarium with a hose.

Using an airstone to remove chlorine

An airstone is also known as an air diffuser. Air from an external air pump is pushed at pressure through a tube that is placed in the tap water. The air leaves the pipe and rises up through the water at great force. An airstone is placed on the end of the tube and breaks up the large bubbles of water into hundreds of much smaller ones so that they rise up to the surface at a less ferocious rate but break up the surface of the water more. This not only allows more carbon dioxide (CO_2) to escape from the water but also makes it possible for more oxygen to enter it. It will also drive off the chlorine from the water, in the form of gas, into the atmosphere. However, any chloramines in the water will remain, because they are not in gas form.

Using carbon to treat tap water

Carbon removes chlorine, chloramine, and metals from water, so it may also be regarded as a dechlorinator. For this purpose, it is used as a prefilter in reverse osmosis (RO) units (see page 84). It will become saturated and therefore needs to be replaced frequently—about once a month—to prevent it from leaching the chemicals and metals back into the water.

Using dechlorination as a stress reliever

Dechlorinating liquids can also be used as a stress reliever to aid the transportation of fish. Brands containing herbal extracts or *Aloe vera* are added to the water by retailers in preparation for long journeys or when fish that have been delivered after transportation are being acclimatized. Dechlorinating liquids can also be mixed with ammonia detoxifying solutions that come in a single bottle and can be used for emergencies or routinely when changing water. These liquids can literally save the lives of the inhabitants of the aquarium if testing reveals there are high levels of ammonia in the water.

Aquarists can also take advantage of the calming properties of these dechlorinating liquids when introducing new fish to the aquarium.

Treating water using a dechlorinating solution

1. Place a clean bucket under the tap and fill it with the recommended amount of cold water.

2. Use boiled water from a kettle and slowly add to the bucket until the chill has been taken away.

3. Check that the temperature is correct for the species that you keep. Add extra cold or hot water if necessary.

4. Pour in the dechlorinating solution at the ratio directed on the bottle.

5. Agitate the water to ensure that the solution has thoroughly dispersed in the water.

6. Pour the treated water onto a dish in the aquarium to avoid disturbing the decoration.

Water purifiers

Tap water that has been made safe for human consumption is not necessarily safe for use with fish. Many toxic materials may still be present, including metals, herbicides, chlorine, and pollutants. Phosphates and nitrates (see pages 108–9) also cause havoc in aquariums by fueling algal blooms, and they are coming straight out of the tap and into your tank.

Using reverse osmosis units

Reverse osmosis—RO for short—is an easy and practical way of removing the vast majority of contaminants from your tap water—not just chlorine and chloramines as with a dechlorinating liquid (see page 82). It is not a term with which many new aquarists will be familiar, but the process is quite simple. In RO water is pushed at pressure through a special membrane that lets pure water through to one side and leaves pollutants and dissolved solids on the other. The membrane is contained in a cylinder and is first prefiltered by a sediment filter and by carbon to remove the chlorine (see page 82).

The pure water exits the cylinder via a small-diameter hose and can then be collected in a bucket or larger container. The water containing the pollutants is called waste water and again exits via a hose, which can then be connected to a drain. RO water is very pure, with the reverse osmosis units removing 99.9 percent of all pollutants from tap water. For every 1 gallon (4.5 liters) of pure water produced from tap water, there will be about 4 gallons (18 liters) of waste water, but this can still be used to water plants in the garden if you wish.

Fitting an RO unit

When you buy an RO unit, you will find that it has three hoses in three different colors. One hose feeds off the water supply, one is the waste water hose, and the other is the RO water hose. Units are normally fitted underneath kitchen sinks or outside, where the water supply and drainage are easily accessible. They can be fitted by the aquarist with relative ease, but if you do not feel confident enough about doing the fitting yourself, consult a qualified plumber about the installation. If you are put off by the high initial purchase price of an RO unit or by

the thought of altering your household plumbing, RO water is available for sale in drums at specialized aquatic outlets.

Running costs

The amount of waste water produced by RO units may add a little to your water supply costs in the long term, and sediment and carbon prefilters need to be changed periodically. Membranes can last for up to 10,000 gallons (45,000 liters) of water before they need to be replaced, but they can be damaged by chlorine if the carbon prefilters are not changed often enough. You do, however, save on dechlorinating solutions, which would otherwise be added to tap water when you change the water.

Below An RO unit showing the blue inner membrane that demineralizes the water.

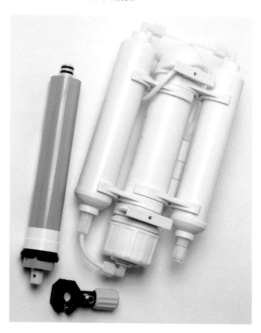

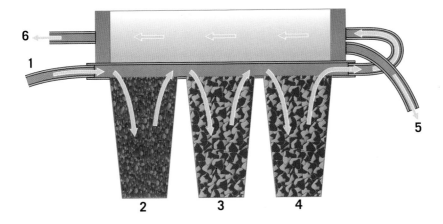

RO unit
1 Tap water feed
2 Sediment filter
3 Carbon filter
4 Carbon filter
5 Dechlorinated waste water
6 Pure RO water

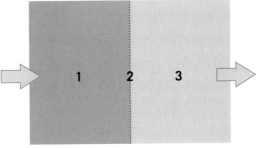

How an RO membrane works
1 Water containing dissolved solids
2 Membrane stops dissolved solids passing through
3 Only pure water passes through

The advantages of pure water

Pure water is an asset to all forms of aquarium fishkeeping, helping beginners and experts alike to achieve success in both establishing and maintaining aquatic life. Water that has been demineralized is very soft and so is a particular advantage to those who keep fish that originate from soft-water habitats such as the Amazon. Elements in the water that affect its pH are known as buffers (see page 105), and these are removed in the RO process. However, buffers, available from aquatic retailers can then be added to the pure water before it goes into the tank to achieve an exact match of pH and hardness with that of the water in which your chosen fish species lives in the wild. This benefits all freshwater and marine species, and RO water's pollutant-free properties are a special bonus when rearing hard-to-keep species and marine corals (see pages 204–5). It should also be used by anyone who is battling with algae, as water changes using normal tap water may be making the situation worse.

Tip

Do not completely fill a tank with RO water without first adding some minerals to it. Its pure, vacuous state can extract salts from fish in extreme cases, and the tank water is liable to become very acidic very quickly. Minerals are available from aquatic retailers.

Preparing to set up a coldwater aquarium

Now that your appetite has been sufficiently whetted and you have a basic understanding of how to prepare water and set up the underwater environment, it is time to set up your first tank. The coldwater aquarium is a good starting point, as it requires the least essential equipment and goldfish are universally available and easy to keep (see pages 127–32). Before you begin, bear the following factors in mind.

Tank size and stocking levels

With adult goldfish averaging 6 inches (15 cm) in length and requiring more oxygen in the water than tropical fish, a larger tank is recommended for their long-term welfare. In our example, the tank used is 24 inches (60 cm) in length, and once the filter has fully matured—within about six weeks of the initial setting up—it will hold four common goldfish or goldfish varieties. For your first aquarium, buy fish that are about 2 inches (5 cm) long. These will be young fish with a long life ahead of them, and they will not be expensive. They will also put less of a strain on the filter than larger fish. Once the fish reach 4 inches (10 cm)

in length, or if you want to increase your fish stock, then a move to suitably larger accommodation is recommended.

Filtration

The chosen filter for our example setup is an internal power filter (see page 35), selected because of its mechanical filtering capacity (see page 38) and because it is easy to fit. An air pump has been added for extra aeration and to provide a stream of bubbles to rise through the water column (see page 42). If the internal filter comes with a Venturi device, then it is recommended that it is used without an air pump.

Shopping list for the coldwater aquarium

- ○ 24 inch (60 cm) glass tank
- ○ cabinet
- ○ internal power filter
- ○ air pump
- ○ air line and accessories
- ○ substrate
- ○ stones
- ○ ornament
- ○ artificial plants
- ○ dechlorinating solution
- ○ light tube
- ○ light starter unit
- ○ hood
- ○ condensation tray (may not be required)

Above This internal power filter can be used with or without a Venturi device, but aeration is recommended.

Water

Coldwater aquariums kept indoors will not strictly be cold all the time. Heated houses and hot summers may increase the temperature to 68–73°F (20–23°C) or even tropical temperatures. Goldfish can adapt to these temperatures over time (an indication of their overall hardiness) and will survive in all but extreme temperatures, so do not panic. Also, if you are changing the water (see pages 170–71), add some water from the hot tap to match the room temperature, as a change to very cold tap water can cause shock and bring on whitespot (see page 180).

The water used is dechlorinated tap water (see page 82), which is perfectly adequate for goldfish and is a cheaper option than RO water (see page 84). If you want the best for the fish, use RO water with added minerals and set to a pH of 7.5. The use of RO water may also help to deter the growth of algae, which can very rapidly build up in the cool, well-oxygenated, plantless environment of the coldwater aquarium.

Above Plastic plants are the only practical choice for goldfish tanks because live plants may be eaten.

Below Pea gravel is a good choice of substrate, as its grains are rounded and will not damage a fish's mouth.

Step-by-step guide to setting up a coldwater aquarium

Before you begin work on setting up, make sure that you have all the equipment on the shopping list on page 86. You should also have a towel to dry your hands and a few extra buckets for containing washed substrates and for filling the tank. Set the tank up during the day so that you can make a trip to your aquatic retailer if necessary. Make sure you have help on hand for lifting heavy objects.

1. Once you have chosen where the aquarium is going to be situated (see page 30), place it in its permanent position and start to add the equipment. The first and most important piece of equipment to be added is the filter. This internal power filter (see page 35) should be placed in one of the rear corners of the tank, just under the surface.

2. Coldwater fish require well-oxygenated water, especially when they are kept in a warm room, so it is a good idea to add additional aeration in the form of an air pump (see page 42). First, connect an airstone (see page 82) to a PVC or silicone air line and fasten it to the side of the tank. When running, the airstone will naturally want to float, so avoid this by attaching it with rubber suckers.

3. Place the air pump on a flat surface near the aquarium. If the pump is placed below the waterline, it is essential to fit a nonreturn valve to prevent water back-siphoning down the air line when the power is turned off.

4. Wash the substrate in a bucket to remove all dust and debris. Then cover the tank bottom with the washed substrate to a depth of about 2 inches (5 cm). The gravel used here is pea gravel (see page 50), which is lime free, so it will not affect the pH of the water (see pages 104–5), and has well-rounded grains, making it safe for goldfish.

5. Add some washed, round stones to the gravel bottom and decorate as you wish. Remember that washed stones are heavy and slippery, so lower them carefully into the tank so that you do not drop them. The stones used are also lime free.

6. This imitation log will add interest to the tank for the fish and for the owner. Goldfish will graze around the bottom of it and loaches (see pages 133 and 147–48) will hide under it. This log has been specially designed to be used in aquariums and is safe to use with all types of fish.

7. Fill the aquarium with tap water and bring it to room temperature with water from a kettle. A temperature between 59° and 68°F (15–20°C) will be fine for coldwater fish like goldfish. Fill the tank to within about 2 inches (5 cm) of the top of the tank.

8. Goldfish eat live plants, so for decoration use artificial plants instead (see pages 58–59). As with live plants, position short ones at the front and tall ones at the back. Leave some room in the tank for the fish to swim freely. Artificial plants can be used to disguise the equipment in the tank.

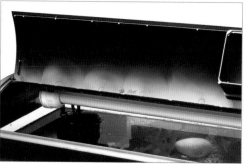

9. Always make tap water safe for the fish by adding dechlorinating solution to the water (see page 82). Some solutions also neutralize heavy metals in the tap water. Calculate the tank volume and treat the water with the dechlorinating liquid, which will get to work immediately. Ideally, leave the tank for a week to allow conditions to stabilize and bacteria levels to increase before you add fish.

10. Choose a light that will bring out the rich colors of the goldfish. A fluorescent tube (see page 46) is the best choice, as they are low in wattage compared with bulbs and have a longer life.

11. Fit the lighting into the hood and place the hood on top of the aquarium. Depending on the manufacturer, your aquarium may or may not need a condensation tray to keep water off the lighting. Check with your retailer when purchasing the setup.

12. The tank setup is now complete. Plug in the filter and air pump and run for a week with no fish. Leave the lights off for the first week, as there are no live plants, which will help to discourage nuisance algae. Stock slowly, starting with two goldfish (see pages 127–32).

Troubleshooting

○ The filter should show signs of clearing the water within a period of around 24 hours. All new aquariums will be slightly cloudy because of the dust particles within the gravel, but you may find that the water goes very milky after about a week, which is known as bacterial bloom. Test the water to ensure that the quality is OK, and it should clear within another few days. The process can be speeded up by adding a specially formulated bacterial bloom-clearing solution.

Preparing to set up a tropical aquarium

The tropical aquarium is a popular choice because there are plenty of fish species available, ranging from tiny fish to suit small tanks, right through to specimen fish and species that provide more of a challenge to the aquarist. In the aquarium, species will exhibit the same behavior patterns that they have in the wild; for example, species that naturally shoal or that are adapted to occupy different areas of the underwater environment will do so in a tank.

Tank size and stocking levels

There is a species to suit all sizes of tropical aquarium, from 12 inches (30 cm) upwards, but for a community of small fish, including several species, and a display of live plants, a tank of 3 square feet (0.28 sq m) is recommended. This will be large enough to accommodate shoals of small fish as well as one or two larger fish with an adult size up to about 4 inches (10 cm) in length. Remember that the emphasis should be on creating a "community" tank, and therefore all the chosen species should happily coexist with each other in the long term. This means that no territorial or predatory fish should be included in the setup.

Filtration

The tank can hold up to 25 small and medium-sized fish when fully stocked (after six weeks or more from the time of the initial setting up), so filtration should be chosen to cope with those demands. A multistage internal filter (see page 35) has been added to our example tank to filter mechanically, biologically, and chemically, if necessary. It will also bring reassurance to anyone who is concerned about external filters springing a leak (see pages 36–37). Multistage filters normally come with carbon filters (see page 40), which will soak up the food added for the plants, so remove it completely before setting up if you are planning a planted aquarium, as in our example.

Below Driftwood is a popular choice for tropical tanks, as it brings a natural look to the tank.

Shopping list for the tropical aquarium

- ○ 3 square foot (0.28 sq m) glass tank
- ○ multistage internal filter
- ○ heater/thermostat
- ○ substrate
- ○ rocks
- ○ driftwood
- ○ dechlorinating solution
- ○ live plants

- ○ net
- ○ thermometer
- ○ plant food
- ○ light tubes
- ○ reflectors
- ○ 2 light starter units or 1 double light starter unit
- ○ hood

Water

The water used in our example tank is dechlorinated tap water (see page 82), but the best choice is to use RO (reserve osmosis) water (see page 84). RO water will keep nuisance algae at bay, which would ruin the plant displays, and it is also physically brighter than normal tap water. Tropical fish come from habitats varying greatly in pH (see pages 104–5), so in a community tank, where several species must be catered to, either choose hardy fish that will thrive in all conditions or choose species that naturally prefer similar water conditions and temperature, of which there are plenty. If your tap water has a pH of between 7 and 7.5, it will be suitable for most species. If it is any higher, many South American species will not thrive, so use RO water and set the pH to the optimum requirements of the fish species.

Plants

The example aquarium will be set up with the dual purpose of growing healthy plants as well as rearing healthy fish. The plant species used, like the fish, are recommended for beginners and should all do well in the conditions provided. Do not stock any fish species that may eat plants, as the display will be quickly ruined. Do not forget also that as well as being fed weekly on liquid fertilizer, plants need the right type of lighting (see pages 48–49) for the right duration (10–12 hours per day), so the use of a timer is recommended.

Above The tank decor will benefit the fish by providing areas of cover, and the live plants aid filtration.

Step-by-step guide to setting up a tropical aquarium

Before you begin work on setting up the aquarium, check that you have all the items on the shopping list on page 93. Make sure you have a towel to dry your hands. An aquarium of this size will need to be lifted into place by two people, one at each end. When you are using several pieces of electrical equipment, as in this case, make sure that you site the tank near a sufficient number of electrical sockets (see pages 30–31).

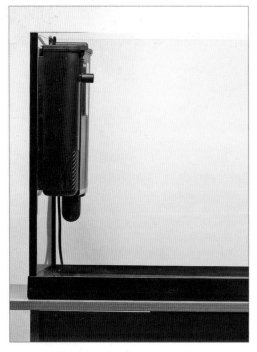

1. Once the tank is in position, add the filter, which in this case is a multistage internal filter (see page 35). Place it at the back of the tank so that the water level in the tank when it is full is between the stipulated levels on the filter box. This filter has a Venturi device fitted (see pages 42–43), which means that it can create its own aeration if necessary.

2. Place a suitably sized heater/thermostat (see page 44) in the compartment inside the filter. Not all filters will have room to accommodate a heater, but if they have, it means that the heater will be protected and will provide a more even heat distribution.

3. The substrate used here is washed silica sand (see pages 50–51), which will provide suitable anchoring for the live plants and is a neutral color, so it will complement rather than compete with the colors of the fish and decoration. Silica sand is lime free and is suitable for all types of freshwater aquarium.

4. This rock pile will provide a suitable refuge for catfish (see pages 154–55) and other fish that like to hide during the day. Position the bottom rock on the base of the tank by clearing an area of sand. This will prevent the rocks from being undermined by fish, causing a rock fall.

5. Driftwood is an ideal, natural product for adding to freshwater aquariums (see page 54) and can be used to mimic fallen trees and driftwood on the bottom of a river. New driftwood will stain the water brown as the tannic acids are leached from within it, but this can be removed by the addition of carbon (see page 40).

6. Half-fill the tank with tap water ready for planting. It is a good idea to bring the water to the correct temperature and dechlorinate it before planting (see page 82). Live plants can be shocked by untreated tap water at the wrong temperature, just as fish can be.

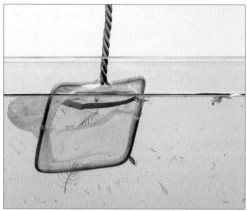

7. Begin planting when the water is ready. Bunch plants should be removed from their weights and planted singly (see page 66). Potted plants should be removed from their pots and the rock wool teased away from the roots (see page 67). Plant tall species at the back and short species at the front (see page 78). Plant quite heavily to help combat the growth of nuisance algae.

8. Fill the tank up to the top with water that is of the correct temperature. The live plants should straighten up towards the surface, and any that start to float should be replanted. Use an aquarium net to remove any shed or floating leaves from the surface of the water.

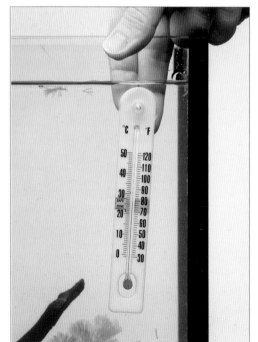

9. Fit a thermometer to the inside of the glass and plug in the filter and heater/thermostat. The heater/thermostat should now regulate the temperature to the required setting.

10. Add plant fertilizers in the form of liquid or substrate tablets (see page 66). A heavily planted tank designed to grow plants to form a beautiful underwater garden should also have some additional CO_2 fertilization. Some plants are hardy enough not to need CO_2 and will grow well using good lighting and liquid food alone.

11. Fit light tubes that encourage plant growth (see pages 48–49). This hood uses two, but some hoods can accommodate more. If your hood takes only one light tube, fit a high-output tube to maximize available light in the aquarium for the plants. Plug the lights into a timer and set it to come on for 10–12 hours per day.

12. The new tank is now complete. All equipment should now be plugged in, and the tank should be left to mature for a week before any fish are introduced. The plants will soon settle in, and some fast-growing species will head up to the surface of the water in a short space of time. Test the water before adding any fish just to make sure that there is no ammonia or nitrate in the water (which can sometimes occur even without the presence of fish) and that the pH is within the desired range (see pages 100–1).

Troubleshooting

○ Before introducing substrates to an aquarium, make sure that they are thoroughly rinsed to remove traces of dirt and debris. Failure to do so may result in cloudy water for weeks afterwards.

○ Make sure that the chosen filtration system can cope with your intended fish when they reach adult size. Having to buy a larger filter later on will be a false economy.

○ Test the aquarium water to make sure that it is safe before you add your first fish, as well as regularly afterwards. The first six-week period after setting up is when the water conditions are at their most unstable.

Getting the tank ready

A mature filter is a key part of the success of any aquarium system. All new filters, no matter how good they are, are sterile when they are first fitted and will need beneficial bacteria to grow inside them if they are to break down fish waste effectively.

Preparation

For any filter and tank to mature, the water must first of all be free of any chlorine and chloramines. These additives are placed in drinking water to kill bacteria, making it safe for human consumption, but they also have a negative effect on filter bacteria, so should be neutralized by using a dechlorinating solution (see page 82). Although these get to work almost right away, you should leave the filter running for 24 hours before adding any filter bacteria for safety.

Types of bacteria

Raw fish waste contains ammonia, and this is converted into nitrite by a strain of bacteria called nitrosomonas. Nitrite is then converted by nitrobacter bacteria into nitrate (see page 108). Nitrate is then utilized by growing plants or removed through water changing. As a filter matures, nitrosomonas and nitrobacter expand in number in both the filter media and on the surfaces of aquarium decoration.

Below This sponge is covered not only with dirt but also with invisible bacteria. A cleaning in old tank water is all it needs to maintain it.

Tip

Filter bacteria are aerobic and will benefit and increase in number when given lots of oxygen. In heavily stocked tanks the use of extra aeration will benefit fish and filters alike (see pages 42–43).

A newly set up tank will not contain either strain of bacteria in any sufficient amount until the first fish are added. Once fish have been introduced, nitrosomonas can then grow to consume the ammonia, followed by nitrobacter to consume the nitrite. Many problems with new tanks occur when there is more ammonia being produced by the fish than there are bacteria to consume it (see pages 112–13).

Bacteria cultures

These are of great benefit to the aquarist and have helped to save the lives of many early fish introductions. They come in bottles and can be found alongside water treatments in aquatic retail outlets. They consist of millions or even billions of beneficial bacteria in a concentrated form that is ready to be poured into tanks.

This boost of bacteria can shorten the time that a tank takes to mature, helping to lower levels of nitrite and ammonia that are on the rise in new tanks, so that the process is completed in five weeks or less rather than the usual six weeks. Established tanks can also benefit from weekly additions of bacteria, which can also help to break down detritus and control algae.

Some brands will need to be refrigerated after opening to keep the bacteria healthy, whereas others have had food added to prolong the colonies' shelf-life.

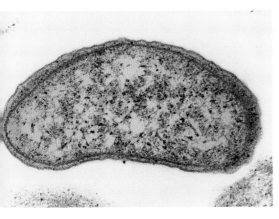

Above Microscopic bacteria are at work in the millions in a mature filter, breaking down waste produced by fish.

Hardy fish

A tank can be made ready for more fish by adding a few hardy fish to begin with. Species of fish that will tolerate ammonia and nitrite are added after one week and fed as normal. The maturation process will begin when a test kit (see page 100) indicates the rise and fall of ammonia levels, then of nitrite, resulting in maturation. When fish are added, the functional bacteria can quickly expand in number to accommodate the additions and prevent further increases in levels of ammonia and nitrite.

The use of hardy fish combined with slow stocking is a tried-and-tested method of tank maturation and is recommended by experts the world over.

Fishless cycling

This process is becoming more popular because it does not put any stress on even hardy fish and can allow heavy initial stocking. Raw ammonia, which is normally used for bleaching hair, can be bought from pharmacies. This raw ammonia is then added at a controlled rate to the tank on a daily basis, along with rigorous daily water testing. Ammonia and nitrite will rise and peak in the normal way and more ammonia can be added to simulate a high number of fish in the aquarium.

When all the ammonia is being consumed by the filter bacteria, and further testing shows no increase, the tank can be considered as mature and fish can be added the next day. Do not continue to add ammonia once fish have been added. Fishless cycling is the best way to mature a tank from the fishes' point of view and should be used when additional numbers of fish are introduced to the tank.

Below A platy is a hardy tropical fish frequently recommended by stores as a suitable first fish.

WATER QUALITY
Why test the water?

The importance of water testing cannot be underestimated. Today science can give us answers to questions such as, Why has my fish died? Poor water quality is the biggest killer of aquarium fish and also contributes to illness, so regular use of a test kit is critical.

How test kits work

Water testing can tell us so much more about how the tank is running than is possible with the naked eye. Water can be crystal clear and yet still contain extremely high levels of toxic ammonia and nitrite (see page 106), as well as nitrate and phosphate (see page 108). The pH and hardness of aquarium water (see page 104) are also impossible to tell just by looking, so a test kit can be used to determine whether particular pollutants are present and whether subsequent action should be taken.

Test kits work by using reagents that change color, which can then be cross-referenced against color charts. Usually each reagent will test for only one parameter, such as pH, and so a kit will include several different tests.

Using test kits for water preparation

It is especially important to use a test kit when you are setting up a new tank and using untreated tap water to find out how many fish the filter bacteria can cope with, whether the pH drops over time, and how quickly nitrate builds up. This determines when the water should be changed and if it is safe to add new fish.

Using test kits for problem solving

If a fish dies or becomes unhealthy, the tank water should always be tested to check the water quality. Long-term problems, such as nuisance algae and poor plant growth, can also be put down to

Below left Liquid test kits are the most accurate and will also contain the highest number of tests.

Below middle Tablet tests are simple to use and come with test tubes and charts, like a liquid test.

Below right Dip strips are a quick and inexpensive method of regular water testing.

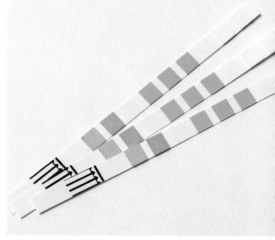

Which test kit?

TYPE OF TEST KIT	FEATURES	PROS	CONS
Dip strip	Several tests come combined on a disposable strip. Squares impregnated with reagent change color when immersed in the tank water. The resulting color is then matched with the corresponding color on the chart.	Cheap. The quickest and easiest test kit to use.	They do not always test for ammonia and can be the least accurate.
Tablet	Tablets come in foil strips. A tablet or tablets is/are dropped into a test tube of tank water and crushed or shaken until dissolved. The resulting color is then matched with the corresponding color on the chart.	Each tablet is a measured quantity, so cannot be overdosed. Easy to use.	Each kit on average contains only 20 tests.
Liquid	One or several drops of a bottled reagent are added to a test tube of tank water. The resulting color is then matched with the corresponding color on the chart.	Accurate and can test for the widest range of parameters. Can provide the most tests per kit.	Can be overdosed, causing a false result. Reagents can be messy and need frequent shaking.

substandard water quality. Even if everything in the tank looks fine, test the water weekly. Just as a thermometer is used to check that a heater is working properly, a test kit can be used to prove that your filter is working not just mechanically but biologically.

Types of test kits

The three most popular forms of test kit are dip strip, tablet, and liquid. Combination test kits, which are called master test kits, consist of multiple tests for several key parameters. Master test kits often represent a saving compared with purchasing separate test kits and can supply a year's worth of tests in certain circumstances. Master test kits are also recommended for the beginner.

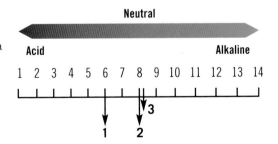

pH levels in the aquarium
1. pH 6 is the lowest pH that should be achieved in the aquarium
2. pH 8 is the highest pH that should be achieved for freshwater fish
3. pH 8.2 is the constant pH needed by marine organisms

Dealing with pollution

Polluted water is the biggest cause of fish death. In fishkeeping terms, polluted water does not just mean water that has been contaminated. It can also mean that the water is polluted with biological pollutants, such as ammonia and nitrite (see pages 106–7). The ultimate effect of pollution on the aquarium is the death of your fish, but illness and loss of condition can also be caused.

Dilution and filtration

In nature, contaminants and pollutants in the water are primarily dealt with by the vastness of the body of water. In the aquarium, which is tiny by comparison, pollutants build up and can be effectively removed only by water changing (see pages 170–71). Filtration is an ingenious advance in pollution control in aquariums (see pages 32–33) by harnessing bacteria to do the work of converting harmful substances into less harmful ones. Aquariums without a filtration system are disasters waiting to happen as pollutants constantly build up to near fatal levels before being removed by a water change.

No body of water as small as the average aquarium exists in nature and supports a permanent colony of fish. It is sometimes said that killifish survive in small pools in the wild, so do not need filtration. This is not the case. The fact is that the body of water they inhabit is much larger when the fish are developing and feeding and pollutants are dealt with by bacteria, water changes in the form of rainfall, and plants.

When the water starts to shrink in size, the pool becomes unable to support fish and they die. They have adapted to the conditions by spawning before the environment gets too harsh, and the subsequent fry will grow in the new pond that develops the following season. So killifish, like all fish in aquariums, must be kept in filtered tanks to keep them alive, and without filtration they may not even live out their short, natural lives.

Added benefits of water changes

Changing the water is the simplest way of dealing with pollution, but it can also benefit fish health in other ways. Some cyprinids, including goldfish (see pages 127–32 and 148–53), emit growth-inhibiting hormones into the water to stop themselves and their offspring from outgrowing their environment. In the aquarium regular water changes will dilute these hormones, allowing the fish to grow to their full potential.

Algae control

The subject of algae is one that crops up frequently in this book. It is important to keep algae under control first and foremost because it is unsightly. We keep fish in glass boxes so that they can be viewed and appreciated. Algae spoils the view into our aquariums by covering all the surfaces in a green film. It can prove to be very stubborn and difficult to remove, causing the aquarist extra work and a reduction in pleasure derived from the fish. Algae is one of the main reasons that people leave the hobby, because algae removal becomes a tiresome and time-consuming chore and the aquarium fails to look

Left Cloudy water may mean that it is time for the filter to be maintained and for the water to be changed.

as it did on the day when it was set up. Regular maintenance will keep the tank free of algae and help you retain your interest in the fish and the environment they inhabit.

Tank maintenance and pollution control

You will need to take time out of viewing your fish every month to maintain the tank and lessen the effects of pollution. The easiest way to carry out all the necessary tasks is to combine them. The chart below sets out a timetable for these routine jobs, with an estimation of the average time involved for a tank of about 22 gallons (100 liters) of water.

Right If water is polluted, small fish like this tetra will often be the first to die.

Monthly maintenance timetable

TASK	ACTION	TIME TAKEN
Filter maintenance	Turn off the filter, clean the impeller (see page 172) with a brush, and clean the sponge media in old tank water.	5 minutes
Algae wiping	Scrub the four inside panes of glass with an aquarium-safe abrasive pad.	5 minutes
Gravel vacuuming/ water changing	Use a gravel vacuum and siphon tube (see page 169) to remove detritus from the substrate. Fill a bucket with dirty tank water and discard. Continue until the gravel is clean and about 30 percent of the aquarium water has been removed.	10 minutes
Water replacement and conditioning	Fill an empty bucket with tap water, bring it to the required tank temperature with water from the hot tap, check the temperature with a thermometer, and add water conditioner. Pour the water into the tank.	10 minutes
Water testing	Fill test tubes with tank water, add reagents, then wait and check the results (see pages 100–1).	20 minutes
Tank cleaning	Clean splash marks from cover glasses and light tubes and wipe the exterior glass with a cloth. Dust the hood and cabinet.	10 minutes

Total time taken per month = 1 hour

pH and hardness

The pH of water is the factor that most novice fishkeepers think is the most important to test for. In fact, ammonia and nitrite (see pages 106–7) are more important, but the three are linked. Along with pH goes the hardness of water. Testing for pH will determine how acid or alkaline the water is, and the hardness will determine whether or not the water contains minerals.

The importance of pH

It is necessary to know the acidity or alkalinity of the water if you are going to place fish in it. Like pollutants, pH is colorless, so the only way you can ascertain the pH of water is to test it. The pH scale ranges from an extremely acid pH 1, through neutral pH 7, which is neither acid nor alkaline, to extremely alkaline pH 14. Fish across the world have adapted to inhabit waters with a pH of 4–9, but those living close to one end of the scale would certainly perish if kept at the other end. The oceans are constant with regard to pH; marine fish will not tolerate a pH outside of the usual 8.2 in which they live.

The effects of pH

The major factor that is affected by pH is the toxicity of ammonia. Ammonia is less toxic at a low pH and more toxic at a high pH. This means that fish that live in waters with a high pH, such as marine fish, will be more affected by low levels of ammonia than if it were present in a tank containing acid water and soft water, freshwater species.

The pH of water can also affect the condition and the breeding potential of fish. Very few species will breed at a pH that is very different from the one to which their bodies have adapted through evolution in the wild.

How to change pH

The best way to lower the pH of freshwater is to replace it with purified water, such as water purified by a reverse osmosis (RO) unit (see page 84). Check first that any substrate or decoration used is inert and is not causing the rise of pH (see pages 50 and 56). The other way of lowering pH is to use water-softening resins in the aquarium. The effects of resins are less on water that is alkaline and hard because hard water has something called residual buffering (see opposite). A natural way of lowering pH is to use peat, but again its effects are far less on hard water, and it is best used on water that is already around neutral with a pH of about 7.

Below Marine fish are used to a constant pH of 8.2, and they will not tolerate any other conditions.

Above Tropical freshwater fish have adapted to live at different pH levels, which are provided by the type of habitat in which they live.

pH crash

This is a term used to describe a sudden drop in the pH of freshwater aquariums. It occurs when water has not been changed for a long time and all the residual buffering of the original tap water has been exhausted. Biological processes from the filter acidify the water, and with no buffer, the pH drops to as low as pH 4.

To remedy pH crash, simply replace a proportion of the tank water with dechlorinated tap water (see page 83), since this is mostly hard and full of buffers (see below), but do it carefully and change only about 10 percent per day until pH values are restored.

Hardness, softness, and buffering

Hardness and pH go hand in hand. Water with a pH higher than 7 (alkaline) is regarded as hard, and water with a pH less than 7 (acid) is called soft. It is the elements and minerals within water that determine its pH and hardness. Hard water has high concentrations of dissolved minerals; soft water has very few.

To make soft water hard, you can simply add minerals or introduce decor that contains calcium. Calcium will precipitate into the water as dissolved solids. Decor that increases and

Tip

Always find out from the aquatic retailer the pH values of their tanks. This way you will be able to acclimatize your newly purchased fish more effectively.

maintains hardness includes coral sand, tufa rock, ocean rock, and sea shells (see page 52). However, if we wish to make hard water soft, the dissolved mineral content has to be removed, which is much less easy. Treating the water with a reverse osmosis (RO) unit is again by far the best method (see page 84). If the minerals in hard water are not physically removed in this way, they remain in the water and counteract the effects of anything added to try to lower pH and hardness, such as peat granules (see page 40) or even acid. The ability that minerals have to set and maintain pH in water is known as buffering. Minerals are available in powdered forms from aquatic stores, and different mineral concentrations can be bought premixed to instantly mimic an environment and pH and hardness level. A pH of 6.2, 7, or 8.2 can therefore be achieved artificially.

Ammonia and nitrite

The pollutants ammonia and nitrite can be bad news if they are present in a tank containing fish, invertebrates, or corals, and they are common in new tanks with immature filters. Ammonia and nitrite are invisible killers, but between them they kill more aquarium fish than anything else. A test kit will tell you whether either pollutant is present in your tank.

Ammonia

As we have seen, this is produced by the waste products that fish excrete and also by uneaten food or dead and decaying fish.

Toxicity

Ammonia is the most toxic pollutant that is commonly tested for in aquariums (see page 100), and it is more toxic in water with a high pH (see page 104). Any levels above zero are considered hazardous to livestock.

The effect on fish

If they are exposed to ammonia, fish can become irritated and lethargic. It may cause lack of appetite, gasping at the surface of the water, and death. Some hardy fish that have been exposed for extended periods may show signs of bleeding in the fins and redness around the gill

> ## Tip
>
> **Ammonia-removing solutions are available from aquatic retailers. They instantly detoxify ammonia and change it into harmless ammonium.**

area. Exposure can also be linked to ailments such as fin rot (see page 181).

Removing ammonia

If the test shows that the level of ammonia in the tank water is very high, carry out a 50 percent water change every day until it lowers (see pages 170–71). Stop feeding the fish for a few days, as this may be making the problem worse. Add plenty of filter bacteria (see pages 38–39), but do not maintain the filter, as more beneficial bacteria may be lost. Look for uneaten food or dead fish and remove them. Growing aquarium plants will utilize ammonia as a fertilizer but should not be relied on for this purpose.

Nitrite

Nitrite is produced by nitrosomonas bacteria when they consume ammonia (see page 98). It can take longer to disappear in new aquariums and is commonly a factor in "new tank syndrome" (see pages 112–13).

Toxicity

Nitrite is the next most toxic pollutant after ammonia and should always be kept at zero.

Left When filter bacteria are added to the water, ammonia and nitrite will be consumed naturally.

Pollutant problem diagnosis and treatment checklist

POLLUTANT	SYMPTOMS	REASON FOR OCCURRENCE	CONFIRMATION	REMEDIAL ACTION
Ammonia	Lethargic or dying fish; fish not feeding; fish gasping at the surface; fish with reddened gills and eroded fins	A lack of bacteria in the system due to a new filter; overfeeding; inadequate filtration; overstocking; rotting fish corpse	A test kit showing any level of ammonia above zero	Change 50 percent of the water; stop feeding the fish; look for any dead fish; add a liquid ammonia remover, add plenty of liquid filter bacteria booster over the next few days
Nitrite	Lethargic or dying fish; aberrant swimming behavior; gasping at the surface; fish not feeding	A lack of filter bacteria in the system; a new tank; improper filter maintenance; overfeeding; overstocking	A test showing any level of nitrite above zero	Stop feeding; add filter bacteria; add salt and change water if keeping all but the hardiest fish, such as platies (*Xiphophorus maculatus*) (see page 159)

The effect on fish

Fish that are exposed to nitrite will show a loss of appetite and become lethargic. Gasping at the surface of the water can also be an indication of nitrite being present. High nitrite levels will cause death in most species, so should be avoided at all costs.

Removing nitrite

To treat nitrite, first stop feeding the fish. Add plenty of filter bacteria and check for any dead fish and uneaten food. With high nitrite levels, change 50 percent of the water every day and do not maintain the filter. Aquarium salt can be used to bring down levels of nitrite.

Right Aquarium salt can be used to detoxify the effects of nitrite in the water.

Nitrate and phosphate

Nitrate and phosphate are lesser evils than ammonia and nitrite (see pages 106–7) in that they are far less toxic, but nitrate levels can rise to hundreds of times that of nitrite, and this does commonly manifest itself as a problem in aquariums. Phosphate on its own or combined with high nitrate is a common factor in tanks with nuisance algae, and levels should be kept close to zero.

Nitrate

Nitrate is produced by nitrobacter bacteria as they consume nitrite in the filter (see page 98). It can be utilized by healthy plants or absorbed by nitrate-removing resins, but the most common and best way to remove nitrate from tank water is by changing the water (see page 170). Regular partial water changes are the key to keeping nitrate levels low, but make sure that the source of new water, such as tap water, is not too high in nitrate itself. If levels are higher than 40 parts per million in the tap water, use RO (reverse osmosis) water instead (see page 84).

Safe levels

Aim for a nitrate level of 40 parts per million or less in freshwater and 10 parts per million or less in marine aquariums containing corals. Nitrate is being added all the time by the filtration system, so test weekly to keep nitrate in check. In badly maintained aquariums, levels of 150 parts per million are not uncommon.

Old tank syndrome

Tanks that do not receive regular partial water changes and that do not have a group of healthy live, growing plants will go through changes that will not be immediately obvious to the owner. As is commonly the case, the water will stay as clear as ever in the tank, but nitrate levels will rise, forcing the resident fish population to acclimatize themselves to it, or otherwise die. The pH levels will lower and even crash because acid comes from the filter and the organic load of detritus builds up (see page 105). Then fish are purchased but die within about 24 hours of being introduced to the tank. The fish are taken back to the retailer by the disgruntled owner, who explains that all the other fish in the tank are fine. This is a classic case of "old tank syndrome." The acidic water with a pH of 4 or 5

and the nitrate level of 100 plus parts per million have caused too much of a shock to the new fish that were being kept in the aquatic shop at a higher pH and much lower nitrate level. The other fish seemed fine because the process had been a gradual one and occurred over months, not hours. The solution is to test the tank water before purchasing fish (see pages 100–1), and if in doubt as to its suitability, ask the retailer.

Below Nitrate and phosphate levels build up over time and are invisible to the owner.

Pollutant diagnosis and treatment checklist

POLLUTANT	SYMPTOMS	REASON FOR OCCURRENCE	CONFIRMATION	REMEDIAL ACTION
Nitrate	Prolific algal growth; buildup of detritus; newly purchased fish not doing well	A heavy biological load on the filtration system, which is being converted by the filter, but not diluted enough by water changes; it can also be introduced in high levels from tap water	A test kit showing levels of 100 ppm or more	Change the water with RO (reverse osmosis) water (which is virtually nitrate free) or tap water with nitrate levels below 20 ppm; vacuum the substrate thoroughly and clean mechanical filter media; add live plants to the system wherever possible
Old tank syndrome	Newly purchased fish dying within days of purchase when added to a well-established tank with long-term fish residents	Insufficient water changes since being set up have caused nitrate levels to spiral and pH and buffering values to drop	A test kit showing nitrate levels above 100 ppm and a pH below 6	Carry out a series of water changes using tap water to lower nitrate levels and restore pH values; also vacuum the substrate to remove any detritus and clean filter media
Phosphate	Prolific algal growth	Phosphates introduced to aquarium from many sources, including tap water, fish food, and fish waste	A test kit showing a level above zero	Switch to RO water; add live plants to the system; add a phosphate-removing resin; cut down feeding wherever possible

Phosphate

Phosphate is present in every living thing but is very low in natural bodies of water. In the aquarium, phosphate can be added through tap water, fish food, and fish processes, and can build up. High levels of phosphate, unlike ammonia, nitrite, and nitrate, will not kill the fish themselves but will cause havoc by feeding algal blooms.

To remove phosphate, plant lots of fast-growing plants or use a special phosphate-removing resin. To keep levels as low as possible, use tap water that is low in phosphate or RO (reverse osmosis) water. Remove any detritus and clean mechanical filters regularly (see pages 169 and 172–73). Feed dry food that is low in phosphate and check that any plant fertilizers are free of phosphate, too.

The nitrogen cycle

The nitrogen cycle is taught to many of us in science lessons at school, but as with many subjects and topics, you probably wondered how useful it would be to you in later life. The answer is that when you become a fishkeeper and set up an aquarium, the nitrogen cycle is paramount to the success of the system. So those science lessons may benefit your understanding and your fishes' well-being.

How the cycle works

Fish produce ammonia through their respiration and bodily functions. Ammonia, however, is highly poisonous to fish, and if it is not dealt with can cause their premature death. Nature can give us a helping hand because a strain of bacteria called nitrosomonas breaks down ammonia and converts it to nitrite. However, nitrite is also toxic to fish; but there is another strain of bacteria called nitrobacter, which in turn converts nitrite into less harmful nitrate (see page 98).

This cyclical conversion of waste products by bacteria is a continuing and necessary process in any mature aquarium, and the fish would not be able to survive in such a confined artificial space without it. What links nitrate back to the fish is the fact that live aquatic plants consume nitrate as part of their own life cycle. Some fish, in turn, consume these plants, and so the whole cycle begins again.

Aiding the nitrogen cycle

On its own the nitrogen cycle would not be particularly effective in the average aquarium because of the high density of fish in relation to the volume of water and the planting. We therefore aid the process by providing a home for many more bacteria than would naturally live in the environment. The biological filter is a home for bacteria that has been engineered by us to cram millions of them into a confined space. The way we do this is to use materials, known as media, that have a very porous structure and a very large surface area (see pages 38–39). We feed the bacteria with a constant supply of oxygen and food in the form of fish waste and they break down the waste for us.

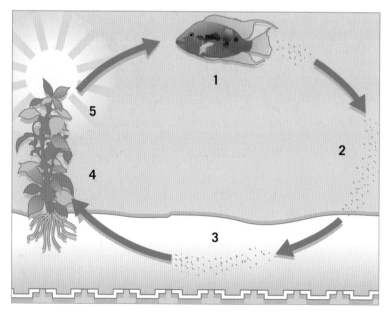

How the nitrogen cycle benefits fish and plants
1 Fish consumes oxygen and produces waste (ammonia)
2 Bacteria convert ammonia into nitrite
3 Bacteria convert nitrite into nitrate
4 Plant consumes nitrate
5 Sunlight enables plant to photosynthesize and produce oxygen and clear water for fish

Above A heavily planted tank is nearly capable of looking after itself and may require fewer water changes.

The continued importance of dilution

In heavily planted aquariums nitrate can be dealt with solely by the plants, but again, because these are confined bodies of water, they will still need to be replaced on a regular basis. Changing the water (see pages 170–71) will add minerals and pH buffers (see page 105) to the tank. It will also remove debris, hormones from fish (thereby encouraging the fish to grow) and phosphates, and clean stained water. Therefore, even with the nitrogen cycle in full swing, continue a regular water-changing regime of about 30 percent every two weeks.

A break in the cycle

If the nitrogen cycle is always present in our tanks, why do fishkeepers experience problems with ammonia, nitrite, and nitrate? The answer is that the bacteria as well as the fish need to be taken care of if they are to do their job properly. If you choose a filter with a large media capacity (see pages 34–37), it will be able to hold more bacteria, which can subsequently

Tip

If you are relying on plants to remove nitrate from the system, don't prune them too heavily because it may upset the delicate balance of the aquarium.

break down more waste. In addition, while bacteria reproduce at a phenomenal rate, if lots of fish are added to a tank at one time, it may take several days before there are enough bacteria present. If the filter capacity is not large enough in the first place, there may not, in any case, be sufficient room in the filter for extra bacteria to live.

If the problem is rising nitrate levels, there are not enough plants growing in the system to consume all the nitrate being produced. This will be the case in all but the largest aquariums with the lightest fish stocking, so, as mentioned above, changing water is the best solution to keeping levels low.

Dealing with new tank syndrome

New tank syndrome is the term used to describe the all-too-frequent problem of stocking a newly set up aquarium with too many fish too quickly. Toxic ammonia and nitrite build up because there are not enough friendly bacteria in the tank to consume and break down the waste that is being produced by the fish. The fish that are in the aquarium may become lethargic and go off their food, and at worst, the occupants may die if levels continue to rise and are not remedied.

How to prevent new tank syndrome

New tank syndrome can be best avoided by following the advice given here.

When you set up the aquarium, use a dechlorinating liquid or tap water purifier to remove chlorine and chloramines from the tap water (see page 82). Chlorinated tap water is not only harmful to fish, but will also prevent the buildup of all types of bacteria, including the ones that you are trying to encourage to colonize your filter. Once the tank is full of water, switch on the filter, and leave it running continuously for the future. By doing this, you will ensure that friendly bacteria will begin to multiply in the filter media within only a few days.

Leave the aquarium without any fish for at least a week and add some liquid filter bacteria to the tank, following the instructions on the bottle. This will provide millions of extra bacteria in the aquarium, and they will help to

What is fish waste?

Fish waste is the term for the pollutants that are excreted from a fish's body. Fish produce waste all the time, not only in the form of visible droppings, but they also urinate and produce ammonia from the gills while they are breathing.

break down waste when the fish are added. Choose hardy fish, like platies and danios, and add only a few each week. It is tempting to add lots of fish at a time, but this way the bacteria levels can multiply at a healthy rate and so catch up with the amount of waste that is being produced by the fish.

Below Platies are quite tolerant of less-than-perfect water conditions and may live and breed as normal.

Below Neon tetras may be the first to succumb to poor water quality in a community tank.

Above Danios, like platies, are tolerant of a range of temperature, pH, and water quality.

Above Tiger barbs should be added only to mature tanks, although they are often on the wish list of new tropical hobbyists.

Feed only small amounts once a day for the first few weeks. This will be fine for a few, small fish and will prevent large amounts of uneaten food from polluting the water. Remove any uneaten food or dead fish immediately with a clean net, as they will soon break down, causing excess ammonia in the water.

Do not maintain or clean the filter media for the first four weeks after installation, because this may disturb the developing bacteria.

New tank syndrome FAQs

Q How do I know for sure if my tank is going through new tank syndrome?
A Use a test kit to read accurately how much ammonia or nitrite is in the tank water (see page 100). Anything above zero will cause stress and discomfort to the fish.

Q What can I do to get rid of it?
A Stop feeding the fish for a day or two, which will cause less waste production. Add some liquid filter bacteria to the tank to boost the filter's capacity to break down waste. If the fish are dying, then carry out a 50 percent water change every day until the levels are noticeably lower (see pages 170–71), continuing to test the water to monitor the quality.

Q Can I still add new fish while I have new tank syndrome?
A Definitely not! The new arrivals will be even more susceptible to the high ammonia and nitrite levels and may die within hours of being added to the tank.

Q Are there any hardy fish that are best adapted to cope with new tanks?
A Yes, danios and platies (*Xiphophorus maculatus*) (see pages 151–52 and 159) are noted for their hardiness and tolerance of nitrite. Neon tetras (*Paracheirodon innesi*) and tiger barbs (*Barbus tetrazona*) (see pages 143 and 150) are not. Danios are the best choice for tanks less than six weeks old because of their hardiness and their ability to do well in the less-than-perfect conditions of an immature tank.

CHOOSING YOUR FISH
Evolution of fish species

With a huge number of fish species in existence, there is one to suit every preference. In the millions of years that freshwater and marine species have lived on the planet, they have evolved to fill every feeding niche possible and to overcome the many obstacles that have stood in the way of their survival.

Environmental influences

Fishes are widely distributed through rivers, lakes, and oceans, which are linked, or have been linked in the past. Fish populations that occur in lakes that have become cut off from it begin to adapt to their new environment and can become genetically distinct from the ancestral river populations. Many species of fish occur nowhere else in the world and are adapted to suit the particular environment they inhabit. This means that they are especially vulnerable to potential future harm from habitat destruction or from overfishing, and these endangered fish populations can be described as fragile.

Walkers

Some species of fish have learned and evolved over time to overcome the physical barrier that is dry land. Walking catfish of the genus *Clarias* can wriggle their elongated bodies and push themselves forward over land with the use of their pectoral fins. This natural adaptation has enabled them to survive when their pools have dried up. Bichirs (*Polypterus* spp.) and snakeheads (*Channa* spp.) have also adapted to breathe air out of the water and to move from one pool to another in their native lands.

Jumpers

Nature has also equipped many species with the ability to jump out of the water. This could be the result of the fish escaping from predators underneath them in the water or of their taking advantage of flying insects above the surface of the water. The problem with fish that like to jump is obvious: without a tight-fitting lid, your prize specimens may end up on the floor.

Spitters

The archer fish (*Toxotes jaculator*) is one fish that has taken jumping for insects one stage further. It has developed a way of knocking insects from branches overhead by spitting a jet of water very accurately from some distance below. This adaptation is quite unique among fish species, and the fish can even take into account the refraction of light from underwater in relation to that in the atmosphere to achieve a near-perfect shot every time.

Archer fish can be kept in captivity in a special setup that accommodates overhanging vegetation so that the fish can behave as it does in the wild. These fish are found in estuarine waters, where freshwater rivers mix with the salt water from the sea. This means that the tank water for these fish has to be of a similar constitution, making what is known as a brackish setup.

Helpers

Through experience, aquarists have found that certain species have a beneficial role to play in aquarium life. Species of the *Loricariidae* catfish family, for example (see pages 154–55), can remove unsightly algae from the glass and decoration in the tank and have become popular for that reason alone. Snails are a popular addition to the aquarium, but some, like the Malayan snail (*Melanoides tuberculata*), can become a pest and reach plague proportions in a very short time. Here again, we are able to put to effective use the adaptations of some species of fish to eat snails. Loaches (see pages 133 and 147–48) eat snails when they come across them in the aquarium and so are an

Above The Amazon River system is a huge ecosystem that contains unique fish and animal species.

Above right The habitat available and types of food will influence the evolution of fish species.

Right Coral reefs are perhaps some of the most specialized ecological niches in the world.

extremely useful addition to the tank if there are lots of unwanted snails that are proving troublesome to keep in check.

A well-run aquarium will contain a combination of helpful species to deal with such things as algae buildup and nuisance snails. In exceptional circumstances aquariums containing sufficient algae-eating fish will be stripped of nuisance algae in a few weeks, and moreover, plant leaves and decoration will remain clean and thus benefit the appearance of the tank as a whole.

Where aquarium fish come from

The fish that we keep in aquariums originate from all over the tropical and temperate areas of the world. Many of the tropical fish that we keep were chosen because of their coloration or appearance and not because they taste good. Fish kept as pets are termed ornamental, and the practice of keeping ornamental fish is by no means new and shows human beings' affection for beautiful things.

The ornamental fish trade

Most tropical and coldwater fish are now farmed in the millions to supply the pet trade, and only a small percentage are taken from the wild. Taking fish from the wild is still often regarded as a sustainable practice, as many obstacles stand in the way of large-scale fishing, such as flooding, remote location, and the fact that tropical fish shoal in relatively small groups compared to the huge shoals that are found in the sea.

Descendants in the wild

For a species to be successful, it must be able to feed and procreate at a speed that is equal to or more than losses sustained from predation and other factors. All species kept in captivity have descendants that originally ran the gauntlet of

Below The harlequin is a wild type fish that is now linebred for color variation.

Alien invaders

The movement of fish and animals around the world by man can cause problems for native flora and fauna if they are accidentally or intentionally released. A species from another country may do exceedingly well in a habitat that was previously unavailable to it, and if it does do well, it may displace the endemic population of fish. The endemic fish may have evolved without competition and may well be threatened by the new species. In some parts of the world, the movement and sale of exotic species are controlled to avoid ecological catastrophes.

life in the wild and succeeded. Through selective breeding of many tropical and coldwater species in captivity, even more variety has been created by linebreeding.

Linebreeding

This is a skill that man has developed and honed since ancient times, when dogs, cats, and cattle were selectively bred for certain characteristics that could benefit the lives of human beings. Linebreeding of ornamental fish is purely to enhance certain naturally occurring, desirable characteristics in a particular species, such as fin length or coloration, and to make them even more pronounced, such as longer fins or brighter colors. There are many types of fish that have been altered in appearance through linebreeding from their original wild form, such as platies (*Xiphophorus maculatus*), guppies (*Poecilia reticulata*), and discus (*Symphysodon* spp.) (see pages 159, 158, and 147). Many have coloration that is so gaudy that if the species were to be released back into its original habitat, it would most certainly be spotted by a predator and eaten.

Weakened strains

Linebreeding does have its problems, however, because to produce a fixed strain of what is not a very prominent characteristic in the wild fish, the fish showing the most potential to carry that characteristic are mated, but they are often related. The problem with mating related fish is that genetic diversity is lost, and defects are consequently common in the descendants. Therefore, fish that look very different from the original wild type are often much weaker and less hardy, and may be associated with various physical defects. These can be visible on the fish, such as a deformed spine, bent head, strangely shaped mouth, or a shortened body. But several invisible weaknesses may also be present, including sterility and a reduced resistance to disease.

If you are breeding fish at home, make sure that you purchase parent fish from different sources and thus different blood lines. This will go some way to ensure that healthy offspring are subsequently produced.

Top The long fins of most angelfish are not a result of linebreeding and are similar to their wild ancestors' fins.

Bottom Linebred discus come in many different colors that would render their camouflage useless in the wild.

117

Where fish live in the aquarium

As we have seen, ornamental fish originate in a wide range of habitats and come to us in a myriad of colors and shapes. It is now up to you, the aquarist, to decide what you like and to consider where in the tank they will live. A community aquarium will usually contain fish that swim in all levels of the tank to provide movement and color from top to bottom.

Surface dwellers

The surface-dwelling species have adapted to live where they do so that they are the first to reach any food that hits the surface of the water. Being visible from above comes at a high price because it means that you will be visible to predators from above and below. Hatchetfish, which are members of the Gasteropelecidae family, are typical surface-dwelling fish, which originate from the Amazon. They have deep bodies with a flat back and upturned mouth for surface feeding. They are camouflaged when viewed from above the waterline, as their coloration is brown or grey, but what do they do to avoid predators that lunge at them from underneath? The answer is to leap from the water, covering a surprising amount ground, to land some distance away. The hatchetfish (*Carnegiella strigata*) (see page 139) has adapted to accomplish this feat by developing huge breast muscles and pectoral fins to aid flight.

These adaptations give the fish its characteristic hatchet shape and hence its common name. Other surface-dwelling fish that are suitable for the home aquarium include live-bearers such as guppies (*Poecilia reticulata*), platies (*Xiphophorus maculatus*), and mollies (see page 158).

Midwater fish

The advantage of swimming in midwater in the wild is that you are at a distance from predators at the bottom and from the top, and it is a position that is occupied by a huge number of fish species, including tetras (see pages 139–44), barbs (see pages 149–50), rasboras (see page 153), rainbowfish (see pages 156–57), gouramies (see pages 135–36), and more. The barbs, gouramies, and rainbowfish will also visit all water levels in search of food, but small tetras and rasboras have evolved not to go near the bottom, because in their native waters it is simply too risky.

Left Hatchetfish spend all of their time at the surface, so must be fed floating foods.

Below Rainbowfish mostly swim in midwater and are active swimmers, covering the whole length of the tank.

Above Clown loaches rarely leave the substrate, and its underslung mouth has adapted to allow it to feed there.

This can present a challenge, because when fishkeepers go away on vacation, it is usual to drop a "vacation block" of dry food (see page 162) into the tank and leave the fish with it for a week or so. With the block sitting, dissolving slowly on the bottom of the tank, the tetras—for example neon tetras (*Paracheirodon innesi*) (see page 143)—will not get any food, and a small fish can loose 10 percent of its body weight per day if not properly fed. The solution is to use an automatic feeder in such circumstances, as it can be filled with flakes or granules that will slowly sink through the water column.

Bottom dwellers

The largest group of bottom-dwelling fish are the catfish (see pages 154–55), of which there are hundreds of species available for community aquariums. They are mostly of bland coloration,

with a few exceptions, but it is their strange shape and antics that make them appealing. One of the best choices of bottom-dwelling catfish is the corydoras (*Corydoras* spp.) (see page 138), of which there is not one species that is unsuitable for aquarium keeping, and there are hundreds of them to choose from. They stay small—around 2½ inches (6 cm) when adult— and are best kept in groups of about five. They will eat food that has been left by other fish, but must have a clean substrate in the first place, otherwise their barbules may disappear with bacterial infection. However, they do need to be fed in their own right and do well on a diet of tablet and frozen foods (see pages 164–65).

Other bottom-dwelling fish include loaches from Asia, represented by the clown loach (*Botia macracantha*) (see page 147), which, although one of the larger members of the group, is well behaved and a good snail eater. Many cichlids naturally hug the bottom, too, because they need surfaces to define territory and deposit eggs (see page 190).

How fish live in the aquarium

When you know where in the tank different species will be swimming, it is time to consider how the different species of fish prefer to live with others, and their compatibility with members of their own kind. We like to choose whom we make our homes with, and fish should be given the same chance. Community fish are known for their tolerance of other species and are deservedly popular.

Solitary fish

If a fish lives on its own in the wild, or holds a large territory, then it is unlikely that it will want to live any differently in captivity. The reason why they have become solitary in the wild is almost always related to the proximity of food. A predatory fish will not appreciate other predators in the vicinity snapping up its dinner before it does, and that will include potential mates outside the breeding season and even older offspring. Those with simpler diets, like those that eat algae, will also want to stake their claim on an area, as that will be the area where their food grows. Examples of algae grazers that occupy a territory include red-tailed black sharks (*Epalzeorhynchus bicolor*) and ruby sharks (*Epalzeorhynchus frenatus*) (see pages 152–53).

As a rule, if a fish is territorial or aggressive, the worst choice of companion in the confines of the aquarium is an exact match, because this may spark a turf war, and the older resident will have everything to fight for.

Below Kribensis are good community fish and well behaved until they start breeding.

Cichlid compatibility

Cichlids (see pages 144–47) are often regarded as aggressive and territorial fish, but once they form a mated pair, two matched individuals will happily cohabit. The problem you will have is that often when a male and female are placed together, the basic territorial instinct comes into force, and the stronger fish (usually the male) will chase off its partner. If the male does take to the female, he may often want to spawn within hours of her introduction. The problem with that is that male fish, like many animals, can spawn immediately, but female fish need to be in condition and full of eggs (see page 192). If the female is not receptive, she will be chased away by the male for entering his territory and wasting his time. However, the female has nowhere to go because she is trapped with him in the same tank.

Cichlid pairing is not an exact science, so at the very least, arm yourself with a divider or a spare tank (see page 195). Be aware also that a "community" cichlid, such as a kribensis (*Pelvicachromis pulcher*) or ram (*Microgeophagus ramirezi*) (see pages 145–46), will not be in an accommodating mood if it thinks that its tank

Right Holding tanks in stores may not simulate the
conditions that all species need, so their combinations
of species should not always be copied.

mates are going to eat its eggs or fry, so you
will either need to separate the parents with a
divider or move one of them to another tank
altogether.

Shoaling fish

Shoaling fish are the exact opposite of solitary fish
in that they look for the company of others for
security. Most shoaling fish, such as tetras (see
pages 139–44), are low down on the food chain in
the wild and live by the rule of safety in numbers.
You will also observe at feeding time that a scout
will cautiously dive for food items before the rest
of the shoal follows. A shoal in the aquarium will
mean stocking them in numbers of six or more.
You will be able to observe the natural behavior of
the shoaling fish, and the species will be much
happier as a result.

Nocturnal fish

Many species of fish that we find endearing are
not as happy in the aquarium as we may think
they are. The majority of catfish (see pages
154–55), for instance, are actually nocturnal,
preferring to hide away during the daytime hours.
We make things worse by preferring to have the
fish on view in the daytime and in bright
fluorescent lighting to boot. One form of lighting
that may be suitable for nocturnal catfish is the
blue (moonlight) lighting used by marine
aquarists. It can be used exclusively to simulate
lower lighting levels provided naturally at dawn
and dusk in the world, when the catfish would
normally be active. A few days of lower lighting
levels and late feeding sessions should make for
happier catfish, and it will mean that you will get
to see them without taking away their hiding
places and feeling of security.

To be fair to the fish, we must provide ample
hiding places and areas of subdued lighting
throughout the daytime, and if you are lucky, they
will then be content enough to come out for short
periods of their own free will. Also, provide ample
midnight snacks in the form of sinking catfish
pellets placed in the tank after lights-out.

Community aquariums

A community of fish of different shapes and colors all coexisting in a decorated aquarium is the goal for most aquarists. Out of the thousands of species available, not all will mix with each other, and some must be kept alone. Don't always follow the example of the fish you see in tanks in aquatic stores where space is at a premium and thousands of fish are held in controlled choas that may not work in the long term.

Community fish

A community fish is one that can be kept in an aquarium without causing problems for its tank mates. Community fish are the most commonly kept and stocked by aquatic retailers for that very reason. Examples include small, peaceful fish such as danios (see pages 151–52), rasboras, most tetras (see pages 139–44), and most live-bearers (see pages 158–59). If a fish is termed community, it will happily (and safely) coexist with other community fish.

Noncommunity fish

A fish can be termed noncommunity for a number of reasons. It could be that the fish is aggressive, territorial, or predatory, or simply that it grows too large for most aquariums, needing special quarters. Noncommunity fish tend to be more intelligent than community fish and can be capable of launching premeditated attacks after dark on tank mates. They may also start life very small but grow very quickly, consuming tank mates as they go. An example

Below The silver shark will live in a community when it is small but may eat small fish when it is large.

of a noncommunity species is the popular oscar (*Astronotus ocellatus*) (see page 145).

Noncommunity community aquariums

There are exceptions to every rule, and sometimes it is quite possible to mix species of non-community fish with each other in a large predatory fish community, cichlid community, or oddball community. These mixtures work for some aquarists and not for others and should be attempted only by those with more experience, as well as multiple tanks for relocating species if things do go wrong. The only way to find out for sure whether your proposed community will work or not is to speak to someone who has already successfully kept that species or to discuss it with the staff at a specialty retailer.

Species aquariums

This term applies to aquariums that are set up to contain only one species of fish. That species could be a shoaling species displayed in a group, such as Congo tetras (*Phenacogrammus interruptus*) (see page 143), or it could contain one specimen oddball fish, like a large, predatory catfish (see pages 154–55). For those

who are new to the hobby, the temptation to have a mixture of fish will be great, so either have a species aquarium as a third or fourth setup or keep a mixed community from the outset. An aquarium containing only one species should be considered because it can itself make an eye-catching display.

Above Yellow tangs are well behaved in marine communities and are safe with small fish.

Below Fancy goldfish should be mixed only with each other in order to avoid problems.

Coldwater community

Many people are eager to find coldwater fish other than goldfish that can be mixed with goldfish. Although there are examples of species of tropical fish that are suitable in terms of temperature (see pages 132–33), many species find the flowing fins of fancy goldfish a temptation and therefore nip and harass them. For this reason, it is worth considering keeping either a temperate community of non-goldfish species or a community of various goldfish species. This way, problems should be avoided.

How to buy your fish

Once you have drawn up a shortlist of the possible species you want to include in your aquarium, it will be time to take a trip to your local aquatic retailer. Remember that a brand-new tank will need time to mature fully before you can fill it with its quota of fish, but bear in mind that by being patient and stocking slowly, no fish will be stressed or lost.

Avoiding impulse buying

When you get to your retailer, there may well be many species you have not seen before. Do not be tempted to buy these fish on a whim, as you may know nothing about them. Instead, gain as much knowledge as you can from the assistant, including if possible the full scientific name, and go away to do some of your own research. The worst possibility when you buy an unknown species is that it will turn out to be predatory or aggressive, or both. Some species will grow too large for your tank and will need new living quarters in due course, which again might throw your plans off track.

Hardy fish first

From your shortlist of species, find out which species are the hardiest and best suited to being introduced first into your new aquarium. If they are not immediately available, ask when they will be and if it would be possible to order some in advance. Many species on sale at aquatic retailers are young fish and may not look exactly like the pictures that you will have seen of them when you were making your choice. If the fish are alert and healthy, take the opportunity to buy them when they are small because they will be cheaper and you will also have the pleasure of conditioning them and watching them mature into beautiful adults. In addition, it means that you get to keep them for longer.

Questions for the retailer

Before you make your purchase, ask lots of questions of the staff in the store, since you can learn a great deal in a short space of time.

Questions for you

The retailer should be asking you questions as well, so be prepared to answer them as best you can, including knowing the size of your tank.

Questions to ask the retailer

- How long have the fish been in the store?
- Have they been quarantined?
- Are they wild caught or tank bred?
- Are they suitable for a new tank?
- How long will they be able to survive comfortably in a plastic bag?
- Is there a discount when buying a small group?
- What are they being fed?
- Will they be compatible with the other fish on my list?

Questions the retailer will ask

- How long has your tank been set up?
- Are these your first fish?
- How far away do you live?
- Have you tested the water?
- How large is the tank?
- Is the water the correct temperature?

Above When purchasing fish for the first time, you should ask a number of questions about the fish before you take them home.

Your answers

If you have followed the advice in this book, your answers will be that this is your first aquarium, it has been set up for a week with no fish, and you have tested the water and taken the temperature and the results were all fine and the temperature is as it should be. You will also have the specification details of your tank ready. How far you live from the store will affect how lightly the assistant packs the fish into the plastic bags for transportation.

If you are satisfied that the fish are the ones that you want and that they are healthy, and the retailer is satisfied that you have made the right choice, then the sale can proceed and you will have taken possession of your first fish.

125

Coldwater fish profiles

The common goldfish is held dear by many of us as one of our first pets, often kept from early childhood. Now that you have set up your first aquarium, you can provide the correct environment for your fish, and because they will be placed in a proper aquarium with adequate filtration, it will not be long before you look for suitable tank mates for your first acquisitions.

Goldfish varieties

The common goldfish continues to rank as one of the hardiest fish available, and other single-tail varieties, such as comets and shubunkins, should be just as hardy. Selectively bred forms of goldfish with shortened bodies and fantails, which are known as fancy goldfish, are less hardy. They are also best kept with each other and not kept with single-tail varieties or non-goldfish types. The reason for this is that through linebreeding, fancy goldfish have not only become more sensitive and less hardy than single-tail goldfish, but they are also much poorer swimmers. This can cause problems at feeding time, and if the single-tails decide to mate with them, the female fancies can be chased around the aquarium until they are exhausted.

Other coldwater species

There are a number of other temperate and coldwater species available, but because they are true to their wild forms, they are not docile enough to be mixed with captive strains of goldfish. The exceptions, such as Borneo suckers (*Gastromyzon* and *Beaufortia* spp.) (see page 132), are peaceable but must be given perfect water quality and the correct diet.

Coldwater algae eaters

Many fishkeepers would like to have coldwater algae eaters. There are a few, but unfortunately many of them are not suitable companions for goldfish. You will, therefore, have to remove algae by hand (see page 168). Consider setting up a separate tank for coldwater exotics.

Temperate fish

A species that is termed temperate is one that has originated from a warm but not hot habitat in the wild. Some tropical fish can also be classed as temperate, as they are quite happy living at lower-than-normal tropical temperatures. The zebra danio (*Danio rerio*) (see page 152) is a temperate species because it is happy at temperatures as low as 64°F (18°C).

Tip

Why not set up a tank for temperate species? Such a tank will look just like a tropical setup but will not have a heater. Nearly all plants will tolerate temperate conditions, and most temperate species of fish don't eat plants, making it all the more possible. Mix danios, white cloud mountain minnows, and Borneo suckers for an inexpensive temperate tank.

CYPRINIDS (*Cyprinidae*)

Common Goldfish *Carassius auratus*

Origin East Asia

Size 12 inches (30 cm), usually smaller

Tank size 36 inches (90 cm)

Ease of keeping Easy

Comments This variety has stood the test of time and is still very popular. If kept correctly, these fish are long lived and will grow to a large size. For best results, offer a variety of frozen and dry foods (see pages 164-67) and change the water regularly (see pages 170–71). The common goldfish should be short-finned and have a stocky body and good, vibrant coloration.

Shubunkin *Carassius auratus*

Origin Aquarium strain

Size 12 inches (30 cm), usually smaller

Tank size 36 inches (90 cm)

Ease of keeping Easy

Comments The shubunkin is a calico or nacreous form of the common goldfish, achieved by selectively linebreeding a characteristic that has come from a color mutation. It is available in both a short-finned and comet form. It can be partially scaled or totally scaleless, and a good specimen will have an even spread of color over the body and a strong, healthy blue coloration.

Comet *Carassius auratus*

Origin Aquarium strain

Size 12 inches (30 cm), usually smaller

Tank size 36 inches (90 cm)

Ease of keeping Easy

Comments A comet is a longer-finned variety of goldfish with a more slender shape and a pointed tail. Coloration is the same as the common goldfish apart from a form called the sarasa comet, which has rich red and bright white coloration. Many fish sold as goldfish are actually comets.

Black Telescope Eye *Carassius auratus*

Origin Aquarium strain

Size 6 inches (15 cm)

Tank size 24 inches (60 cm)

Ease of keeping Moderate

Comments The fish was given its common name because of its protruding eyes and black coloration, and it is a popular variety. Older fish will start to turn bronze from the belly up, and old specimens can be susceptible to cataracts. Also available are red telescopes and calico telescopes.

Oranda *Carassius auratus*

Origin Aquarium strain

Size 6 inches (15 cm)

Tank size 24 inches (60 cm)

Ease of keeping Moderate

Comments Orandas are popular because of the hoodlike growth on the head, which develops with maturity. They are available in many color forms, including red, blue, chocolate, black, calico, and red and white. Fish start to develop the distinctive thickening of the skin around the head, called a hood, when they are about 2 inches (5 cm) long.

Ryukin *Carassius auratus*

Origin Aquarium strain

Size 6 inches (15 cm)

Tank size 24 inches (60 cm)

Ease of keeping Moderate

Comments Ryukins are also commonly called fantails, and they may be distinguished from orandas (see above) by their different head shape and the fact that they do not develop hoods. Mature, show-grade specimens become incredibly deep bodied, and a fish 6 inches (15 cm) long may be 5 inches (13 cm) deep. Ryukins are available in calico, red, red and white, and other color forms.

Ranchu *Carassius auratus*

Origin Aquarium strain

Size 6 inches (15 cm)

Tank size 24 inches (60 cm)

Ease of keeping Moderate

Comments Ranchus are even less hardy than other fancy goldfish. They have been bred so that they have no dorsal fin and short pectoral and ventral fins, which makes them poor swimmers. They develop a hood with maturity, and quality, show-grade ranchus are much sought after and expensive. They are available in red, black, green, calico, and red-and-white forms.

Pearlscale *Carassius auratus*

Origin Aquarium strain

Size 6 inches (15 cm)

Tank size 24 inches (60 cm)

Ease of keeping Moderate

Comments Pearlscales are less hardy than other fancy goldfish because linebreeding has weakened them, and they are poor swimmers. The common name derives from the raised cap in the center of each scale. They have round, almost spherical bodies and are available in red, red and white, black, and calico. A hooded form is called the crown pearlscale.

Wakin *Carassius auratus*

Origin Aquarium strain

Size 6 inches (15 cm)

Tank size 30 inches (75 cm)

Ease of keeping Easy

Comments Wakins are twin-tailed varieties of the common goldfish, but unlike fancy goldfish, they do not have the shortened, rounded bodies that restrict activity. They are active, hardy fish and can be kept alongside single-tailed varieties. They are available in red and red and white.

Bubble-eye *Carassius auratus*

Origin Aquarium strain

Size 4 inches (10 cm)

Tank size 24 inches (60 cm)

Ease of keeping Difficult

Comments The fluid-filled sacks on the face of the bubble-eye goldfish horrify some viewers and delight others. This is not a genetically modified fish in the modern sense and has been around for a long time. They are best kept with other bubble-eyes in an aquarium that contains no sharp objects and has a gentle water flow. They feed on floating foods because they cannot see the bottom.

Celestial *Carassius auratus*

Origin Aquarium strain

Size 4 inches (10 cm)

Tank size 24 inches (60 cm)

Ease of keeping Difficult

Comments The celestial is also called the stargazer because of its upward-facing eyes. It is said that the fish were bred in this way to gaze at the emperors in ancient times. They do not have a dorsal fin and are weak swimmers, so they should be kept with other celestials or with bubble-eyes (see page 131).

Borneo Sucker, Hong Kong Plecs *Gastromyzon* and *Beaufortia* spp.

Origin China and Southeast Asia

Size 2–4 inches (5–10 cm)

Tank size 24 inches (60 cm)

Ease of keeping Moderate

Comments Several species are known as Borneo suckers, and deliveries of fish with this name at retailers often contain a selection of different species. Apart from the fact that they prefer cooler water, they are not especially suitable for goldfish aquariums. In the wild they live in shallow streams with a strong water flow and high oxygen levels, and they graze on tiny invertebrates that live in the algae, as well as the algae itself.

Weather Loach *Misgurnus anguillicaudatus*

Origin China

Size 8 inches (20 cm)

Tank size 36 inches (90 cm)

Ease of keeping Easy

Comments Weather loaches behave sufficiently well to be kept with single-tailed varieties of goldfish in aquariums. Their common name arose because their behavior varies with changes in barometric pressure. They can breathe air and will need to surface regularly. They also like to burrow, so provide a deep substrate.

White Cloud Mountain Minnow *Tanichthys albonubes*

Origin China

Size 1½ inches (4 cm)

Tank size 18 inches (45 cm)

Ease of keeping Easy

Comments The white cloud mountain minnow is a pretty, small fish that is well suited to smaller, unheated aquariums. It will breed readily and will not eat its fry. It is too small to be kept with most goldfish, which may eat it, so is best kept in a small shoal on its own. There are forms with long fins and natural fins.

Tropical fish profiles

With species size, variety, and skill levels for fishkeepers of every level, tropical fish are understandably popular, and they can be inexpensive too. If you are a newcomer to the hobby, it would be sensible to start with a community of small to medium-sized fish. This should include fish that swim at all levels of the water and that are colorful and active.

Species variety

The choice of species of tropicals is huge and is getting larger all the time as new species are discovered and new forms are bred. The following profiles highlight the most popular and widely available species. They range in level of difficulty and will provide several species that you can plan to buy once the new tank has matured.

Golden rules

Refamiliarize yourself with the basic rules of fishkeeping to ensure success and satisfaction:

- Always research unfamiliar species before you buy, because retailers will stock species that have the potential to grow to a huge size as well as those that will remain within the normal range.
- Stock your tank slowly and test the water regularly. Never wash filter media under the tap.
- Find a good aquatic retailer and listen to the advice offered, but also carry out your own research and eventually become your own expert. The key to being a good fishkeeper is to know about and fully understand the fish that you are keeping and the conditions they need to thrive.
- Regularly maintain the tank by changing the water and removing algae before it builds up (see pages 168–69).

Tip

If you want to start with a hardy species, platies (*Xiphophorus maculatus*) (see page 159) and danios (see pages 151–52) are good choices. Start with no more than six individuals, feed in small amounts, and monitor the water quality with a test kit (see pages 100–1).

LABYRINTHS (Anabantoidei)

Siamese Fighting Fish *Betta splendens*

Origin Thailand (formerly Siam)

Size 2½ inches (6 cm)

Tank size 12 inches (30 cm)

Temperature 75–86°F (24–30°C)

Water parameters Soft to neutral, pH 6–7

Ease of keeping Moderate

Comments The Siamese fighting fish is a mainstay of the tropical hobby. The aquarium form is more colorful and longer finned than the wild form. Although it has a fearsome reputation, these days it is often the victim of attack itself. It is best kept in a quiet tank, with no boisterous fish, lots of plants, and gentle filtration.

Honey Gourami *Colisa chuna*

Origin Asia

Size 2 inches (5 cm), but often 1½ inches (4 cm)

Tank size 18 inches (45 cm)

Temperature 75–82°F (24–28°C)

Water parameters Soft to neutral, pH 6–7

Ease of keeping Moderate

Comments Males will display their rich coloration only if they are settled into a mature tank. Provide a well-planted tank with gentle filtration and no boisterous tank mates. Offer frozen and live foods to keep them in best condition (see pages 164–65).

Dwarf Gourami *Colisa lalia*

Origin Asia

Size 2 inches (5 cm)

Tank size 18 inches (45 cm)

Temperature 75–82°F (24–28°C)

Water parameters Soft to neutral, pH 6–7

Ease of keeping Moderate

Comments A lovely-looking fish that has now been linebred to produce colorful females as well as males. They are bubble-nest breeders (see page 189), so provide some floating vegetation and a filter with a flow that is not too strong. The male grows slightly larger than the female.

Pink Kissing Gourami *Helostoma temminckii*

Origin Southeast Asia

Size 8 inches (20 cm)

Tank size 48 inches (120 cm)

Temperature 75–82°F (24–28°C)

Water parameters Around neutral, pH 7

Ease of keeping Moderate

Comments This is the pink form of the species; there is also a marble form. The kissing action is more a test of strength than an act of passion, but it has brought the species popularity. Balloon forms, linebred from a genetic deformity, are available but should be avoided.

Pearl Gourami *Trichogaster leeri*

Origin Southeast Asia

Size 4³/₄ inches (12 cm)

Tank size 36 inches (90 cm)

Temperature 75–82°F (24–28°C)

Water parameters Soft to neutral, pH 6–7

Ease of keeping Moderate

Comments A beautiful addition to any larger community, the pearl gourami has subtle coloration and graceful movements. Males have a red patch on the chest and a longer dorsal fin than the females. Keep in groups in a well-planted tank with more females than males.

Three Spot Gourami *Trichogaster trichopterus*

Origin Southeast Asia

Size 4³/₄ inches (12 cm)

Tank size 36 inches (90 cm)

Temperature 75–82°F (24–28°C)

Water parameters Soft to neutral, pH 6–7

Ease of keeping Moderate

Comments The third spot in the patterning is the eye, giving the three spot gourami its name. This species is also available in gold and blue striped forms. Males can be a little boisterous, so keep them in large, well-planted tanks with more females than males. Males have a longer dorsal fin.

CATFISH (Callichthyidae)

Brochis Catfish *Brochis* spp.

Origin South America

Size 3¼ inches (8 cm)

Tank size 36 inches (90 cm)

Temperature 72–79°F (22–26°C)

Water conditions Soft and acidic, pH 6–7

Ease of keeping Moderate

Comments Brochis catfish look like large corydoras and perform a similar role. They are peaceful and make excellent community fish. Provide open areas for swimming and do clean the substrate (see page 169), because a badly maintained substrate may cause bacterial infection and the loss of the barbules.

Corydoras Catfish *Corydoras* spp.

Origin South America

Size 2½ inches (6 cm)

Tank size 30 inches (75 cm)

Temperature 68–75°F (20–24°C)

Water conditions Soft and acidic, pH 6–7

Ease of keeping Moderate

Comments All corydoras are well behaved and peaceful, and they provide the added service of eating uneaten food from the layer of substrate. There are many species in the genus, providing a range of options for the aquarist.

CHARACINS (Characidae)

Marbled Hatchetfish *Carnegiella strigata*

Origin South America

Size 1½ inches (4 cm)

Tank size 24 inches (60 cm)

Temperature 75–82°F (24–28°C)

Water parameters Soft and acidic, pH 6–7

Ease of keeping Moderate

Comments Hatchetfish are strict surface dwellers and are well known for jumping to escape predators in the wild. Luckily, they are much less likely to jump in captivity, but a tight-fitting lid should be used as a precaution. Provide small, floating foods (see pages 166–67) and keep the fish in groups in tanks with surface vegetation.

Glowlight Tetra *Hemigrammus erythrozonus*

Origin South America

Size 1½ inches (4 cm)

Tank size 24 inches (60 cm)

Temperature 75–82°F (24–28°C)

Water parameters Soft and acidic, pH 6–7

Ease of keeping Moderate

Comments This is a South American tetra with a red neon stripe. Keep glowlight tetras in groups of six or more in a mature aquarium with other similarly sized community fish. Although the red band is reflective, these fish do not glow in the dark.

Serpae Tetra *Hyphessobrycon eques*

Origin South America

Size 1½ inches (4 cm)

Tank size 24 inches (60 cm)

Temperature 73–81°F (23–27°C)

Water parameters Soft to neutral, pH 6–7.5

Ease of keeping Moderate

Comments This fish may nip the fins of other fish. It will be fine with other short-finned fish, but should not be kept with long-finned fish such as Siamese fighting fish (*Betta splendens*) (see page 135) and guppies (*Poecilia reticulata*) (see page 158). Keep in a planted tank.

Bleeding Heart Tetra *Hyphessobrycon erythrostigma*

Origin South America

Size 2½ inches (6 cm)

Tank size 36 inches (90 cm)

Temperature 75–82°F (24–28°C)

Water parameters Soft and acidic, pH 6–7

Ease of keeping Moderate

Comments The bleeding heart tetra is a beautiful addition to an aquarium and looks good in a planted tank. Unlike its relatives, the male grows larger than the female and develops an extended dorsal fin. Keep in groups and provide some room for swimming. This species improves with age.

140

Black Neon Tetra *Hyphessobrycon herbertaxelrodi*

Origin South America

Size 1½ inches (4 cm)

Tank size 24 inches (60 cm)

Temperature 73–82°F (23–28°C)

Water parameters Soft and acidic, pH 6–7

Ease of keeping Moderate

Comments A lovely fish that is similar in habit to the neon tetra (see page 143). Keep in groups of six or more in a planted aquarium. Do not add fish under six weeks old to aquariums because they will not tolerate nitrite (see page 106). Female black neon tetras become more rounded and grow slightly larger than males.

Lemon Tetra *Hyphessobrycon pulchripinnis*

Origin South America

Size 1½ inches (4 cm)

Tank size 24 inches (60 cm)

Temperature 73–82°F (23–28°C)

Water parameters Soft and acidic, pH 6–7

Ease of keeping Moderate

Comments The lemon tetra may look quite pale when it is first purchased, but given the right food and conditions, the fish will become much more yellow, with the male gaining a prominent black edge to the anal fin. Keep in groups with other tetras in a well-planted tank.

Red Eye Tetra *Moenkhausia sanctaefilomenae*

Origin South America

Size 2½ inches (6 cm)

Tank size 30 inches (75 cm)

Temperature 75–82°F (24–28°C)

Water parameters Soft to hard, pH 6–8

Ease of keeping Moderate

Comments This species can shoal very tightly, making an impressive display. They are quite robust and can be kept with medium-sized cichlids (see pages 144–47) in a larger tank. They do have small teeth and sometimes nip the fins of long-finned fish. They live longer than smaller species of tetra.

Cardinal Tetra *Paracheirodon axelrodi*

Origin South America

Size 1¼ inches (3 cm)

Tank size 24 inches (60 cm)

Temperature 75–82°F (24–28°C)

Water parameters Soft and acidic, pH 6–7

Ease of keeping Moderate

Comments This fish has even more color than the neon tetra, with the red coloration stretching all along the belly. Cardinal tetras complement any community tank and should be kept in groups of six or more. For best effect, keep them in a well-furnished tank with no boisterous fish.

Neon Tetra *Paracheirodon innesi*

Origin South America

Size 1¼ inches (3 cm)

Tank size 18 inches (45 cm)

Temperature 75–82°F (24–28°C)

Water Parameters Soft and acidic, pH 6–7

Ease of keeping Moderate

Comments This popular aquarium fish is instantly recognizable by its red-and-blue coloration. Keep this tiny fish in groups of six or more in a mature aquarium with no boisterous fish. Keep lighting moderately low and furnish the aquarium with driftwood (see page 54) and plants (see pages 62–75).

Congo Tetra *Phenacogrammus interruptus*

Origin Zaire, Africa

Size Males 4 inches (10 cm), females 3 inches (7.5 cm)

Tank size 48 inches (120 cm)

Temperature 75–81°F (24–27°C)

Water parameters Soft to neutral, pH 6–7

Ease of keeping Moderate

Comments This is the best known of the African tetras and is popular because of its coloration and extended finnage. The fins of the males develop only in a large aquarium where there are no boisterous fish. The females are smaller and less colorful.

Penguin Tetra *Thayeria boehlkei*

Origin South America

Size 2½ inches (6 cm)

Tank size 30 inches (75 cm)

Temperature 75–82°F (24–28°C)

Water parameters Soft and acidic, pH 6–7

Ease of keeping Moderate

Comments Penguin tetras are very striking and appear to swim at an angle. They frequently reach their maximum size in captivity. They are suitable for communities of medium-sized fish and swim in the upper layers of a large tank. There are other types of penguin tetra that also sport a black line in the tail.

CICHLIDS (Cichlidae)

Cockatoo Cichlid *Apistogramma cacatuoides*

Origin South America

Size 2¾ inches (7 cm)

Tank size 24 inches (60 cm)

Temperature 75–79°F (24–26°C)

Water parameters Soft and acidic, pH 6–7

Ease of keeping Difficult

Comments Apistogramma are a large group of colorful dwarf cichlids from South America. They need to be kept in soft water in well-decorated tanks with mature filtration. They eat a variety of small live and frozen foods (see pages 164–67) and should be kept with other small fish.

Oscar *Astronotus ocellatus*

Origin South America

Size 12 inches (30 cm)

Tank size 60 inches (150 cm)

Temperature 75–82°F (24–28°C)

Water parameters Soft and acidic, pH 6–7

Ease of keeping Easy

Comments Although it is one of the most popular tropical fish available, the oscar is anything but a community fish! These fish grow rapidly, eating smaller tank mates along the way. Provide a large tank with suitable power filtration and offer a varied diet of sticks, pellets, and frozen food (see pages 164–67).

Ram *Microgeophagus ramirezi*

Origin South America

Size 2¾ inches (7 cm)

Tank size 24 inches (60 cm)

Temperature 75–82°F (24–28°C)

Water parameters Soft and acidic, pH 6–7

Ease of keeping Difficult

Comments This pretty fish must be provided with the right conditions to thrive. Keep them in pairs in a soft water setup, with plants and driftwood for decoration (see page 54). Offer live or frozen food (see pages 164–67), and keep them with small, nonaggressive fish. Males have an extended dorsal fin ray.

Kribensis *Pelvicachromis pulcher*

Origin Nigeria, Africa

Size 4 inches (10 cm)

Tank size 30 inches (75 cm)

Temperature 75–79°F (24–26°C)

Water parameters Soft to neutral, pH 6–7

Ease of keeping Moderate

Comments A well-behaved and colorful dwarf cichlid, the kribensis occupies the lower levels of the aquarium. Females develop a rounded, red belly when they are ready to spawn. They breed readily in aquariums, the parents protecting the brood. Provide hiding places and potential breeding sites (see pages 188–89).

Angelfish *Pterophyllum scalare*

Origin South America

Size 4³/₄ inches (12 cm)

Tank size 36 inches (90 cm)

Temperature 75–82°F (24–28°C)

Water parameters Soft to neutral, pH 6–7

Ease of keeping Moderate

Comments Angelfish are well behaved when they are small, but adults can become aggressive and eat small fish, such as neon tetras (*Paracheirodon innesi*) (see page 143). Keep them in tanks that are taller than usual to accommodate these tall fish and in groups until a pair has formed.

Discus *Symphysodon* spp.

Origin South America

Size 6 inches (15 cm)

Tank size 48 inches (120 cm)

Temperature 81–86°F (27–30°C)

Water parameters Soft and acidic, pH 6–7

Ease of keeping Difficult

Comments The discus should be provided with warm, soft water of a consistently high quality. Use a reverse osmosis (RO) unit for all water changes (see page 84). Buy fish that are 2¾ inches (7 cm) or more in length and keep them in groups until adult. Feed several times a day on high-protein granules and frozen foods (see pages 164–67).

LOACHES (Cobitidae)

Clown Loach *Botia macracantha*

Origin Southeast Asia

Size Up to 12 inches (30 cm) but usually only half that

Tank size 39 inches (100 cm)

Temperature 77–86°F (25–30°C)

Water parameters Soft to neutral, pH 6–7

Ease of keeping Moderate

Comments These scaleless fish are social creatures that communicate by using a series of audible clicks. Feed with sinking catfish tablets, bloodworm, and frozen cockles and mussels (see pages 164–67). They are also reputed to eat nuisance snails (see page 115).

Coolie Loach *Pangio kuhli*

Origin Asia

Size 4 inches (10 cm)

Tank size 30 inches (75 cm)

Temperature 75–79°F (24–26°C)

Water parameters Neutral, pH 7

Ease of keeping Moderate

Comments These wormlike loaches can access every nook and cranny in the aquarium in order to find food, and they can also bury themselves in the substrate. Notoriously difficult to catch once in the tank, these fish should be kept in groups and fed a diet of sinking foods and bloodworm (see pages 164–67).

CYPRINIDS (Cyprinidae)

Silver Shark *Balantiocheilus melanopterus*

Origin Asia

Size 14 inches (35 cm)

Tank size 60 inches (150 cm)

Temperature 75–82°F (24–28°C)

Water parameters Soft to hard, pH 6–8

Ease of keeping Moderate

Comments Silver sharks are popular aquarium fish, but they frequently outgrow their aquarium and may eat small fish. Silver sharks should be kept in groups in a large aquarium where there is plenty of free swimming space. They are, of course, not related to marine sharks.

Rosy Barb *Barbus conchonius*

Origin Asia

Size 4 inches (10 cm)

Tank size 36 inches (90 cm)

Temperature 64–79°F (18–26°C)

Water parameters Soft to medium hard, pH 6–7.5

Ease of keeping Easy

Comments The rosy barb is an excellent community fish and is also hardy. They are active, undemanding fish, which breed readily in the aquarium. They can be kept in unheated aquariums, and there are many variants available, including neon and long-finned forms. Keep more females than males. Males turn bright red.

Rosyline Shark, Red Line Torpedo Barb, Denison Barb *Barbus denisoni*

Origin India

Size 6 inches (15 cm)

Tank size 36 inches (90 cm)

Temperature 68–77°F (20–25°C)

Water parameters Neutral to hard, pH 7–8

Ease of keeping Moderate

Comments This fish was made popular by the bright red stripe on its body. They are safe to keep in groups, and if they are kept in good conditions, develop tail markings similar to that of a scissortail (*Rasbora trilineata*). Do not keep them in water that is too warm or acidic and provide plenty of oxygen.

Tiger Barb *Barbus tetrazona*

Origin Asia

Size 2¾ inches (7 cm)

Tank size 36 inches (90 cm)

Temperature 72–79°F (22–26°C)

Water parameters Soft to neutral, pH 6–7

Ease of keeping Moderate

Comments The tiger barb is well known in the hobby, partly for its reputation as a fin nipper. To prevent this, keep these fish in groups of six or more and do not combine them with any species with long fins. Decorate the tank with plants (see pages 62–75) and also provide some free swimming space.

Cherry Barb *Barbus titteya*

Origin Asia

Size 2 inches (5 cm)

Tank size 24 inches (60 cm)

Temperature 73–79°F (23–26°C)

Water parameters Around neutral, pH 7

Ease of keeping Easy

Comments The cherry barb is an undemanding species, and it makes a good community fish. Males turn bright red when they are sexually mature, and they will breed in the aquarium. Decorate the tank with wood, rocks, and plants (see pages 52–55 and 62–75) and provide a varied diet. This species is suitable for the beginner.

Siamese Algae Eater *Crossocheilus siamensis*

Origin Southeast Asia

Size 6 inches (15 cm)

Tank size 36 inches (90 cm)

Temperature 75–79°F (24–26°C)

Water parameters Soft to medium hard, pH 6–7.5

Ease of keeping Moderate

Comments Also known as the Siamese flying fox, this species has an excellent reputation as an algae eater. There are several other similar species that are mistaken for the true species, but they are not as well behaved and can be territorial. To tell them apart, note that *C. siamensis* does not have markings on the tail, whereas the other species do.

Pearl Danio *Danio albolineatus*

Origin Asia

Size 2 inches (5 cm)

Tank size 18 inches (45 cm)

Temperature 68–79°F (20–26°C)

Water parameters Neutral to medium hard, pH 7–7.5

Ease of keeping Easy

Comments Pearl danios are excellent community fish and are suitable for beginners. They are tolerant of cooler water and accept all foods. Keep them in groups of six or more and provide swimming space and the flow from a power filter. The species displays subtle coloration and is very active.

Zebra Danio *Danio rerio*

Origin Asia

Size 2 inches (5 cm)

Tank size 18 inches (45 cm)

Temperature 64–79°F (18–26°C)

Water parameters Neutral to medium hard, pH 7–7.5

Ease of keeping Easy

Comments The zebra danio is easy to keep and breed and is suitable for new tanks. It can even be kept indoors in unheated aquariums. Keep six or more in tanks without fish that are large enough to eat them. There are selectively bred forms of this species, including golden, leopard, and long fin. All danios will shoal together.

Red-Tailed Black Shark *Epalzeorhynchus bicolor*

Origin Southeast Asia

Size 6 inches (15 cm)

Tank size 36 inches (90 cm)

Temperature 75–79°F (24–26°C)

Water parameters Around neutral, pH 7

Ease of keeping Moderate

Comments Keep this bottom-dwelling fish singly in a well-decorated tank. If it does not have sufficient cover, the species may become aggressive and territorial. Offer a variety of foods, including tablet foods and algae wafers (see page 167). Do not combine with other species of tropical shark.

Ruby Shark *Epalzeorhynchus frenatus*

Origin Southeast Asia

Size 6 inches (15 cm)

Tank size 36 inches (90 cm)

Temperature 75–79°F (24–26°C)

Water parameters Around neutral, pH 7

Ease of keeping Moderate

Comments This species has several common names, including red-finned shark and rainbow shark, and it is also available in an albino form. Keep singly in a heavily decorated tank with plenty of cover. Offer a variety of sinking foods (see page 167) and do not combine with other tropical sharks.

Harlequin *Rasbora heteromorpha*

Origin Southeast Asia

Size 1½ inches (4 cm)

Tank size 24 inches (60 cm)

Temperature 75–79°F (24–26°C)

Water parameters Soft and acidic, pH 6–7

Ease of keeping Moderate

Comments This pretty fish will grace any community of small fish. Keep them in groups and decorate the tank with plants for cover (see pages 62–75). Females become fuller with age and may spawn on broad-leaved plants when mature. The harlequin is an active species that swims in all areas of the tank.

CATFISH (Loricariidae)

Bristlenose Catfish *Ancistrus temminckii*

Origin South America

Size 6 inches (15 cm)

Tank size 36 inches (90 cm)

Temperature 75–82°F (24–28°C)

Water conditions Soft and acidic, pH 6–7

Ease of keeping Moderate

Comments This is an excellent algae eater and a good community fish, being compatible with both smaller and larger fish. They can be kept in groups and may breed in the aquarium. The male, which looks after the eggs, can be identified by the bristles on the face.

Golden Nugget Plec *Baryancistrus* spp.

Origin South America

Size 4 inches (10 cm)

Tank size 36 inches (90 cm)

Temperature 72–79°F (22–26°C)

Water conditions Soft and acidic, pH 6–7

Ease of keeping Moderate

Comments This very attractive species grazes on driftwood. Keep it in a well-filtered aquarium and offer a variety of foods, including bloodworm, cucumber, and catfish pellets (see page 167). It can be kept in groups, and several similar species are available.

Zebra Plec *Hypancistrus zebra*

Origin South America

Size 2½ inches (6 cm)

Tank size 36 inches (90 cm)

Temperature 73–79°F (23–26°C)

Water parameters Soft and acidic, pH 6–7

Ease of keeping Moderate

Comments This brilliantly marked species is much sought after by aquarists and commands a high price. They have been in danger of being overfished but are now being bred in captivity all over the world. The downside to keeping this catfish is that it will hide for much of the day.

Midget Sucker Catfish *Otocinclus affinis*

Origin South America

Size 1½ inches (4 cm)

Tank size 24 inches (60 cm)

Temperature 75–82°F (24–28°C)

Water conditions Soft and acidic, pH 6–7

Ease of keeping Moderate

Comments This tiny algae eater can remove algal buildup when it is kept in groups. They are active during the day and are good community fish. In the absence of algae, feed them on algae wafers and vegetable matter. They may eat soft leaves of Amazon sword plants (*Echinodorus bleheri*) (see page 72).

RAINBOWFISH (Melanotaeniidae)

Red Rainbowfish *Glossolepis incisus*

Origin New Guinea

Size 6 inches (15 cm)

Tank size 39 inches (100 cm)

Temperature 75–79°F (24–26°C)

Water Parameters Neutral to hard, pH 7–8

Ease of keeping Moderate

Comments The male red rainbowfish becomes increasingly colorful with age and develops a humped back. Their coloration and high level of activity make them excellent fish for large display aquariums, and they are long lived. Keep them in groups with other rainbowfish and provide plenty of space for free swimming.

Boeseman's Rainbowfish *Melanotaenia boesemani*

Origin New Guinea

Size 4 inches (10 cm)

Tank size 39 inches (100 cm)

Temperature 75–82°F (24–28°C)

Water parameters Neutral to hard, pH 7–8

Ease of keeping Moderate

Comments This is one of the most beautiful tropical fish, displaying bright yellow and blue coloration. Keep in groups in larger aquariums with plants and open water. These are active fish, always displaying to each other and frequently spawning, releasing eggs over plants, but then eating them.

Blue Rainbowfish *Melanotaenia lacustris*

Origin New Guinea

Size 4 inches (10 cm)

Tank size 36 inches (90 cm)

Temperature 72–79°F (22–26°C)

Water parameters Neutral to hard, pH 7–8

Ease of keeping Moderate

Comments The blue rainbowfish is a rarity in the hobby, because it is one of the few fish that naturally develops blue coloration. They are undemanding in the aquarium and, if provided with good food and space to swim, will really improve over time. Keep with other rainbowfish in a spacious aquarium.

Dwarf Neon Rainbowfish *Melanotaenia praecox*

Origin New Guinea

Size 2½ inches (6 cm)

Tank size 30 inches (75 cm)

Temperature 75–82°F (24–28°C)

Water parameters Neutral to hard, pH 7–8

Ease of keeping Moderate

Comments This species is almost a perfect aquarium fish: it is peaceful, colorful, and stays small. Males become a more intense blue than females and develop a red edge to the fins. Keep them in groups and provide ample swimming space and a varied diet.

LIVE-BEARERS (Poecilidae)

Guppy Poecilia reticulata

Origin South and Central America

Size Males 1¼ inches (3 cm), females 2 inches (5 cm)

Tank size 18 inches (45 cm)

Temperature 64–79°F (18–26°C)

Water parameters Soft to hard, pH 6–8.2

Ease of keeping Easy

Comments This species has been linebred to produce color forms. As a result, the males and females are now much larger than the original wild fish, but the aquarium strain is becoming progressively weaker over time.

Sailfin Molly Poecilia velifera

Origin Central America

Size Males 4 inches (10 cm), females up to 6 inches (15 cm) but usually 3 inches (7.5 cm)

Tank size 36 inches (90 cm)

Temperature 77–82°F (25–28°C)

Water parameters Medium-hard to hard, pH 7.5–8.2

Ease of keeping Easy

Comments Male sailfin mollies have an enlarged dorsal fin, which they use during courtship. Males can be boisterous if there are not enough females, so keep three females to every male. Mollies benefit from aquarium salt.

Swordtail *Xiphophorus helleri*

Origin Central America

Size 4 inches (10 cm)

Tank size 30 inches (75 cm)

Temperature 72–82°F (22–28°C)

Water parameters Medium-hard to hard, pH 7.5–8.2

Ease of keeping Easy

Comments Swordtails are available in many varieties and are easy to sex, with the male carrying the sword. Keep at least two females to every male. Swordtails have been crossed with platies (*Xiphophorus maculatus*) (see below) to produce hybrids, which can be colorful. Swordtails are hardy and a good choice for the beginner.

Platy *Xiphophorus maculatus*

Origin Central America

Size 2½ inches (6 cm)

Tank size 24 inches (60 cm)

Temperature 64–77°F (18–25°C)

Water parameters Medium-hard to hard, pH 7.5–8.2

Ease of keeping Easy

Comments The platy is available in hundreds of forms, some with longer dorsal fins. It is an excellent fish for the beginner, since it is suitable for new tanks and will tolerate low levels of nitrite. Platies breed in the aquarium and should be kept at a ratio of two females to each male.

How to acclimatize fish

The actual introduction of new fish to your aquarium must be properly carried out; if it's not done in the right way, the fish may die. The parameters and temperature of the water in the retailer's tanks can vary widely from your own, and the water condition can also deteriorate in the plastic bag in which the fish are contained while they are being transported.

Adjusting the lighting

It is good practice to turn off aquarium lights when introducing fish. Fish are often packed in brown paper to cut out the light and to help insulate the plastic bag during transportation, so when you turn on the light in the middle of the night, fish are shocked by sudden bright light and may become stressed. The only acceptable tank light to use are moonlight bulbs if they are fitted to your tank, and all acclimatization should be carried out in ambient room light.

Equalizing the temperature

The bag containing the fish should first be floated, unopened, on the surface of the water for 20–30 minutes to allow the water in the bag to become the same temperature as that of the aquarium. After 10 minutes of this time period, cut the knot off and roll down the sides of the bag so that it floats. At this point you can start gently to add some aquarium water to the bag, which will start to equalize the water parameters.

Water mixing can also be done by adding small amounts of water to the bag using a syringe or dropper, or by using an air line to siphon water slowly in. To do this, place the bag upright in a bucket, below the aquarium.

Adding the fish

After 20 minutes or so, the water in the bag should be the same temperature and chemistry as that of the tank. The fish should then be gently caught with a net and placed in the tank. The environment will be strange to the new fish, so expect them to be shy for about a day. The water in the bag should be discarded.

Post-introduction observation

New fish should be observed hourly to make sure that they are coping and adapting to their new surroundings. If the fish goes out of sight, do not be tempted to look for it right away, as moving decoration to find it will cause further stress. Feeding can be carried out as normal, but only to distract the focus of any existing fish from the newcomers. A new fish may not feed for a day or two until it has settled.

Problems

If the fish displays erratic behavior when it is released from the bag, your first step should be to test the water (see pages 100–1). Levels of ammonia and nitrite should always be zero and nitrate should be low. Check that the fish is not being attacked by tank mates; if it is, it will need to be separated or removed. It makes good sense to have a divider ready or a separate tank when introducing new fish (see page 194). Also check the pH and termperature of the water. If they are not to the fishes' liking, they may be the cause of the problem. If you discover that you have made a genuine mistake while purchasing (such as buying a tropical fish for a coldwater tank), capture the fish, place it in the bag that it came in, and take it back to the store as soon as possible.

Fish guarantees

Some stores will offer a guarantee against their fish dying in your care within a few days of purchase. This, in itself, is a sign of good retailers, as they are trusting that their staff have asked the right questions and ensured that their fish are going to an adequate home in the first place. When you buy the fish, ask if there is a guarantee and what the conditions are. If the fish dies, it is standard practice to be asked by the retailer for the receipt for the purchase and some of your tank water for them to test so that they can check that it is right for the fish. You must also check the health of the fish when you buy it.

Acclimatization

1. Turn off the aquarium lights and float the unopened fish bag on the surface of the water for about 20 minutes.

2. After 10 minutes, cut the knot off the top of the bag, roll down the edges so that the bag floats on the surface, and introduce some of the aquarium water.

3. Use an aquarium net to catch the fish in the bag, cup the net in your hand, and place the fish in the aquarium. Discard the bag water after introduction and observe the fish.

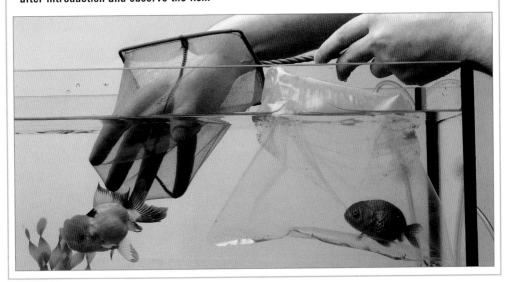

BASIC FISH CARE
Nutrition

Proper nutrition is vital for the long-term survival of fish in aquariums. Try to provide a diet that is varied and interesting to the fish. Offer small amounts of food to small fish and large amounts of food to large fish, and make sure that it is presented to them in a stimulating way. Tetras (see pages 139–44), for example, will hardly ever take food off the bottom and could starve if fed in no other way.

A balanced diet

Feeding should meet all the nutritional needs of a fish on a daily basis. This includes proteins, fiber, and vitamins. Dry foods will contain the correct balance of all these nutrients, but small, live and frozen foods can be comparatively less nutritious per portion, so should be offered more often if used exclusively. Different fish need to be fed different foods at different times. The chart opposite details the feeding requirements of some commonly kept fish species.

How often to feed

Predatory species have a different makeup from prey species, in that they have adapted to be opportunists and have developed expandable stomachs to deal with large, sporadic feeds. For this reason, they should be fed less often and with larger foods. Feeding a large predator daily may cause massive growth but will also shorten the fish's life span.

Small community fish have the opposite requirements and must be fed little and often just to maintain their weight. Their metabolisms are high, and they burn a lot of energy, so should be fed up to three times a day. Dry foods can be fed twice a day, with one feed of live or frozen foods given as a treat.

Feeding in a new tank

Caution should be used when feeding fish in new tanks (see page 112). The manufacturer's directions on a can of dry food may say to feed three times a day, but this can cause problems in a new tank. If ammonia or nitrite is present (see page 100), stop feeding until they have been dealt with by the filter. Despite the advice given above, the immediate welfare of the fish must take priority, and missing a few feeds will not be harmful in the long term if proper feeding is resumed in due course. Feed once a day, filter permitting, and be sure to remove any uneaten food immediately.

Feeding while on vacation

Making appropriate and effective provision for feeding your fish while you are away on vacation can be a problem if you have not been able to make suitable arrangements. Three basic options are open to fishkeepers in this situation:

1. Fill an automatic feeder with dry food, which will be administered at timed intervals during the break. This is probably the best solution.
2. Add slowly dissolving food blocks to the tank (see page 119). These are popular, but not all fish will eat the food inside them, and every tank has a different number and size of fish, making it difficult to determine whether it will be too much food, causing water-quality problems, or too little, leaving the fish to go hungry.
3. Get somebody to feed the fish for you. There is an added advantage to this approach in that filters can be checked and livestock counted at the same time, but the benefits end there. Well-meaning friends and neighbors who overfeed fish are a huge cause of fish deaths while owners are away. The only safe approach is to put the correct portion of food for each day into a bag or container and to label the day that it should be used.

Above Neon tetras need to be fed frequently on small foods in order to stay healthy.

Above Oscars are adapted to eat large foods but require feeding less often.

Fish feeding requirements

FISH SPECIES	SUITABLE FOODS	FREQUENCY
Neon Tetra (*Paracheirodon innesi*) (see page 143)	Crushed tropical flakes; small granules and frozen foods, including daphnia, mosquito larvae, and brine shrimp	Dry food in the morning and evening; frozen foods every other day
Guppy (*Poecilia reticulata*) (see page 158)	Tropical flakes; tablet foods; algae-based foods and frozen foods, including mosquito larvae	Dry foods twice a day; tablet foods available daily; frozen foods every other day
Silver Shark (*Balantiocheilus melanopterus*) (see page 148)	Tropical flakes; pellets; food sticks and frozen foods, including mosquito larvae and larger shrimp, such as krill	Dry foods twice a day; frozen foods once a day. As the fish grows, feed larger food sticks and pellets, and feed frozen food every other day
Oscar (*Astronotus ocellatus*) (see page 145)	Pellets; food sticks; cockles; mussels; prawns and earthworms	Twice a day when small, introducing larger foods, chopped. When larger, feed food sticks once a day and meaty foods every other day
Bristlenose Catfish (*Ancistrus temminckii*) (see page 154)	Algae wafers; cucumber; mosquito larvae; driftwood (see page 54)	In the absence of sufficient algae, feed algae wafers every day and mosquito larvae every other day. Cucumber can be fed weekly

Live and frozen foods

The feeding of whole, natural foods is of great benefit to fish and they are, after all, what fish thrive on in the wild. Given the chance, fish will not just consume but gorge on these foods until their bellies look as if they are going to burst. Fish fed on a variety of frozen, live, and dry foods will undoubtedly grow at a better rate and show better coloration and condition.

Live foods

Live foods can be caught from natural bodies of water such as ponds but are more commonly purchased in small portions from aquatic retailers. The sealed bags in which they are contained will cause the foods to perish if they are not used up quickly, so find out when the delivery arrives at the store each week and plan to buy it on that day.

There are three different kinds of live food available for aquarium fish:

1. Bloodworm, or red mosquito larvae, found in cold freshwater—most suitable for freshwater fish
2. Daphnia, found in cold freshwater—most suitable for freshwater fish
3. Brine shrimp, found in warm saltwater—most suitable for freshwater and/or marine fish

Tip

Heat causes live foods to perish even more quickly, so if you are intending to keep the food for a few days, put it in the refrigerator.

Benefits of live food

Live food can benefit all types of fish because they are complete foods and are presented in bite-sized portions for small to medium species. Some difficult species of fish will eat nothing else, making live food invaluable for those that are new to captivity. Live foods also make great conditioning foods, and an increase in feeding them may encourage spawning (see page 192).

Fish as food

The practice of using live fish as food for other fish is unnecessary in captivity and should be avoided. Even the most difficult species can eventually be persuaded to take dead (frozen fish) foods with a little perseverance on the part of the aquarist. Dead foods can be tied to fishing line and dangled or pulled through the water to mimic the action of a live fish, which normally does the trick. After all, this subterfuge works effectively when it is used by fishermen in the wild to catch predators, and they are surrounded by live fish!

Frozen foods

These are dead foods that can be kept in the freezer indefinitely. You get more for your

Left Bloodworms are very popular food for tropical and coldwater fish and are available live or frozen.

money than with live foods, and once thawed out, they will be consumed with just as much vigor by fish. They also have the advantage of being free of parasites and disease, which cannot be guaranteed with any live food.

Smaller foods come in blister packs averaging 24 cubes of food per pack. The foods are packed in foil on one side, so are simply popped out when it is time to feed. Larger foods, such as frozen fish and shellfish, come in one single large block.

Defrosting

When you are transporting frozen foods, try to keep them as you would food for human consumption. Thawing and refreezing should be avoided wherever possible. To defrost for feeding, take a small amount of aquarium water and place the frozen cubes in the water. Placing the food under the aquarium lights can help to accelerate thawing. When the food is thawed, mix it into the water to form a soup and pour it into the tank. The fish will race after the food as it is pushed around the tank by the filter flow.

There is an alternative method of defrosting, which should always be used for preparing brine

Tip

Dying or diseased fish should definitely not be used as food, as they will pass on the ailment not just to the predator but also to the water in which it is living.

shrimp, as the salt is removed in the process; otherwise it would increase the salinity of the tank water over time. Place the cubes in an aquarium net and rinse them under the tap. The food will be defrosted and rinsed within seconds, and therefore ready to feed.

Freeze-dried foods

Freeze-dried foods have existed for a long time but are slowly going out of fashion. Natural food, like bloodworms or Tubifex, are dried to a crisp and can then be packaged and placed on store shelves like flakes or granules. Contact with the water then rehydrates them.

Below Proprietary fry food is used in combination with tiny live foods to help young fry to grow.

Below Freeze-dried river shrimp have had the moisture removed from their bodies.

Dry foods

The other main type of fish food, and the most popular, is dry food in the form of flakes, pellets, tablets, granules, and food sticks. It is big business and, thanks to research into pet nutrition, aquarium fish can be fed exclusively on dry food for their whole lives and do very well indeed. Every nutrient that a fish requires can be added to dry foods to help keep your fish healthy.

Benefits of dry food

One of the main reasons for feeding dry foods is convenience. The foods come sealed in cans and can be used at will by the aquarist. Dry foods are also complete foods, and fish can do better on dry foods than some frozen foods, because dry foods can be nutritionally balanced, vitamin enriched, and otherwise supplemented and enhanced in a controlled, precise way. Cans of dry food can also be purchased from supermarkets, making them highly accessible.

Flakes

The most popular form of dry food by far is flakes. It does not resemble any food that species encounter in the wild, but a huge number of fish will happily eat it in captivity. The composition of flakes makes it available to fish of all swimming levels, because when it first hits the water, it floats; then after a few seconds it softens, takes on water, and begins to sink slowly to the bottom, satisfying midtank and bottom feeders as it does so.

Flakes are available for coldwater, tropical, and marine fish and come as a mixture of several different colors of flake. The colors represent different nutritional supplements, such as red flakes for color enhancing, for example, and green flakes for vegetable matter. A mixed flake can be regarded as a staple food, containing a little of everything, and this should be fed on a daily basis. Specific flake types are also available to enhance color or to encourage growth.

Below Flakes are the most widely used dry food in the world and eaten by most fish.

Below Pellets are better for offering to large fish, as they are more of a mouthful.

Sticks and pellets

These are aimed at larger fish that prefer to eat bigger mouthfuls of food. Sticks float on the surface for some time and are easily removed with a net if not eaten within a short period of time. They do soften when they hit the water and will also be nibbled by some smaller fish. Pellets are heavier than sticks and will put bulk on a larger fish if they are offered regularly. As pellets contain a great amount of food, fewer should be fed and all uneaten food should be removed. Not all larger fish will take sticks and pellets at first, but they generally prefer them once they have got used to them.

Granules

These have been specially designed to fall slowly through the water, making them acceptable for midwater feeders (see page 118), such as discus (*Symphysodon* spp.) (see page 147). They are hard at first, but soften when wet, and can be fed exclusively to promote growth and color. Again, they are often initially ignored if introduced to unfamiliar fish, but will eventually be readily accepted.

Below Tablets sink to the bottom, making them suitable for all bottom-dwelling fish.

Tip

Some tablets can be stuck to the glass, making them a treat for all tank mates.

Tablets

Tablet foods are of great advantage to aquarists that like to keep bottom-dwelling fish such as catfish and loaches (see pages 133, 138, and 154–55). These fish will often miss out on floating foods, which will be quickly taken by midwater and surface-dwelling fish (see page 118). It is also a misconception that bottom dwellers can live exclusively on uneaten food and algae in the lower layers. They need food in their own right, and many tablet foods are designed especially for them. When dropped into the water, they quickly reach the bottom and can be added last thing at night for nocturnal species.

Algae water

These are sinking foods suitable for algae-eating fish. They have a very high vegetable content.

Algae wafers

These are usually aimed at sucker-mouth catfish and other bottom-dwelling fish, but they are eaten with vigor by nearly all fish and even fish that usually feed from the surface (such as guppies). Make sure that the wafers go to the intended species by feeding them after lights-out at night or by dropping the wafers down a tube right into the catfish's usual hiding place.

Tank cleaning

Tank cleaning is an essential part of the hobby of fishkeeping. Over time, waste products and algae inevitably build up in the aquarium and must be physically removed by the owner. A lack of maintenance will not only leave the tank looking unsightly and ruin any display in the aquarium, but may also seriously affect the long-term health of the fish.

Algae wiping

The first area that will need cleaning will usually be the glass. The fluorescent light used to illuminate the aquarium (see page 46) will encourage green algal growth on the inside of the glass, and this should be removed.

The easiest way to remove algae is with an abrasive pad. These are available from aquatic retailers and are guaranteed safe to use in aquariums. To clean the inside of the glass, place your arm in the tank and sweep the pad across the glass. The majority of the algae should wipe off effortlessly, but some areas will require a little more pressure from scrubbing. Be aware that the surface of the pad should be free from any sand or gravel, which, if pushed and scraped along glass or acrylic, may cause scratches. To avoid this, gently slide the bottom gravel to one side when cleaning near the bottom and regularly check the surface of the pad.

Scrapers

There are also many forms of scraper available to tackle stubborn or hard-to-reach algae. The experienced aquarist will usually have an array of cleaning implements to deal with all situations. A very useful form of scraper that is regularly used is called an algae magnet. This device consists of two powerful magnets in a plastic casing, designed to grip either side of the pane of glass. The exterior magnet comes with a soft, polishing pad, while the interior magnet, which is placed inside the aquarium, is fitted with a coarse pad for scraping. Once fitted to the glass, the outer magnet can be slid along the outside of the glass, and it drags the inner magnet and scourer across the inside of the glass, cleaning the surface as it goes.

Algae magnets have proved to be very popular over the years, as algae wiping has been made more enjoyable with their ease of use. The

Left An abrasive pad is a simple but effective tank cleaner and should be used regularly to rid the glass of algae that has grown on the tank.

Below An algae magnet allows you to clean the glass inside the tank without getting your hands wet.

experienced magnet-handler will be able to turn corners and even attract a fallen magnet to the outer glass without having to get their hands wet.

Gravel vacuuming

Gravel vacuuming is an essential part of aquarium maintenance and is more important than algae wiping because it can have a positive effect on water quality. In addition, cleaning dirty gravel will improve the appearance of your tank. In any substrate, fish waste and detritus will build up among the particles and contribute to polluting the water. This trapped waste can harbor nitrates, which should be controlled and diluted (see page 108), and if it is not regularly removed, the waste can even block the gravel entirely, causing gas to build up and the substrate to turn rotten. To counteract this, disturb and clean the substrate about every two weeks. For best results, use a vacuum, which can be connected to a siphon tube and powered purely by the siphoning action of the tube. They are also available as separate devices powered by either electricity or a battery. A siphon-powered vacuum will remove water at the same time, while an electric or battery vacuum both have the option of solely removing dirt and returning water to the tank.

How to use the vacuum

A gravel siphon works by connecting a wide-bore plastic tube, about 2 inches (5 cm) in diameter, to a normal siphon tube and hovering over the gravel at close range. The suction should be sufficient to lift the gravel partway up the tube, releasing the dirt, but then allowing the heavier gravel to drop back down to the bottom. Start at one end of the tank and drag the siphon over the entire substrate until all the dirt has been removed. Gravel vacuuming should be carried out as part of a water change (see pages 170–71), and a correctly sized vacuum should result in about 25 percent of the aquarium water being removed into buckets at the same time.

Right This battery-powered gravel vacuum can collect debris in a cloth bag for easy removal.

Tip

Combine gravel vacuuming with algae wiping and filter maintenance as part of your twice-weekly maintenance regime.

Water changing

Water changing will vary depending on the type of aquarium you are keeping—tropical, coldwater, or marine—and whether you use tap water or purified water (see pages 82–85). Water changes are an essential part of fishkeeping and, if done properly, cannot be overdone. Remember that in nature the biggest form of filtration is dilution (see page 102), since waste products are dissipated by the vastness of the body of water; even the best filters are incapable of removing nitrates and replacing essential minerals in your fish tank.

Frequency

It is advisable to replace about 25 percent of the aquarium water every two weeks, as this should help to keep nitrates low (see page 108). If you are using tap water for the changes, test it to make sure that the pH and hardness are to the liking of your fish (see pages 104–5). Check also

Tip

The most effective way to keep a tank clean is to combine water changing with filter maintenance, algae wiping, and gravel vacuuming (see pages 168–69).

Below Gravel vacuums are really useful equipment, and every aquarium owner should use one.

that the nitrate level in the tap water is sufficiently low. If the nitrate is reading at 40 parts per million or over, it could actually be contributing to a rising nitrate level in the main tank, and if this is the case, you should consider finding alternative water sources or purifiers. If you are in any doubt about the suitability of your local tap water, consult your local authority.

Equipment

Set aside some clean buckets and siphon tubes especially for water changes and do not use them for any other purpose, such as washing the car. If you are using large containers to store water, check that they are made from suitable food-grade plastic, because some plastics may cause your fish to die if the chemicals leach into the water. Keep stored water in the dark to stop algal blooms forming and run an airstone into it

Tip

One natural source of tank water is rainwater. It is naturally soft and devoid of minerals, but should be filtered through carbon (see page 40) to remove any traces of pollutants. If you are collecting run-off rainwater from a roof, check that the roof is made from a suitable clean, inert material.

to keep it fresh (see page 82). If using reverse osmosis water, an airstone placed within it can help to keep the pH stable. If left for too long without aeration, it may become very acidic.

Tank water dos and don'ts

Take note of the following points to help you avoid problems in your water-changing routine. Incorrect water changes may do more harm than good.

Do

✔ If you are using purified water with all the chlorine and minerals removed (see page 84), first add a mineral additive to replace essential electrolytes, then bring the water up to the appropriate temperature using a heater/thermostat and thermometer (see page 44).

✔ If using tap water (see page 82), bring the water up to the appropriate temperature by using water from a hot kettle or a spare heater. Use a thermometer to check that the temperature is the same as that in the main aquarium.

✔ If you are preparing water for a reef aquarium (see page 214), use only hot water that is free of copper. For this

reason, water from the hot tap is generally regarded as unsafe.

✔ Always dechlorinate water before adding it to the main aquarium (see page 82). Untreated water can kill beneficial bacteria on all surfaces, such as gravel and decorations, as well as in the filter.

Don't

✗ Add water that is too cold. It may cause stress and give your fish an outbreak of whitespot (see page 180).

✗ Add water that is too warm. It will affect oxygen levels in the tank and may kill filter bacteria.

Filter cleaning

Cleaning filters is not as easy as it sounds. Pump impellers and shafts must remain intact during cleaning, and beneficial bacteria should be left undisturbed as much as possible. Tap water should be used only on mechanical media and never on biological media (see pages 38–41). External filters (see pages 36–37) must remain primed, and the whole operation, combined with a water change (see page 170), should go smoothly to avoid stressing the fish.

Washing sponges

To wash sponges, first turn off the filter. As sponges are mechanical filters, they are usually filthy, and when you remove it, it will be covered in dirt and detritus.

Mechanical function only

If the sponge is being used in combination with specific biological media, it can be washed in untreated tap water. It does not have to be thoroughly cleaned, but most of the visible dirt should be removed. When it is clean, inspect the state of the sponge, which may have become quite compacted due to the pulling action of the pump. If, after squeezing, it does not return to its original shape and has become ill-fitting in the filter, this is a sign that it should be replaced.

Dual biological and mechanical function

If the sponge is working biologically as well as mechanically, only wash it in old tank water to keep bacteria levels high. If it does need replacing, cut the sponge in half and use half the old and half the new for the next few weeks until the new sponge has been colonized with bacteria. Never use a completely new sponge, because ammonia and nitrite levels will rise.

Impeller cleaning

The impeller is what drives the water inside the pump, and it is accessed by removing a disk under the head unit. The impeller, which resembles a small propeller, spins on a shaft inside a central column and can be gently lifted out, because it is held in place only by magnets. The shaft on which the impeller spins may be

Below Wash mature sponges in water that has been removed from the tank during cleaning.

Below If you need to replace the old sponge with a new one, cut it in half and use half old and half new.

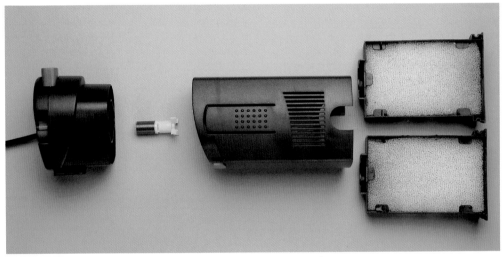

made of steel or ceramic. If it is ceramic, take care that you do not break it, because it will be brittle. The shaft will be stuck into rubber nipples at either end for vibration dampening, and it can also usually be removed. Check first that the shaft is in one piece and second that the nipples have not perished with age. Replacements can be ordered from aquatic retailers.

The impeller can be cleaned with an old toothbrush or an impeller brush under the tap. Cleaning the impeller will lengthen the life span of the pump—in fact, many people are unaware of their existence and go to the expense of buying a new pump when all that is required is cleaning the impeller.

Top The impeller is the driving force of any power filter and should be kept clean.

Bottom This internal power filter provides easy access to the impeller and comes with two sponges for alternate cleaning.

Chemical and biological media

Carbon and other chemical media should be removed and replaced when they are exhausted. None of them is essential, but each has a benefit. Carbon should be replaced every four to six weeks. Biological media, such as ceramics, can be plunged into a bucket of old tank water to remove the worst of the debris, then replaced in the filter.

Emergency contingencies

If something goes wrong with the equipment in your aquarium, it can be worrying. Aquarium fishkeeping systems are entirely dependent on electricity to keep the fish alive. If you are faced by a situation in which there is a technical problem or failure, the key is to stay calm so that you can think about what to do as quickly and effectively as possible.

Heater failure

If the heater/thermostat fails in the off position (see pages 44–45), you should take a look at the thermometer reading. The room temperature in modern houses is around 68°F (20°C), so do not panic—if that is the temperature of the water, it is not cool enough to kill tropical freshwater or marine fish. If you are concerned that the water will drop to a lower temperature, wrap the tank in blankets, which should conserve enough heat.

If the heater fails in the on position, and you come home to find your fish in a distressed state, unplug the heater but make sure that it has cooled before you remove it from the tank, as it may shatter otherwise. If you have an air pump or Venturi device on your filter (see

pages 42–43), turn it on to full power. Siphon off about 50 percent of the tank water and change it for new water that is slightly colder than usual (see page 170). Add the water slowly so that you do not shock the fish, and the fish should recover.

If the water is very hot and the fish look as if they are going to die, they are best removed and placed in a bucket of conditioned tap water of the correct temperature. Place an airstone in the water (see page 82) and they should recover.

Filter failure

Symptoms of filter failure can range from obvious signs such as no water flow or no air flow, to cloudy water and gasping fish. If the

Below During a power loss replace a proportion with new water and pour it in from a height to create oxygen.

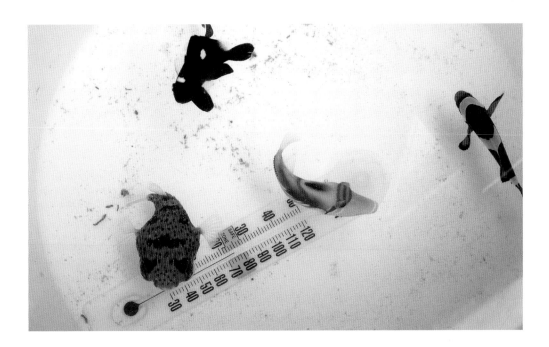

Above These fish have been placed in a bucket until the problem in the main tank is rectified.

fish are gasping, this is probably an indication of low oxygen levels as well, so add an air pump (see page 43) or, failing that, carry out a 50 percent water change and vigorously add water to the tank to create more oxygen by pouring it in from a height. If the filter pump has stopped, first of all check the inlet to make sure that it is not totally blocked. Second, check that the impeller is not totally blocked and check that the shaft on which it spins is in one piece and not broken (see page 173). If the shaft is broken, it may be a part stocked by your retailer that you can easily replace.

If the filter is beyond repair (remember also to check the fuse), the best solution is to buy the same model and swap the old mature media for the new. That way what is left of the bacteria may be saved. In the event of filter failure, check the water several times a day to give you an idea of what is happening. Water testing can tell you much about your tank, and it may, literally, save lives (see pages 100–1).

In the event of filter failure, avoid feeding the fish, as they produce more waste immediately after feeding, which may poison them if the filter is not working to eradicate it.

To aid tank recovery

- In any situation that may have caused your fish stress, do not feed them. They may not eat the food under the circumstances, but if they eat it or not, it will end up as ammonia in one way or another, which will only add to your problems.

- Add tap water conditioner containing herbal extracts to help lower stress in your fish (see page 82).

- Add Zeolite or liquid ammonia remover to the water (see pages 40 and 106).

HEALTHCARE

Fish anatomy

Getting to know your fish by observing them is one thing, but you need to be knowledgeable about their fins if you want to be able to identify the sex of many species, and body characteristics can offer clues about what the fish eats and where it swims in the water column.

Fins

Fins are used for propulsion and maneuvering. A fish can push itself slowly forwards using only its pectoral fins, but for bursts of speed the pectoral fins are held flat against the body, and the big push comes from the tail, or caudal, fin.

Fins can also offer a clue as to the sex of the fish. Fins are often longer and more colorful in the male of the species so that it can display and attract a female. Live-bearing fish, such as

guppies (*Poecilia reticulata*), take fin adaptation one step further, with males developing a modified anal fin, called the gonopodium. This tubular fin carries sperm to the female fish, and males practice insemination. It is the ease with which males mate without prior female consent that makes it necessary to keep more females than males in the same tank, otherwise females will be mated with several times a day, causing exhaustion.

Anatomy of a fish

1 Brain	16 Eye
2 Gill slits	17 Gill cover
3 Olfactory bulb and nerve	18 Lateral line
4 Tongue	19 Dorsal fin
5 Heart	20 Caudal peduncle
6 Liver	21 Caudal fin
7 Intestines	22 Anal fin
8 Reproductive organs	23 Ventral fin
9 Anus	24 Pectoral fin
10 Genital opening	25 Barbels
11 Ureter	
12 Kidney	
13 Spinal column	
14 Fin ray supports	
15 Neural spine	

Position of fins

1 Dorsal fin
2 Adipose fin
3 Caudal fin
4 Anal fin
5 Pelvic fin
6 Pectoral fin

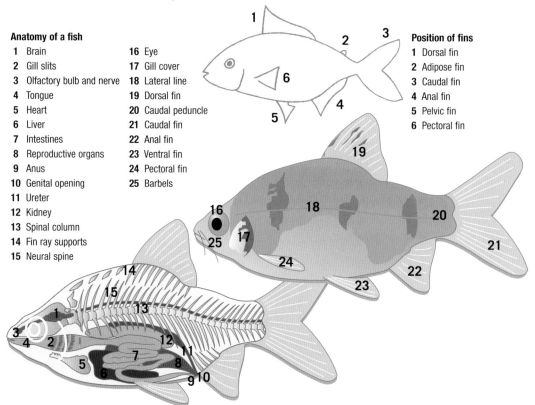

Only characins (see pages 139–44) and salmonids carry an adipose fin—a small fin between the dorsal and caudal fin. It has no primary function and does not aid swimming.

Mouth position

The position of the mouth is a clue to where the fish naturally eats. Upward-facing mouths are termed as superior and are adapted for surface feeding. Downward-facing mouths are called inferior and are adapted for bottom feeding; centrally positioned, forward-facing mouths are called anterior and are adapted to take food from the middle of the water column.

Mouth size

If a fish has a big mouth, it will usually be predatory. A predatory fish is opportunist and will take fish up to a third of its size. The

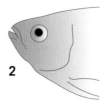
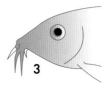

Mouth positions
1 Middle-positioned is called anterior
2 Upward-positioned is called superior
3 Downward-positioned is called inferior

stomach of a predatory fish is elastic so that it can expand to cope with huge, sudden meals. Predatory fish only give a real indication of their spacious mouths when they yawn.

Whiskers

The whiskers on a catfish (see pages 154–55) can also give an indication of its diet. Bottom-feeding catfish, such as *Corydoras* spp. (see page 138), have small, downward-facing barbules for sifting sandy bottom material. Combined with a small mouth, they indicate that the catfish eats only small food items and not fish.

Wide, horizontal barbules on the side of a wide mouth are a sure sign of a catfish that likes to eat small fish, such as pimelodids.

The flattened, disk-type mouths of Loriacariidae catfish do sometimes contain teeth, but they are only able to rasp away at wood. Loriacariidae are not adapted to catch and swallow prey fish, so they are safe to keep with small fish. They can, however, devour dead fish with great speed and efficiency.

Mouth sizes
1 A small mouth and short barbules are for foraging on the bottom
2 A mouth made for rasping
3 A wide mouth and long whiskers for sensing prey indicate that the fish is a predator

What makes fish healthy?

Many fish diseases can be avoided by keeping your fish healthy in the first place, but a major factor that can have a detrimental effect on the immune systems of fish is stress. Stress is responsible for, or linked to, many fish deaths and is a more common problem than many aquarists believe. Stress can be caused by a number of factors in the aquarium, and these are noted below.

Causes and signs of stress

There are obvious factors that cause stress to aquarium fish, such as aggression from other fish and overcrowding, but there are also invisible causes, such as poor water quality or the wrong water conditions. To check for signs of stress, use a test kit to give a clear idea of how the system is running (see pages 100–1). Second, use your eyes to look for indications of rapid gill movement, reluctance to feed, and a change of behavior.

Treating stress

Some water conditioners contain aloe vera or herbal extracts and have been shown to reduce stress (see page 82), especially when you are introducing or transporting fish, but normally the cause of the stress must be removed if the fish is to recover.

Below Remove any uneaten food from the aquarium in order to avoid water-quality problems and stress.

Avoiding stress

Properly research the species that you are keeping and check their eventual size and long-term compatibility. If you keep soft-water species with hard-water species, for example, one or none of the species will be truly happy in the long term, causing stress.

Seemingly minor factors, such as having the light on for too long, vibration from loud music, or unsuitable hiding places and retreats, can stress many species.

Feeding

Once you are satisfied that stress is not a factor in your tank, you can concentrate on the long-term health of your fish. Proper feeding of aquarium fish can do wonders for their health, and a well-fed fish can naturally fight off many diseases. So, be sure to follow the advice below when you are feeding your fish.

- Feed brand-name foods manufactured by reputable companies. Take time to research so that you know that you are feeding the correct type of foods, such as algae wafers for algae eaters, for example (see page 167).
- Feed small fish small portions and often, because they have fast metabolisms.
- Feed large fish more substantial meals less often (see page 162).
- Keep food fresh, and where possible, do not buy loose dry food because it will already have lost much of its nutritional value (see pages 164–65).
- Remove any uneaten food immediately, as it will disintegrate and adversely affect the water quality.
- Provide a varied diet of fresh, frozen, and dry foods to your fish wherever possible, as this will provide interest for the fish as well as optimum nutrition.

Water quality

Providing good water for your fish is paramount and vital for their long-term health, so remember to adhere to the following rules.

Above Overcrowding can be a direct cause of stress in the aquarium.

- Choose an adequately sized filter that will allow for the future growth of your fish (see pages 34–37).
- Never wash biological filter media under the tap, because all the good bacteria will be lost and toxic ammonia will rise (see page 38).
- Choose a maintenance regime, such as changing 25 percent of tank water twice weekly, and stick to it (see page 170).
- Provide the right type of water for your fish, such as soft water for South American species (see page 104).

Fish stocking

The wrong stocking can have dire consequences on your fish and affect their long-term health, so consider the following points when you are choosing your fish.

- Only buy fish that you are sure you can adequately house. Some fish grow to be huge, and it can be easy to underestimate this when you are buying them.
- Don't stock fish too heavily. It is tempting to try to create a visual display with as many different fish as possible, but this can cause stunting, parasite infestations, and oxygen deprivation, as well as a very heavy load on your filter.
- Keep shoaling fish in groups and keep solitary fish on their own.
- Provide the right lighting conditions for the fish at all times—some are sensitive or unaccustomed to bright light (see pages 46–47), and this can cause stress.
- Stock slowly with compatible fish from the outset. Do not keep predators with prey fish, even if you buy them when they are small.

What's wrong with your fish?

Fish ailments are as common as human ailments and can have a number of causes. One of the factors that contributes significantly to fish illness is the lowering of the immune system through stress. Stress can be caused primarily by poor water quality but also through social factors, such as bullying or overcrowding (see page 178). Some of the most common are described here.

Types of illness

Illness in fish can be divided into two main categories, parasitic and bacterial, and in either case the fish must be treated with the correct medication in time if it is to survive.

Parasitic infection can come from newly introduced fish that are carrying parasites. Alternatively, a small population of parasites within the aquarium, which would normally be held at bay by the resident fishes' immune system, can take hold when a fish becomes stressed and susceptible.

Bacterial infection can also be caused by stress or carried by fish, but can also be secondary to the effects of a parasite infestation.

Common fish ailments

The following is a guide to the most commonly occurring ailments in aquarium fish, how to spot the symptoms, and the recommended treatments. Whitespot and fish lice are parasitic infections; the remainder are bacterial problems.

Whitespot

Whitespot is easily recognizable because the fish becomes covered in white spots about the size of a pinhead. The condition is caused by parasites on the fish and normally starts as faint scatterings of spots on the fins, which quickly work their way across the body. If it is allowed to spread to the gill area, the condition can become fatal. Whitespot is largely stress related and is the result of the fish being given a

Below Whitespot covers the fish's body and fins and is fatal if not treated in time.

Below Fish lice are a large external parasite that hold on to the host fish with a sucker.

Above Dropsy affects all sorts of freshwater fish and appears out of nowhere.

Above Fin rot is a bacterial infection that is usually caused by poor water quality.

quick chill (during water changing, for instance) or if the fish has been exposed to poor water. Turn the heater to maximum to raise the temperature of the tank water to 86°F (30°C). The whitespot parasite is severely weakened at high temperatures and may not be able to carry out its life cycle. Also, apply an anti-whitespot treatment. If caught early, whitespot is easily cured with medication.

Fish lice

Fish lice, or *Argulus*, are nasty-looking external parasites, which are commonly found on newly imported goldfish. They use a specially developed sucker on the underside of their flattened bodies to fasten onto the fish and feed on their blood, growing up to ½ inch (1.2 cm) in diameter, before falling off to lay eggs. If left untreated, *Argulus* can reach plague proportions in an aquarium and will severely weaken or kill their hosts. They are easily removed by hand and disposed of, but you should also use a treatment specially formulated to kill off fish lice eggs or juveniles.

Dropsy

Dropsy can be caused by bacterial infection and is one of the most easily identified ailments, as it changes the appearance of the fish quite dramatically. Affected fish swell up with fluid to the point at which the scales become raised like those on a pine cone, and the eyes protrude. The condition often arises from nowhere but has been linked to species being kept in less-than-perfect conditions. It is rarely cured and often proves fatal. Use a specially formulated treatment for dropsy.

Fin rot

Fin rot is caused by bacteria that are always present in aquarium water. Fish become susceptible to fin rot when they are kept in poor water conditions, and it is common on fish kept in unfiltered tanks or bowls. If left untreated, the disease will erode the fins, especially the tail, and can enter the body of the fish, causing death. Symptoms include loss of fins and white and red patches on the fins. Treat with an anti-fungal fin rot treatment.

Above Fungus can come from physical damage and poor water quality.

Above Pop eye can be caused by a number of factors and may result in one or both eyes protruding.

Fungus

Fungus on fish is caused by fungal spores that are present in aquarium water. It can be identified by white, cottony growths on the fish and commonly takes hold only on damaged areas of the fish's body. Damage can be the result of improper handling or aggressive spawning techniques. It can also be caused by periods of extreme stress brought about by poor water quality. The danger with fungus is that it can go deep into the body of the fish and may be beyond treatment if action is not taken early on.

Pop eye

Pop eye can be recognized by one or both eyes protruding abnormally. Its cause can be related to a number of factors, but it will rarely spread to all fish in the tank and normally stays isolated to one or two fish. It will need to be treated with a specially formulated medication for pop eye, and the affected fish should be kept under observation to make absolutely sure that it is not the early stages of dropsy (see page 181).

Ulcers

Ulcers are common in coldwater fish, such as goldfish that have been exposed to a sudden rise of temperature or other stresses, like poor water quality. Symptoms are red, eroded areas that go through the outer layer of skin and look like burns. Treat the problem with an anti-ulcer treatment, which will also help to prevent further secondary infection. Even if the ulcer is halted, recovery is slow, as new tissue must be grown and this can take some time.

Swim bladder disorder

This is very common in fancy goldfish (see pages 127–32). Symptoms include increased buoyancy, causing the fish to float and in some cases to turn upside down. The fish normally look otherwise unaffected, but will suffer long-term stress from the disorder. There is a swim bladder disease, but the most common reason for such problems in fancy goldfish is that the swim bladder is bent against the spine, a defect that has been caused by breeding them to have shortened bodies.

Above Ulcers need to be treated to prevent further infection, and tissue regrowth is slow.

Above Swim bladder problems in fancy goldfish can be the result of a number of contributing factors.

The factors that seem to acerbate the problem include warm temperatures and dry foods that are full of air when eaten. A simple remedy is to change the fish's diet to sinking foods and feed frozen daphnia for a week to act as a laxative.

Because of the way that they have been bred, many fancy goldfish are susceptible to buoyancy problems—the shorter and fatter the fish, the more likely it is to be affected.

Tip

Many fish ailments are avoidable if you practice proper fish husbandry, maintenance, and feeding. If fish do become ill, treating them sooner rather than later is the key to a successful recovery, along with proper diagnosis in the first place. Very few fish die of old age, and if water quality is not the reason, it is usually disease. Fish can also come down with secondary infections as a result of being ill the first time around, so observing the fish carefully in the weeks after illness, and quarantining for a period, are the best options.

Using medications

When you have properly diagnosed a disease, you should take prompt action to remedy it. Medications can be dangerous if they are misused, so be sure to follow the guidelines below. All medications used should be specifically for fish in aquariums and purchased from a specialty aquatic retailer. Keep fish medications out of the reach of children.

Testing the water quality

A fish will not get better if it is being kept in water of poor quality. Indeed, the water quality may have been a factor in the fish becoming ill in the first place, so always check the quality of the water before you start (see pages 100–1).

Ensuring the correct dosage

To treat an aquarium with a medication, you must know the size of the aquarium before you add anything. Underdosing can render the medication ineffective, and overdosing may risk the health of the fish and deplete filter bacteria. See page 24 for advice on calculating the volume of your tank. Some brands of aquarium treatment also have a reference chart to help you calculate tank volume.

Ensuring the right treatment

Medications vary from being wide-range general bacterial and parasite treatments, through to particular chemicals aimed at treating a specific ailment. If you are not sure what is affecting your fish, always get a second opinion from someone with expert knowledge or experience. Time is of the essence with fish ailments, because a small fish with prominent symptoms may have only hours rather than days to live.

Safety precautions

Medications should always be handled with care, because they can be hazardous to human health. When you are handling any medication, avoid contact with your skin and eyes. For safety, the use of latex gloves is recommended, as treatments can be messy to use. Professionals also wear goggles for protection. Always read the directions on the packaging carefully before administering any treatments to make you aware of any dangers involved.

Keep all medicines out of the reach of children, but if a treatment is swallowed, seek immediate medical attention and tell the doctors what type of treatment is involved. Always avoid inhalation.

When using any medications, remove carbon and Zeolite from the system because they will absorb medications (see page 40). Turn off ultraviolet sterilizers if fitted (see page 210) and make sure there is plenty of oxygen in the water because many medications deplete oxygen.

The most effective treatments are often those used in their raw form. The chart opposite is a guide to the most widely used chemical treatments for aquarium fish and their specific benefits and drawbacks.

Below Calculate the tank's volume before using treatments. Some treatments come with a chart.

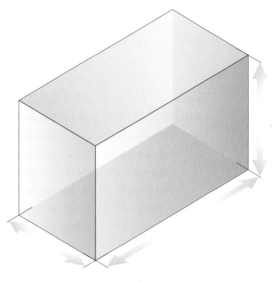

Analysis of raw chemical treatments

RAW CHEMICAL	PROS	CONS
Malachite green	An effective treatment for fungus and protozoan parasites	More toxic at low pH levels and is a carcinogen
Formaldehyde	Treats skin parasites and body flukes; can be used in conjunction with malachite green	Can strip oxygen from the water and is also more toxic at a low pH
Potassium permanganate	Effective against parasites and bacterial infection	More toxic at high pH and may affect filter bacteria
Acriflavin	Effective against bacterial infection	If used too often, it will remove background levels of bacteria essential for the fish's immune system function
Salt	Detoxifies nitrite and aids gill function; kills some parasites	None; but soft water species will not benefit from long-term exposure

Below left Make sure that filtration is working effectively because it may be the cause of the sickness if it is malfunctioning.

Below middle Make sure the water is strongly aerated because oxygen levels can be depleted by treatments.

Below right Remove carbon or Zeolite from the system when using medications.

Tip

Prolonged use of any medication can make it less effective. Only treat when you have to.

Setting up a hospital tank

Having a spare aquarium that you can use as a hospital tank is an excellent idea, and one that you should really consider when keeping any community of fish. Not only can it be used to hold and treat sick fish, but it will be useful for quarantining new purchases until you are satisfied that they are 100 percent healthy and disease free. Practicality is the only requirement for a hospital tank.

Recommended size

A hospital tank does not need to be large—an 18 inch (45 cm) and 24 inch (60 cm) tank should be adequate for freshwater and marine fish respectively. Neither does it need to look attractive—it is merely there to serve a practical purpose, so a secondhand tank or an old, scratched tank would be fine.

Equipment required

The tank should be fitted with the same range of equipment as a normal aquarium, including the essential filter (see pages 34–37) and a heater/thermostat for all tropical fish (see page 44)—see the shopping lists below—but that is where the similarities end. A substrate is not necessary, as no live plants will be grown in the tank because they can harbor parasites and bacteria. Lighting should at best be subdued (see page 46), because a newly purchased fish kept on its own will be nervous, and low lighting has the added benefit of limiting algae buildup and consequently requires less maintenance. Carbon or other chemical filter media should also be omitted (see pages 40–41), because if medications are administered, you need to be sure that they remain present long enough to do their work, and they would be quickly eradicated by such media. For marine aquariums, leave out the protein skimmer (see pages 206–7), as this will also remove any treatments from the water.

For both a tropical and marine hospital tank, use water from the main aquarium unless acclimatizing a fish to a new pH and hardness.

Maturing filtration

All filters used in hospital tanks should be pre-matured, either in the main tank or by being left to run continuously in the hospital tank (see pages 98–99). Failure to mature filtration ready for fish will cause a secondary and major problem, and that is water quality. The last thing you want is a fish that is fighting against both disease and bad water!

Shopping list for a tropical hospital tank

- 18 inch (45 cm) glass tank
- heater/thermostat
- thermometer
- test kit
- air-powered sponge filter
- air pump
- cave or flowerpot (for shelter)
- plastic condensation tray
- polystyrene tiles (for cushioning)

Shopping list for a marine hospital tank

- 24 inch (60 cm) glass tank
- heater/thermostat
- thermometer
- test kit
- internal power filter
- cave or flowerpot (for shelter)
- plastic condensation tray
- polystyrene tiles (for cushioning)

The aquarium should be set up on a permanent basis so that if you do discover a sick fish in the main tank, it can quickly be moved to the hospital tank with the minimum of fuss and discomfort. This may seem to be a lot to ask because aesthetically it will not look very appealing, but if you keep one or several tanks, it should get quite a lot of use, if only to quarantine new purchases or raise young fry. You can also use the hospital tank to quarantine live plants because they frequently come with nuisance snails attached, and a few days of close observation can stop a future snail infestation in the main display tank.

Hospital tank

1 Heater thermostat to keep temperature constant
2 Thermometer to check temperature
3 Flowerpots used as shelter by nervous fish
4 Air-powered foam filter for freshwater tanks with small fish
5 External power filter for large freshwater or marine fish
6 Bare-bottomed tank to improve hygiene and cleanliness

Above Use only plastic plants in hospital tanks because they can be removed and sterilized.

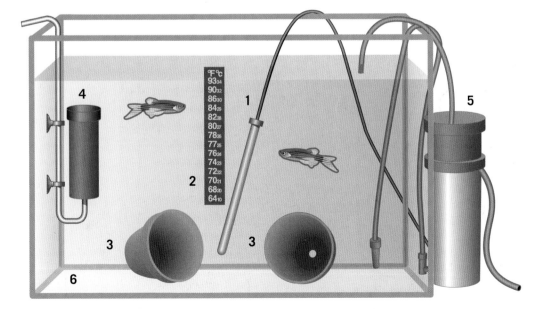

FISH REPRODUCTION

Breeding methods

Different species of fish reproduce in different ways, all of which work perfectly in the natural environment. However, your fish need special equipment if they are to successfully spawn in a breeding tank. Here are the most common methods of spawning used and the tank setups that will help make it happen.

Egg scatterers

The majority of community fish kept in aquariums use egg scattering to reproduce. It is common with fish of all sizes and means that spawning can commence quickly and without creating much attention from predators. The method relies on strength in numbers.

Days before spawning, the female fish will become ripe with eggs and will look decidedly plump. The males will darken in coloration in an attempt to look their best. The act of spawning occurs when the male and female rub against each other, with the female releasing eggs into the water. The male fertilizes them by releasing sperm at the same time. Spawning often occurs annually in nature and will be triggered by an influx of food or a change in temperature.

The eggs are often adhesive and will naturally stick to plants and overhanging roots or will fall in between gaps in rocks or gravel. Examples of egg-scattering fish include most tetras, barbs, and rainbowfish (see pages 139–44, 149–50, and 156–57).

Tank setups for egg scatterers

If you wish to breed egg-scattering fish, you will need to set up an aquarium specially to facilitate the breeding. The reason for this is that in the normal community aquarium, the parents and other fish species would eat the eggs as soon as they are scattered and none would survive. Also, the fry are tiny, and if they did manage to hatch, they would be eaten by other fish or sucked into the filter.

There are two main ways that fishkeepers can successfully spawn and rear egg scatterers:

Method 1

As previously mentioned, scattered eggs are adhesive and species such as tetras (see pages 139–44) naturally swim through vegetated areas as they spawn, with the eggs sticking to plants and fine, feathery roots. This can be mimicked in the breeding tank by making some spawning mops.

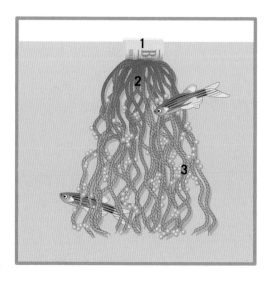

Tank for egg scatterers (method 1)
1 Cork makes the spawning mop float
2 The mop is simply made from strands of wool
3 Adhesive eggs stick to the wool mop

These mops can be created simply by wrapping knitting wool around some stiff cardboard several times. One end is then tied into a bunch and the other cut with scissors, forming a mop.

Mops will float from the surface if tied to a piece of cork or plastic, or they can be weighted down with plant weights. To catch the eggs, a combination of floating and sunken mops can be used. Alternatively, you can use natural spawning mops in the form of the feathered leaves of *Cabomba* and *Myriophyllum* (see pages 70 and 74).

Method 2
Another way to collect the eggs of scatterers is to fit a mesh about 3 inches (7.5 cm) above the bottom of a bare-bottomed tank. Plastic gridding, called eggcrate, can be placed in the tank in one big sheet so that the adults are kept away from the

Tip

Place young fish in the main aquarium only when they are about 1 inch (2.5 cm) long. If they are any smaller than that, they may be eaten.

eggs once they have scattered them. The holes in the grid must, of course, be small enough to prevent the fish from swimming through them. The adults can be removed after spawning and the fry raised in the spawning tank.

A variation on this method is to use a layer of marbles across the bottom of the tank. The eggs fall between the gaps onto the tank base, making them inaccessible to the adults. However, the former approach means that the grid can be removed more easily. Examples of species that can be bred using this method include barbs and danios (see pages 149–50 and 151–52).

Bubble-nesters
Bubble-nesting is an advanced spawning method that is used by anabantoids (see pages 135–37). The male constructs the nest by blowing hundreds of bubbles, which stick together on the surface in a thick foam. The male entices a female under the nest where they spawn together in a tight embrace. The eggs fall to the bottom, but are picked up by the male and are placed in the nest. The male tends the nest.

A tank set up for bubble-nest construction should consist of a bare-bottomed aquarium half-filled with water. This helps the male to find and replace the eggs that fall out of the nest. The nest often needs support, so floating plants can be used along with a standard bunch plant to stop the nest from floating away.

Anabantoids possess an organ called the labyrinth organ, which enables them to breathe atmospheric air. The point at which the young fry develop this organ is crucial. Air above the

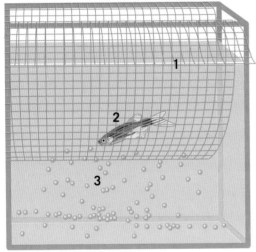

Tank for egg scatterers (method 2)

1 Mesh or egg crate is suspended in top half of the tank
2 Adult fish are conditioned and placed above mesh where they spawn
3 Eggs fall through the mesh and cannot be eaten by the adult

1 Half-fill tank with water
2 Floating plants help to secure nest
3 Feathery plants may also be used in nest building
4 Bubble-nest may protrude above the surface
5 Clear bottom for parent fish to identify and retrieve any fallen eggs

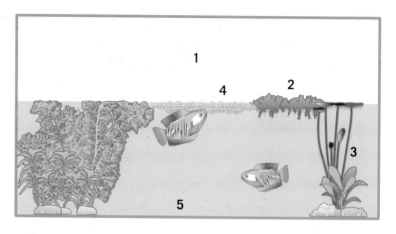

water's surface must be warm enough or the fry may die, so fit a lid that keeps the space between the water and the top of the tank warm.

Egg depositors

Egg depositing is an advanced method of spawning because the parents partake in parental care of the eggs and fry. Most cichlids are egg depositors (see pages 144-46). Where the eggs are placed varies from species to species, but angelfish (*Pterophyllum scalare*) (see page 146) prefer to lay on the leaves of Amazon sword plants (*Echinodoraus bleheri*) (see page 72), but discus (*Symphysodon* spp.) (see page 147) prefer vertical surfaces. Central American

cichlids, such as the firemouth (*Thorichthys meeki*), will dig pits and choose several potential spawning and nursery sites before secretly spawning but may move the fry frequently once hatched.

Cichlids will show marked aggression towards all other fish species when protecting eggs and fry, so they should be placed in an aquarium on their own before spawning, with plenty of potential spawning sites provided in the form of caves, plants, rocks, and flowerpots. Very often they will spawn in a place other than where you intend them to spawn so that you cannot see the eggs. One or both parents will tend the fry for up to a month.

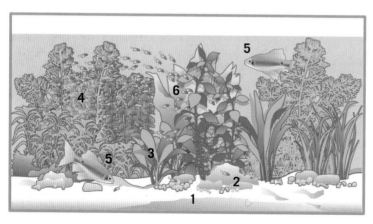

Tank for egg-depositing fish

1 Substrate should be deep so that parent fish can dig pits in which to place fry
2 Rocks provide possible spawning sites
3 Leaves may also be used by some species to lay eggs
4 Planting will provide cover for fry and possible grazing sites
5 Only the adult breeding pair should be placed in the tank prior to spawning
6 Fry are herded together when they have become free swimming. They are protected by the parents.

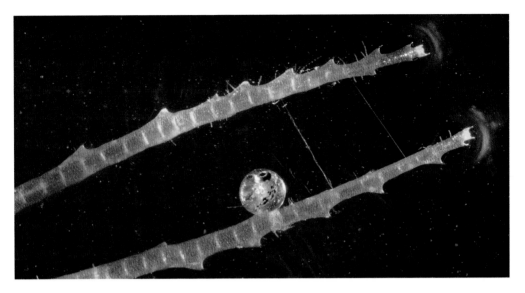

Above This close-up picture reveals an adhesive fish egg stuck on to the leaf of a fine-leaved aquarium plant.

Live-bearing fish

The ability of some species to produce live young is quite remarkable and has made them very successful. Guppies (*Poecilia reticulata*), platies (*Xiphophorus maculatus*), mollies (*Poecilia* spp.), and swordtails (*Xiphophorus helleri*) are all live-bearers (see pages 158-59), and most female fish are already pregnant when you buy them. The males constantly mate with females and so should be outnumbered to prevent females from being harassed. A pregnant female will look very plump and may display a dark patch on the lower belly called a gravid spot (see page 193). It is hard to know exactly when they are going to give birth, so females should be placed in a breeding trap or breeding tank one at a time when they start to get big.

Breeding traps, although common, are more stressful on female fish and are simply too small for pregnant females. A breeding tank should be simply furnished with lots of feathery plants in bunches for the fry to retreat into once the female has given birth. Once she has done so, she can be put back into the main aquarium and the fry grow on.

Tank for live-bearing fish

1 Breeding trap of mesh can be used to hold pregnant female fish
2 Pregnant female fish
3 Feathery plant offers cover for newly born fry
4 Fry swim through mesh and away from female when they are born

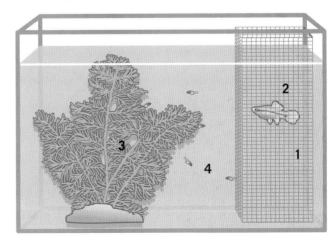

Conditioning and breeding signs

Conditioning is a very important aspect of breeding fish in the aquarium, and without it they may never breed. To condition a fish for spawning involves giving it extra-special care to get it into perfect condition and health and to try and encourage it to reproduce. Fish can be conditioned in two ways: by proper feeding and by providing the right water conditions. Fish in top condition can also be considered for showing at your local fish club.

Feeding

As we have seen, in terms of the way in which they reproduce, fish can be divided into two groups—egg layers and live-bearers—but in both cases, as in human pregnancy, the act of reproduction can be an exhausting and energy-demanding process. Extra energy demands are also put on male fish during breeding.

Female fish

To feed fish in preparation for spawning activities, it is important to understand their nutritional needs and what foods can meet them. Egg and fry production use up lots of protein and energy, so foods should be offered more often and of a higher protein content. If your fish usually receive mostly dry foods (see page 166), offer much more live and frozen foods (164) because these complete tiny animals are perfect for providing an extra nutritional boost to aid the reproductive process.

Male fish

Males will also need a higher protein content because courtship can involve much displaying, chasing, and sometimes even fighting, which all take a big toll on energy. Males also need to look their best to entice females, so introduce some color and growth foods (see page 166). Bear in mind that fish breed in the natural environment only when times are good and the prospective parents can be sure that there will be enough food for the young fish as well.

Water conditions

The right water conditions are crucial when encouraging fish to spawn. In nature, invisible triggers cause the fish to change their normal routine and start to think about breeding. Change of temperature plays a big role in the reproductive cycle of many species. Coldwater fish, such as goldfish (see pages 127–32), spawn when the weather gets warmer. Some tropical species are triggered by the coming of the rains, which means that the weather becomes cooler. Again, goldfish are triggered by early morning sunlight on the tank, whereas some tetras (see pages 139-44) have eggs that are light sensitive, in which case the tank should be blacked out.

It is, therefore, important to research the particular requirements of the species that you intend to breed and to make provisions for them as far as possible. A key factor is to ensure that the water is of the correct pH and hardness (see pages 104–5). Soft-water fish will not usually breed at all in hard water and vice versa.

Other specific needs

In the case of egg layers, you will also need to consider what method of spawning your chosen species uses, because without the correct support they may not spawn. Egg depositors, such as cichlids (see pages 144–47), should be provided with surfaces on which to deposit eggs, and bubble-nesters need something to which they can anchor their nest (see page 190).

Breeding signs

So how do you know when your fish are sexually receptive or are about to spawn? The most obvious signs are changes in coloration and behavior, but there are differences in the ways that different species reproduce and spawn. So let us again divide the two types of reproduction into egg layers and live-bearers.

Egg layers

As we have seen on pages 188–90, these can be divided further into egg scatterers and egg depositors. As an example, in the case of the

Above Male and female fish taking time out together is a sure sign of sexual activity.

egg-scattering tiger barb (*Barbus tetrazona*) (see page 150), breeding is signaled by the males becoming darker in coloration with dark red fins, while the females grow larger around the belly region. The shoaling action becomes more frenzied, and the males will pursue ripe females up and down the tank, displaying their coloring and speed. The act of spawning will occur when the two sexes stop momentarily and quiver their bodies at one another—sometimes you may be able to see the eggs as they are released.

Egg depositors, such as the kribensis (*Pelvicachromis pulcher*) (see page 146), will form pairs and become more antisocial. They will be noted by their absence at the front of the tank, as a pair finds a secret spawning site among the decoration. Their spawning will remain out of sight, but signs will be erratic behavior towards other fish and increased coloration.

Tip

Make sure that tank mates are not putting your fish off mating. For example, catfish may eat the eggs at night, and territorial fish may keep interrupting spawning rituals and the depositing of eggs.

Live-bearers

There are no other signs of breeding behavior other than the obvious ones of male fish pursuing and inseminating females, which will happen many times in a day, and females become very plump before giving birth weeks later, some having a dark patch, or gravid spot, on the belly.

Breeding tanks

A breeding tank can be a tank intended to hold breeding adults or a tank in which you can raise young fish that have been bred in the main aquarium. Its size will depend on the species, but most fish will breed in or be raised in a 24 inch (60 cm) tank. The tank does not have to be elaborate because it is merely there to serve a purpose and is not intended as a display tank.

Basic requirements

The fundamentals for any breeding tank are to have the water at the right temperature and pH for the chosen species to breed, and to have the right spawning aids for that species, such as flat rocks on which eggs can be laid, or bushy plants for scattering eggs into (see page 188–89). The filtration should be mature enough to keep the water quality consistently perfect and be able to cope with an influx of several hundred fry, all being regularly fed. Any filtration should also be fry friendly in that the powerful action must not be able to suck them in. The filter chosen by many breeders is a simple air-powered foam filter (see page 34).

Shopping list for a breeding tank

- ○ 24 inch (60 cm) glass tank
- ○ cover glass/condensation tray
- ○ heater/thermostat
- ○ thermometer
- ○ air-powered foam filter
- ○ air pump
- ○ air line and accessories
- ○ test kit
- ○ spawning aids (flowerpot, bush plant, etc.)
- ○ fry foods
- ○ divider (for some pairs, if necessary)
- ○ water (usually taken from the main tank)

Breeding traps

The breeding trap is mainly for use with smaller species of live-bearing fish, such as guppies (*Poecilia reticulata*) and platies (*Xiphophorus maculatus*) (see pages 158–59). Pregnant females are placed in the trap in the main tank a few days before they give birth. When the fry are born, they drop through a slot in the bottom of the trap where they are safe from predation from the mother. Once she has finished giving birth, the female can be placed back in the main tank, and the fry can be reared in the trap, the removable compartments being taken out first. The breeding trap is an effective method of separation for live-bearers, but is too small for rearing the fry in the long term.

Net traps

The net trap is a small nylon net tied around a plastic frame which clips inside the tank. It can be used to separate fish temporarily or to hold fry, but it is too small to raise fry in the long term. If large fish are being kept in the main tank, they may suck small fry through the holes in the net.

Tank dividers

A tank divider is a plastic frame that can be placed in the tank to split it in half (or two dividers can also be used to make three separate compartments). Its clear, perforated screen allows water to flow through it, but it keeps adults or fry separate from each other. These are a useful aid to breeding and raising some species in the main tank, such as cichlids (see pages 144–47), which form mated pairs before laying eggs but may split up at any time and begin fighting. Dividers have the advantage over nets and traps in that they can be used for separating medium to large species on a longer term basis. However, manufactured dividers will not fit all sizes of tank.

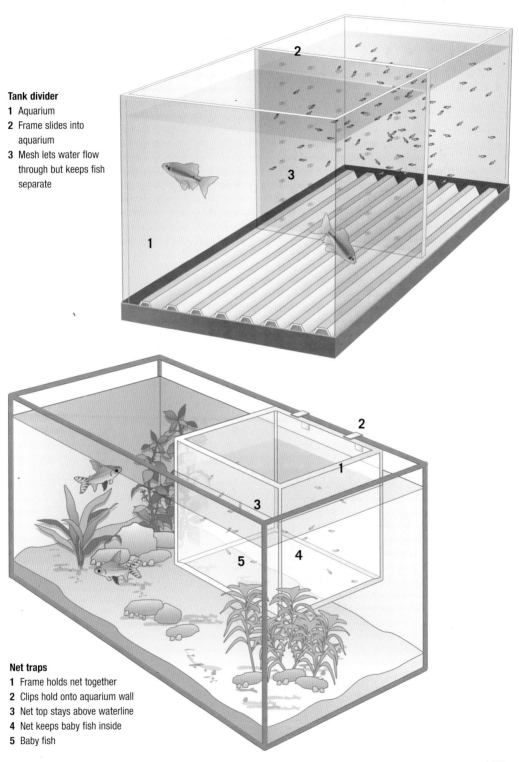

Tank divider
1 Aquarium
2 Frame slides into aquarium
3 Mesh lets water flow through but keeps fish separate

Net traps
1 Frame holds net together
2 Clips hold onto aquarium wall
3 Net top stays above waterline
4 Net keeps baby fish inside
5 Baby fish

Caring for baby fish

Breeding your fish can be very rewarding and a personal triumph, but baby fish need extra care if they are to reach adulthood. Newborn fry are tiny in comparison with their parents and will need special foods that they can fit into their mouths and that will aid growth. Baby fish will also need to be fed more frequently than adult fish.

Protection from predation

Small fry will obviously need protecting from predation from larger fish, but even fry that are a few weeks older than a subsequent batch may turn on and eat the younger ones. Therefore, it is important to keep fry of different ages apart from each other.

Below These tiny cichlid fry are protected by their parents but will quickly starve if not fed tiny foods.

Feeding requirements

The aquarium environment is low in natural fry foods, whereas in the wild, fry swim through a rich soup of available foods all day long. The largest fry are those that are born live, such as guppies (*Poecilia reticulata*) and platies (*Xiphophorus maculatus*) (see pages 158–59), and

Above Discus produce nutritious mucus on their flanks for their fry to feed on.

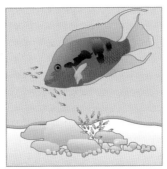

Above Cichlids may herd their fry around the aquarium to help their youngsters find food.

Above The fry of mouth-brooding cichlids are often large enough to take adult foods right away.

those that have been mouth-brooded, such as some African cichlids. These may well take crumbled-up adult flake (see page 166). They will, however, need feeding more often—three or four times a day.

The smallest fry are those that have hatched from eggs of fish, such as tetras (see pages 139–44), and those that have hatched from bubble-nesting species, such as gouramies (see pages 135–37). They will be too tiny to accept even powdered flake, so need to be fed special liquid foods—fry foods that contain tiny food particles in suspension—or a naturally cultured "soup" called infusoria (see below).

Types of fry food

These are the main options available for feeding fry, from do-it-yourself to ready-prepared foods.

Infusoria

Infusoria looks like nothing more than green water, but it is what fry would be swimming through and consuming in the wild. It consists of organisms that are very simple in structure and form the basis of the food chain. It is perfect for tiny fry and can be cultured in a spare aquarium.

To create infusoria take a small glass tank and place it on a windowsill. Fill it with aquarium water, a lettuce leaf, and an apple snail (*Pomacea canaliculata*). The snail will consume the lettuce leaf and its droppings will act as a fertilizer. The light from the window in combination with the

fertilizer will cause the water to turn green, and tiny organisms will appear in the water that feed on green water. These can then be fed to fry.

Baby brine shrimp

Adult brine shrimp are a popular food for adult fish and are available frozen and live (see page 164). Newly hatched brine shrimp are perfect for small fry and are available frozen from aquatic retailers or can be cultured at home using a brine shrimp hatching kit. If culturing your own, it is advisable to have several hatches running at different intervals in order to ensure a constant supply.

Specially formulated fry foods

A range of high-grade fry food products is available from your aquarium retailer, offering the appropriate nutritional content and particle size for fry of all types. The foods have emerged as a result of manufacturers developing fry foods for fish used in science and aquaculture. These foods can be very effective and offer a practical alternative to do-it-yourself food cultures.

Other, more common fry foods are available in stores and are popular with all hobbyists who raise fry. They are liquid solutions that are squirted into the water around where the fry are swimming. The fry swim through the liquid food, consuming it as they go. They are graded for two sizes of fry—egg-layer fry and live-bearer fry—but fry from egg layers can also be fed live-bearer food.

MARINE FISH CARE
Marine basics

Marine fish can be more delicate, more expensive, and less forgiving than most freshwater fish, but they are also unique in their coloration and behavior. The marine aquarist can, for example, delight in watching the symbiosis of a clownfish (*Amphiprion ocellaris*) (see page 233) nestling into an anemone, a creature that is equipped with stinging tentacles to catch and devour most other species of fish.

Species to avoid

Some marine animals are far more challenging, and therefore the aquarist should not attempt to keep them. A large percentage of marine fish species, mainly due to their feeding requirements, do incredibly badly in aquariums. Seahorses, for example, do not have stomachs and need to feed continuously on enriched mysis shrimps. Many butterflyfishes (see page 236) are specialized coral polyp eaters and will not survive on anything else. Because of their nomadic nature, some species are not adapted to cope with bumping into obstacles such as aquarium walls and are better left in the sea.

An extra dimension

Live corals add another fascinating dimension to marine fishkeeping. For decades corals were thought to be plants and not animals. In a relatively short space of time aquarists have mastered the practice of keeping corals successfully in captivity, and many species can even be cultivated with relative ease.

Conservation issues

Marine conservation is a factor that affects everyone, and moral questions are often raised about the capture of marine fish from the wild. Ninety percent of all marine fish available have been caught in the wild. Very few marine species have been spawned and reared in captivity.

Top Seahorses are popular worldwide but are a challenge to keep, as they often have feeding difficulties.

Bottom Live corals are unique to marine reef-keeping and have created a hobby all their own.

But the debate is not totally one-sided. The capture of marine fish with small hand nets by local fishermen is considered sustainable, and it is said that this generates a better understanding of the importance of maintaining healthy reefs for the future. Horror stories of cyanide being used to capture fish are mostly a thing of the past, and no reputable marine importer would ever buy such fish, which lessens demand. The marine aquarists are not the only group that takes marine life from the reefs, however. A far greater negative impact on natural reef life comes from dynamiting for the building trade, and even the capture of reef fishes to provide food for farmed tuna.

Future developments

It is possible for the discerning marine aquarist to keep totally captive-bred fish, such as clownfish (*Amphiprion ocellaris*) (see page 233), as well as totally captive-raised corals, and as knowledge and experience is gained, more will be achievable and advances made. For instance, it has been found that a segment can be taken

from a healthy coral growing in the wild and then grown on independently of the parent coral. This process is known as fragging and could well revolutionize the marine hobby in the future.

Responsible marine fishkeeping

It is essential when keeping marine fish and invertebrates to take your considerable responsibilities very seriously. Great care should be taken to ensure that captive marines remain alive and healthy. Corals and anemones can live for decades if not centuries, so to lose such a creature inside ten years should be considered a failure and not a triumph. If you decide to stop keeping marines for any reason, surrender them to your retailer, who will be capable of relocating them properly. If you keep losing a particular species, give up and move on to something less difficult.

Below If you cannot provide proper care and a long-term commitment to marine organisms, leave them in the store.

Marine systems

The way in which marine fish and corals are kept in captivity has been changing over time. The fact that they all need warm saltwater that is both free of pollutants and well oxygenated is universally acknowledged, but how those pollutants are disposed of is a matter for debate. Some of the most common methods of disposal are discussed below.

The Berlin system

One of the most effective methods of keeping marine animals in a tank was developed in the late 20th century. Known as the Berlin system, it consists of a tank with powerful lighting, powerful water movement, which turns over the complete tank volume more than ten times an hour, live rock (see page 213), and a large protein skimmer (see page 206). There is no internal or external filtration.

The live rock handles the bulk of the biological filtration because inside its porous structure, aerobic and anaerobic bacteria break down ammonia, nitrite, and even nitrate (see pages 106–9). This may seem confusing to newcomers, as this book hitherto has stressed the prime importance of filtration for all aquariums. The features of the Berlin system are that the skimmer acts as a pre-filter, removing vast quantities of organic waste, and the live rock breaks down the rest using bacteria. So the filtration is, in fact, present, but in a different form. Think of live rock as large chunks of biological media (see page 40) being presented with food and oxygen by the large water flow, which is just what happens inside a filter.

Refugiums

Corals need food as well as powerful lighting and water movement. In the ocean, food comes in the form of plankton, which is the collective name for tiny invertebrates, larval life forms, and eggs that float around the ocean like soup. In the marine aquarium, planktonic life comes out of live rock but is removed by the otherwise beneficial skimmer or quickly eaten by fish. To generate more plankton in a system and to create more food, a tank can be joined to the main tank using pipework, and placed underneath the main tank in the cabinet. The

Tip

A protein skimmer is still the most popular and quickest way of removing organic waste from the system, and it should be an essential item of equipment for all new aquarists setting up a successful first marine tank (see page 206).

extra tank, known as a sump tank, can also be used to hold the heater/thermostat and a skimmer, if used.

Live rock and live sand, which is mature sand from the main aquarium, can be placed in the sump tank, and plankton will start to grow without risk of predation from the fish. When the numbers of plankton build up significantly, the pump in the sump tank draws them in and shoots them into the main tank where they are consumed by fish and corals. The advantage of the safe haven underneath is that only excess plankton finds its way to the main aquarium and is not overgrazed by the fish. A sump tank used for the breeding of plankton is known as a refugium.

Advanced refugium systems

Refugiums can also be used to grow marine algae called *Caulerpa*, which would otherwise be eaten in the main tank. When it grows, *Caulerpa* can take up excess nutrients, such as nitrate and phosphate, and can then be harvested, removing it from the system. *Caulerpa* can normally be quite difficult to grow, so experts have found that by lighting the sump tank with a fluorescent tube for

Above A superb marine display such as this is normally aided by the addition of an effective protein skimmer.

24 hours a day, it grows more quickly and is less likely to fail.

Tanks containing refugiums with live sand, live rock, and healthy *Caulerpa* produce lots of plankton, are low in nutrients, and have even more success with corals. Some systems using successful refugiums eliminate the protein skimmer because all organic waste is being dealt with in the sump tank.

Marine fish

The compatibility of marine fish species in the aquarium can be compared with that of freshwater fish (see pages 122–23) in that there is a huge diversity of species available to the aquarist, from large to tiny fish, predators and prey, solitary and shoaling fish, as well as aggressive and placid fish. They will not mix, and care must be taken when selecting fish.

Community fish

Creating a community tank is similar to mixing tropical fish, either in groups of a single species or a variety of species. Begin by researching the species you would like to keep and find out what its feeding requirements are, what size tank it requires, and whether it will suit your system. Bear in mind that some species that live in groups on the reef may not happily coexist if kept in groups in the aquarium. This may be because the species congregate together in nature only to breed, after which they disperse, or the vastness of the ocean provides them with a much larger natural territory and the tank is simply not large enough for them to keep out of each other's way.

Reef-friendly fish

Fish that congregate around a coral reef in nature will all be there for different reasons. As well as providing hiding places, the corals on a

reef are constantly under attack from fish that have become specialized to feed from them. The mobile invertebrate life on the reef is also part of the food chain, with crabs, shrimp, and starfish appearing on the menu. Fish that are safe to be kept with almost all mobile and sessile (fixed) invertebrates in the aquarium (see page 204) can be classed as reef friendly.

Only fish

A fish-only marine aquarium is exactly that (see page 216). It is a term used for aquariums that do not contain corals and marine invertebrates, either because the fish species kept will destroy them or simply because fish are the focus and invertebrates are not desired. Some of the most beautiful marine fish, such as butterflyfishes (see page 236) and large angelfish (see page 232), are not reef friendly and so must be kept in a fish-only environment, so do not feel that if you take the fish-only route, you will be missing out.

Below Chromis, which are peaceful and hardy, are the best choice of fish for beginners.

Above Research fish species fully before adding them to the aquarium, as they may not mix.

Right As a general rule, don't mix larger fish with small ones, as they may get eaten.

A fish-only aquarium can contain live rock and run as a Berlin system (see page 200), or it can use an external filter and a protein skimmer (see pages 206–7). In both cases, the skimmer is important to obtain and retain optimum water quality. Popular decorations for fish-only aquariums includes ocean rock, tufa rock, and fake corals (see page 212).

First fish

All marine fish are sensitive, but some species are the preferred choice for new setups. Clownfish (*Amphiprion ocellaris*) (see page 233) are quite hardy, reef friendly, and readily available, so they make a good choice as first fish. By choosing a pair in the aquarium store,

one will become a male fish and one will grow larger and become a female. Tank-bred clownfish are an even better choice, because they are hardy fish and have no impact on the natural reef.

Another group of marine fish that are regularly chosen for new setups are damselfish (see pages 233–35). They remain small and are colorful and hardy, but many species become territorial and aggressive over time, so these fish are actually best left until last. However, one species of damselfish, the green chromis (*Chromis viridis*) (see page 233), is not aggressive and instead prefers the company of a small shoal of five or more individuals, so it makes an excellent choice of first fish.

Marine invertebrates

Invertebrates represent the biggest challenge for the marine aquarist, because if they are to thrive, the conditions of a coral reef in the wild must be replicated in the aquarium, with exactly the correct water chemistry and environment. Invertebrates can be separated into two groups—those that can move and those that cannot.

Mobile invertebrates

This massive group includes shrimp, crabs, starfish, snails, sea slugs, and more. Colorful species are used as added decoration in the tank, but many offer an added purpose of providing a service to the reef. Turbo snails (*Turbo castaneus*), which are not actually very fast moving, and small red-legged and blue-legged hermit crabs (*Pylopagurus* spp.) are a must for the new reefkeeper, because they carry out the important task of grazing algae from live rock. There are hundreds of different types of marine algae, but only a few, such as purple coralline algae (*Hydrolithon boergensenii*), are desirable. Some algae that grow in new aquariums are highly unsightly and can quickly ruin an attractive tank. Hermit crabs and turbo snails can be stocked at the rate of one per 1 gallon (4.5 liters) to help prevent algal buildup and will, of course, eat any leftover food as well.

Other mobile invertebrates perform useful tasks in the marine aquarium, such as the well-known cleaner shrimp (*Lysmata grabhami*) (see page 251). This white and red shrimp crawls over the fish, removing parasites and bits of old skin along the way, thus helping to keep the fish healthy at the same time as helping itself to a free meal. And all this fascinating natural behavior can be observed from the comfort of your living room!

Sessile (immobile) invertebrates

These include corals, which are a feature of reef aquariums (see pages 244–49). There are both hard and soft corals to choose from, and many reef aquariums contain a combination of the two for an authentic-looking underwater scene.

Below Cleaner shrimp are a popular invertebrate and bring with them a benefit to the tank.

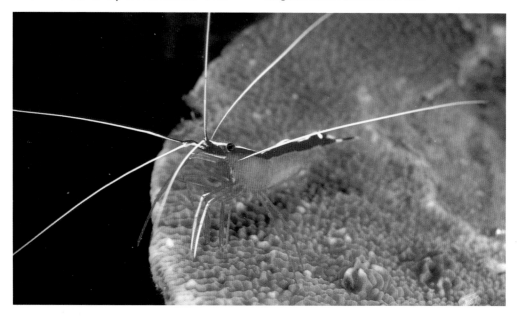

Above Clams are much sought after due to the coloration of their mantles but are not for beginners.

Above Starfish are instantly recognizable by their form and are available in many different colors.

Soft corals

These are generally less demanding than hard corals and are more suitable for the beginner and for new tanks. All soft corals like to be placed in an area with good lighting and moderate-to-strong water flow. Corals can be placed next to each other, but they should not touch each other, because different species will sting and try to kill each other to keep a stake on the available light.

Hard corals

These are so called because they form skeletons that actually make up the reef structure in the wild. They are also generally harder to keep, needing even more light and water flow than soft corals. They are also more demanding of mineral supplements, which they need in order to build their skeletons. Only experienced aquarists should attempt to keep hard corals.

The dangers of copper

All marine invertebrates will die if exposed to levels of copper in the water. Many fish parasite treatments contain copper specifically for that reason, as marine parasites are actually tiny invertebrates, so never use copper-based treatments in reef aquariums and avoid using hot water from the tap, which may contain traces of copper. For peace of mind, use RO (reverse osmosis) water (see page 84) and bring it up to the appropriate temperature using a heater/thermostat (see page 44).

Protein skimmers

Also known as a foam fractionater, a protein skimmer is a type of pre-filter that is commonly used in marine aquariums. It may be initially viewed as an expensive, non-essential extra, but it can make a huge difference to the well-being of the tank.

Above A protein skimmer should be high on the shopping list and a must-have piece of equipment.

How they work
Tiny air bubbles rise up a chamber to the surface of the water. As they go, each one becomes coated in a small amount of saltwater, which will contain, among other biological substances, proteins. The mass of bubbles at the surface start to sit on top of each other, causing a foam to rise above the surface. A baffle in the chamber allows the foam to well up very slowly and rise over into a collection cup. The protein-rich foam that has been collected is then discarded.

Advantages
Part of a protein molecule is made up of ammonia. Normally, as we have seen previously (see page 98), ammonia in the tank is broken down by bacteria into nitrite and then nitrate, which is removed by changing the water. A marine aquarium needs to be as free as possible of all three pollutants, so a protein skimmer can help to solve the problem at the source. Less protein means less subsequent ammonia, nitrite, and nitrate. Algal cells also stick to the bubbles, so effective protein skimming can also help to clear up nuisance algae from the aquarium.

All types of marine aquarium will benefit from the extra filtration and water purification that a skimmer provides, and many of the world's best marine aquariums rely heavily on protein skimming. Effective skimming benefits both fish-only and reef aquariums (see pages 216 and 222).

Disadvantages
One disadvantage of skimming is that it can remove good bacteria as well as bad, which means that it is unwise to skim a new tank, as it will need all the bacteria that it can get in order to mature. Another disadvantage is that it can remove tiny plankton from the water, which corals would naturally feed on in the wild. Good skimmers can be expensive and will not fit every design of aquarium. All internal and external hang-on models will need to have the collection cup above the surface of the water, which may cause problems in fitting them inside the hood.

Hang-on protein skimmer

1 Inlet strainer
2 Power head
3 Venturi inlet
4 Air/water mix collects proteins
5 Collection cup
6 Phosphate remover or carbon
7 Outlet for water to aquarium
8 Extra media container

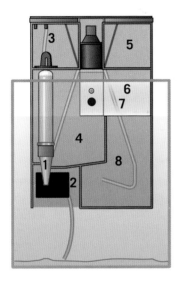

The art of effective skimming

Several factors can increase the effectiveness of a protein skimmer:

○ Contact time. The amount of time that the bubbles stay in the chamber before reaching the surface can increase the amount of protein that they pick up.

○ Bubble size. The smaller the bubble, the greater the surface area in relation to its volume.

○ Foam. The foam pouring into the collection cup should be as "dry" as possible—that is, the bubbles collecting at the top of the chamber should be coated with only a little saltwater, and the rest should be smelly, brown residue. A wet skim means that too much water is being collected with the foam and that the waste is not being effectively separated.

Skimming FAQs

Q Can you overskim?
A No. A good skimmer can only make a positive contribution to the upkeep of a pristine marine aquarium.

Q Can you run a marine tank without a skimmer?
A Yes, but the results are not generally as good. Without a skimmer, the system will run at what is termed "nutrient rich," meaning that the water has more ammonia, nitrite, nitrate, and proteins in it, which together can cause nuisance algae and adversely affect corals. Some corals, such as knobbly mushrooms or mushroom anemones (*Discosoma florida*) (see page 244), have been known to do better without a skimmer, but there is also evidence to the contrary.

Q Should the skimmer be on all the time?
A Yes, but you should turn it off when you treat the water with liquid coral food because otherwise the skimmer will remove it. Turn the skimmer back on about an hour after feeding.

Marine lighting

Lighting for marine aquariums differs from lighting for freshwater tanks in both its intensity and spectrum because of the different nature of the light in these contrasting environments in the wild. Different forms of marine life also have varying requirements for lighting, which must be clearly understood to ensure the success of the aquarium.

Blue-spectrum lighting

Modern reef aquarium lighting is a combination of high-intensity lighting and blue spectrum lighting to imitate that in the natural reef. Marine lighting is high in the blue end of the spectrum and low in the red end, with even so-called marine white light appearing slightly more blue than standard fluorescent lighting. This is because when sunlight shines through a depth of water, all the red part of the spectrum is removed, and consequently, all marine life has adapted to this type of light. When reefs are described as shallow, they may still be over 33 feet (10 m) in depth, which means that the light is already being filtered by the time it actually reaches the corals. Freshwater lighting, conversely, is the opposite of marine, and plants have adapted and evolved to process the red spectrum that shines through shallow riverbanks and ponds.

Lighting can also provide the mood for the marine tank and set the scene. Lots of blue spectrum lighting can create the effect of a deep-water reef or it can be used at lights-out to simulate moonlight.

Lighting for corals

Most of the corals that we keep in aquariums are from the shallower areas of coral reefs, and these are exposed to the full glare of the tropical sun. Therefore, these conditions need to replicated in the tank environment. Corals have evolved to harness the power of the sun by harboring photosynthetic algae called zooxanthellae in their tissues. This algae is a primary source of energy for the coral, and without it they cannot survive. Through years of research and development, artificial lighting has been specially tailored to meet the needs of corals kept in aquariums, helping to ensure their long-term well-being.

Different lighting requirements

Some species of marine fish are nocturnal, but most of the fish that we keep will need moderate to bright lighting for 10–12 hours a day. Other invertebrates are not fussy when it comes to lighting, so they can be kept in moderate to brightly lit aquariums. If an aquarium contains corals, light it brightly for 10–12 hours a day.

Bright lighting

Bright lighting can be achieved by the use of several high-output fluorescent tubes (see page 48) or with metal halide lighting, which is the brightest of all (see below). Their power is measured in watts and their spectrum (or color temperature) is measured in Kelvin. When choosing lighting for reef aquariums, use a combination of fluorescent tubes with Kelvin between 10,000 and 20,000 or, for aquariums 24 inches (60 cm) or more deep, the better option is to use metal halide or T5 lighting, again with a spectrum between 10,000 and 20,000 Kelvin.

T5 lighting

T5 was originally a reference to the diameter of the light tubes used, that is ⅝ inches (1.5 cm); standard 1 inch (2.5 cm) diameter light tubes are called T8. T5 lighting has been developed for marine aquarium use to obtain more output from fluorescent tubes for not much more wattage. Its suitability for use with reflectors has also increased (see page 46), because when it is encased in a reflector, the thinner T5 tube reflects less light back on itself and more into the aquarium. Two T5s with reflectors can be as bright as four T8s so can represent a significant saving in lighting costs.

Metal halide lighting

Metal halide lamps are used by many forms of industry because of their high light output. This

Above Multiple light tubes will be necessary over a reef tank to benefit the corals.

Right A major drawback with lots of artificial light is that heat is produced, and a fan may be necessary.

was recognized by the hobby, and specially designed spectrum lamps were developed for aquarium use. They have a high energy consumption, with lamps of 150, 250, and 400 watts being common, but they do provide a type of light that looks similar to sunlight and are very popular as a result. Metal halide lighting is the most expensive form of lighting available to the aquarist, but it also has the advantage of being the brightest. The downside of metal halide lighting is that the bulbs run at a very high temperature and can contribute to rising temperatures in the marine tank. They also need to be suspended at a height of at least 8 inches (20 cm) above the water level for that reason, meaning that the light has to be suspended from the ceiling above the tank.

Sterilizers

A sterilizer holds a special kind of ultraviolet light tube, hence its common abbreviation to UV. This is harmful to certain undesirable organisms in the aquarium, so it can be used to deal effectively with green water, bacterial blooms, and parasite manifestations.

How do they work?

The light tube is placed in a special clear tube called a quartz. The quartz is then held at each end by rubber O-rings and placed inside a chamber. Water is pumped inside the chamber, but does not touch the light tube, which remains safely dry inside the quartz. The water that enters the chamber is exposed to the UV light and consequently algae, bacteria, and some parasites and disease pathogens are killed off by it. The water then exits the chamber and travels back into the aquarium via a hose.

Benefits

Because of the effect that they have on small organisms that are exposed to it, UVs can be used to tackle a number of problems in the marine aquarium. First, they can be used in tanks that are suffering from water clarity problems. Second, they can help to keep down the number of parasites in the tank water, so are of particular benefit when keeping fish that are prone to ailments such as whitespot (see page 180).

How to fit a UV sterilizer

Normally, UVs are fitted inline with an external filter. The filter hose is cut and connected to the inlet and outlet hose tails of the UV. In the absence of an external filter or if a UV is used in a reef aquarium, a unit can simply be fitted by connecting it to a hose from a power head (a universal underwater pump).

Using your UV sterilizer effectively

The amount of time that the water spends exposed to the light is critical. If the water flows too quickly past the light, the contact time will not be long enough to successfully kill the organisms. For this reason, all manufacturers will specify a maximum flow rating that should not be exceeded. If the water flows more slowly than specified, it is not a problem, because an even greater contact time will have been achieved.

UV bulbs degrade very quickly and should be replaced at least every 12 months. The bulbs should not be handled unless you are wearing gloves, as their effectiveness can be damaged by fingerprints. Quartz tubes should also be cleaned and replaced occasionally. They are very brittle and so should be handled with care.

Safety precautions

If the bare tube is exposed when lit up, it should not be viewed with the naked eye. Most UVs have opaque hose tails that will glow in the dark. This is a sure indication that the bulb is on. Tubes that have recently been lit should be allowed to cool before they are removed.

Choosing a model

Because of the benefits that a UV offers, you cannot overdo the size of unit that you choose. In commercial applications such as fish retailers and wholesalers, huge banks of UVs are used together to provide effective sterilization of system water and to prevent any pathogens from passing from tank to tank. They also greatly benefit freshwater systems, and a variation on the UV sterilizer, called a UV clarifier (or UVC), is used universally on outdoor ponds to stop green water.

Tip

When you are buying a UV sterilizer, choose the largest model available, as UV sterilization cannot be overdone.

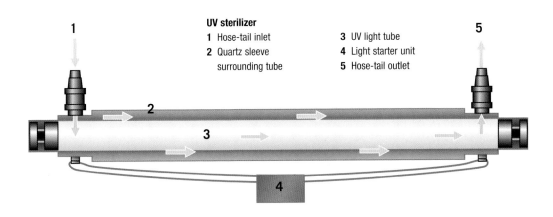

UV sterilizer
1 Hose-tail inlet
2 Quartz sleeve surrounding tube
3 UV light tube
4 Light starter unit
5 Hose-tail outlet

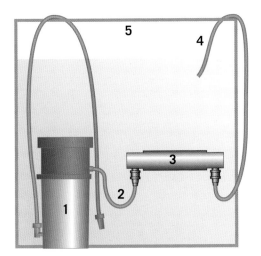

Fitting a UV option 1
1 Exernal filter
2 Flexible hose
3 UV unit
4 Outlet hose
5 Main aquarium

Fitting a UV option 2
1 Power head
2 Flexible hose
3 UV unit
4 Outlet hose
5 Main aquarium

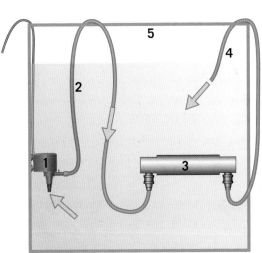

Marine decoration

The materials used to decorate marine aquariums differ from those used for freshwater aquariums, so make sure that you are buying the correct ones for your setup. Some freshwater decor, such as driftwood (see page 54), will leach unwanted tannins and acids into the tank water and break down in the marine environment. Some other materials, such as some rocks, may contain metals hazardous to marine life and must be avoided at all costs.

Aesthetic considerations

The vast majority of marine fishkeepers choose to try and create a complete, realistic imitation of the beauty of the ocean. The best way to do this is to use materials that have actually come from the ocean, such as coral sand and ocean rock. The use of such materials will not only result in an authentic effect, but will also be safe for the fish and invertebrate life in the aquarium.

Choosing materials

To help you make the right choice of materials, the lists (right) will guide you as to what is and what is not safe to use in a marine tank. The safe materials listed can be used in marine fish-only or reef aquariums (see pages 216 and 222) and can be used exclusively or in conjunction with live rock (see opposite).

Safe materials

- ○ tufa rock
- ○ ocean rock
- ○ shells
- ○ coral skeletons
- ○ aragonite sand

Unsafe materials

- ○ driftwood
- ○ some lava rock
- ○ rocks containing metals
- ○ nonaquatic ornaments
- ○ painted shells and coral

Below Coral sand is the most widely used marine substrate and buffers pH and hardness values.

Marine decoration FAQs

Q What is live rock?

A Live rock is rock or rubble that has been taken from the sea around coral reefs.

Q Why is it called live?

A Because its outer surfaces are covered in many different forms of microscopic life, from algae and tiny worms to sponges and tiny coral polyps. More importantly, its inner surfaces are colonized with beneficial bacteria, which break down ammonia, nitrite, and nitrate (see page 98).

Q Does collecting it harm the natural reef environment?

A No. Live rock is rubble-collected after storms and can even be farmed. It is not broken off the reef by man.

Q Is it expensive?

A Yes. It can be five or six times more expensive than standard tufa or ocean rock, but the benefits to the marine aquarium outweigh its relative high cost.

Q Is there anything that I should look out for when buying live rock?

A Make sure that it has gone through a process called curing. When live rock is cured, any dead matter that is connected to the rock is removed and it is placed for several weeks in well-oxygenated vats. This replenishes beneficial bacteria and gets the rock bacteria working properly again.

Q Can I obtain any other "live" materials?

A Live sand is available, which is similar in its properties to live rock. It is full of good bacteria, which will get to work in your tank and will also contain tiny colonies of invertebrates and plankton.

Q When do I put live rock or live sand in the tank?

A Both can be placed in the aquarium once it is filled with prepared saltwater of the right temperature and salinity (see page 214).

Right Not all lava rock is safe to use in marine aquariums, so it is best avoided.

Tip

If you use seashells and coral skeletons, make sure they have not been painted or glued and used as souvenirs in the tourist industry. If so, they may contain hazardous contaminants or may be benefiting a trade that is having a negative impact on the natural environment.

Preparing saltwater

The thought of mixing saltwater every time a water change is carried out puts off many people and is the reason some people never try marine fishkeeping. However, it is a relatively simple process and is within the capabilities of any fishkeeper. First, always heat the water before adding the salt, and then use a hydrometer to check the level of salt.

Heating the water

Freshwater comes in the form of tap water or purified water, such as RO (reverse osmosis) water (see page 84). It is also available as rainwater, but this is not recommended for use in marine tanks.

• If using tap water, first bring it to the appropriate temperature using either water from a hot kettle or by using a heater/thermostat (see page 44). Use a thermometer to measure the temperature, which should be 75–77°F (24–25°C).
• If using RO water, add some mineral replacement (available from your aquatic retailer), then bring the water to the appropriate temperature using a heater/thermostat.

Buying salt

There are two basic types of salt—synthetic sea salt, which is made in a laboratory, and desalination salt, which is the by-product of making drinking water from seawater. Both are equally acceptable for use in the tank. Always purchase salt for marine use from an aquatic retailer, as it is not the same as ordinary table salt.

When adding the salt to the tank water, buy more than you need for the following reasons:
• Salt is cheaper when bought in larger quantities.
• It often makes less saltwater than stated on the packet.
• You will always need salt for water changes.
• You may need salt in an emergency situation, so it is always worth keeping some in reserve should the need arise.

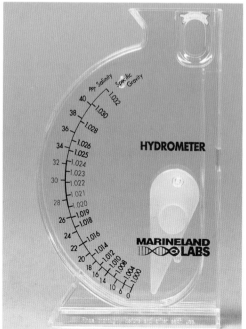

HYDROMETER

MARINELAND
LABS

Water heating FAQs

Q Why can't I use water from the kettle with RO water?
A The tap water in the kettle will contain all the nitrate and phosphate that you are trying to eradicate by putting it through an RO (reverse osmosis) unit. You could put RO water in the kettle, but not if the kettle contains lime scale.

Q Why can't I use water from the hot tap?
A Water running through copper pipes may contain copper in suspension, which is harmful to marine invertebrates and some fish. In hard-water areas, copper pipes become lined with calcium carbonate, so the water may not touch the copper, but you can't be sure, so don't risk it.

Left Saltwater is measured using a hydrometer. Water should be at the correct temperature when measured.

Mixing saltwater

1. Obtain a clean bucket and fill it with water. If using tap water, add a dechlorinating solution at the same time (see page 82).

2. Place a heater/thermostat in the bucket and leave it until the temperature reaches 75–77°F (24–25°C).

3. Check the temperature with a thermometer and, once it is correct, start adding the salt a little at a time.

4. Use a hydrometer (see opposite) to check the rising salinity and stop when a level of 1.024 has been reached.

5. Place an airstone or power head in the bucket and leave until all the salt has dissolved into the water— this can be overnight.

6. Once all the salt has dissolved, leave the water for 24 hours before adding it to the aquarium.

Adding salt

The amount of salt that you need to add can be calculated by weight—add 1¼ ounces (35 g) of salt to every 1¾ pints (1 liter) of aquarium water. Alternatively, add the salt 9 ounces (250 g) at a time and use the hydrometer to check the salinity until the desired 1.024 is reached.

Measuring salt levels

Use a hydrometer to measure how salty the water is. These come in the form of floating glass tubes or boxes with a swinging needle. The latter is easier to use for a beginner and will not break as easily. Check the salt level again once all the salt has dissolved.

Preparing to set up a marine fish-only aquarium

The fish-only aquarium is often the best choice for beginners because you can focus all your efforts on ensuring the well-being of the fish. The fundamental differences between setting up a marine fish-only tank and a tropical tank are that salt should be added to the water (see page 214) and a protein skimmer should be used (see page 206).

Tank size

The minimum tank size for any marine fish-only aquarium is 36 inches (90 cm) long. The marine tank needs to be a stable environment; tanks smaller than this will fluctuate in temperature, and the water quality will vary more quickly. Remember that marine fish should be stocked at a much lower density than tropical and coldwater fish, and this size tank will hold only six small fish when fully mature.

Filtration

With no live rock to be added to this example setup, the bulk of the filtration is to be carried out by an external power filter (see page 36). Choose an external over an internal filter, because it will have a larger media capacity and will take a variety of filter media. The filter should be filled with sponge for mechanical filtering, ceramic media for biological filtering, and carbon for chemical filtering. Choose a model that is oversized for the setup with a powerful turnover of water.

Protein skimmer

The addition of a protein skimmer will help with filtration, because by removing a lot of organic waste from the system, it will help to keep the by-product of biological filtration (nitrate) at a low level. It can also help keep down algae. Air-driven skimmers are the cheapest type available and work simply by connecting them to an air pump (see page 43), but a skimmer should not be skimped on and the external hang-on type of skimmer is more powerful and more effective.

Decoration

This is the one type of marine tank in which it is feasible to use shells and coral skeletons as decoration, but as previously mentioned (see page 212), choose your sources carefully so that you do not create demand for such products. Coral sand or coral gravel is suitable as a substrate, but do not layer it too deeply, as it may hold phosphate and nitrate if it is not cleaned regularly (see 168).

Live rock (see page 213) can be used in the fish-only aquarium and will benefit filtration and water quality. However, 44 pounds (20 kg) or more of live rock can be costly, and the purpose of this example fish-only setup is to show that such an aquarium can be created simply and cheaply.

Ocean rock has been used for this setup, as it is a natural marine product and has an interesting shape.

Shopping list for a marine fish-only aquarium

- ○ 36 inch (90 cm) glass tank
- ○ external filter
- ○ heater/thermostat
- ○ protein skimmer
- ○ coral sand
- ○ ocean rock
- ○ barnacle cluster
- ○ marine salt
- ○ hydrometer
- ○ thermometer
- ○ light tubes
- ○ light starter units
- ○ hood
- ○ test kit

Above This pile of ocean rock helps to conceal the majority of the equipment that is fitted behind it.

Right Fake corals made from resin are a good choice for the fish-only aquarium.

Step-by-step guide to setting up a fish-only aquarium

Once you have assembled all the items on the shopping list on page 216, you can begin setting up the tank. If this is your first attempt at setting up an aquarium, bear in mind that you are under no time pressure, so take it slowly. It will take a week or more before your first fish can be added. Follow these steps for a trouble-free setup.

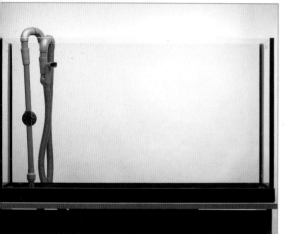

1. All marine fish need very good water quality, and to ensure that you can provide this, opt for an external power filter (see page 36). The pipework should be connected to the rear corner of the tank. Fit the inlet to draw water from just above the base of the tank. Fit the outlet to just under the surface of the water. Trim the pipes as necessary for a good fit.

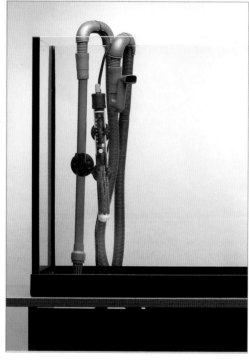

2. Place the heater/thermostat on the rear glass above the bottom and be sure it is fully submerged. Either place it diagonally or vertically in an area of strong water flow. A heater guard should be considered if placing next to rockwork or if keeping fish with powerful teeth. Set the heater to 75°F (24°C).

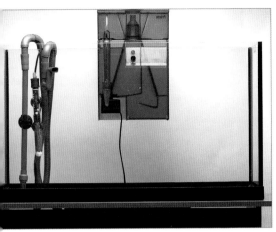

3. Fit a protein skimmer to the tank to act as a prefilter (see page 206). This model hangs on the back and pours water back in across a wide lip. Find out which type of skimmer will fit your tank and hood, as all makes of aquarium will vary in design.

4. Add coral sand to a depth of 2 inches (5 cm) to the base of the tank. Prewash it in a bucket of tap water to remove all debris and dust. Coral sand is a decorative product for marine aquariums that will also buffer the pH and hardness of the water (see page 105).

5. Ocean rock is a dense, marine rock suitable for use in marine reef and fish-only aquariums (see page 212). It is used in this tank to create most of the basic aquascape. Build it up directly off the bottom of the tank to avoid rock falls. Tall rock piles can also be leaned against the back glass for extra stability.

6. These giant barnacle shells are suitable for this sort of aquarium and are a natural marine product. Make sure that they have not been painted or glued and that they are free of any dead matter. Arrange them to provide hiding places for fish and position them on stable areas of rock.

7. Mix the saltwater in buckets and pour it into the tank. Pour it over a dish or over the rockwork to avoid disturbing the sand. Even sand that has been properly cleaned may still cloud the water. Fill the aquarium to within 2 inches (5 cm) of the top.

8. Install a thermometer to check the temperature of the water and monitor it to check that the heater is holding the desired level. Choose a thermometer that is accurate and easy to use.

9. Use a hydrometer (see page 214) to check the salinity of the water. Remember that the hydrometer calibrates with water of the correct temperature, so it should be used with a thermometer. Newly mixed saltwater may become more salty as the last salt dissolves, so leave the checking of the salt level until a few days after filling.

10. With no corals or invertebrates needing special lighting, the choice of light is not essential. However, marine tanks should be lit with marine lamps to give the blue effect of the tropical oceans (see page 208). This hood takes two tubes, so add one marine white fluorescent tube and one marine blue.

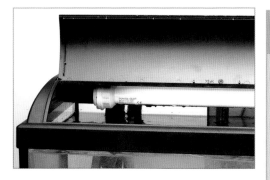

11. Fit the lights into the hood with the blue tube at the back. A section of this hood has been removed to accommodate the protein skimmer. Do not turn the skimmer on for some weeks after filling, as it may remove useful filter bacteria in the early stages of maturation.

12. The setting up of the tank is now complete. Leave for a week before adding any fish. Marine fish are more delicate than freshwater fish, so check and double check all water parameters (consult your aquatic retailer, if necessary) before adding fish (see page 161). From your list of preferred species, choose the hardiest and most peaceful species first.

Aftercare

○ Do not despair if the aquarium is cloudy and bubbles appear on the front glass. The water may take several days to clear and the bubbles will disappear over time.

○ To help mature the aquarium, add plenty of filter bacteria in the first few weeks.

○ Leave the lights off to discourage algae until the fish are added.

Preparing to set up a marine reef aquarium

The reef setup can be the most spectacularly beautiful aquarium but also the most challenging. A period of keeping freshwater fish is strongly recommended before you consider setting up a more complicated reef tank. This will help you to familiarize yourself both with the basics of fish behavior and the rigorous management of water quality.

Tank size

The minimum tank size for a reef tank containing fish is one with a volume of 40 gallons (180 liters) of water. It is not appropriate to specify a tank length because reef aquariums need to be taller and wider than normal in order to provide an effective aquascape and room for the corals. The tank used in this example setup is 39 x 16 x 16 inches (100 x 40 x 40 cm). The water needs to be even more stable than a fish-only setup, so be prepared to use cooling equipment or fans in hot weather.

Right Power heads provide water movement in the main aquarium, which benefits the corals.

Shopping list for a marine reef aquarium

- ○ 40-gallon (180-liter) glass tank
- ○ power heads
- ○ heater/thermostat
- ○ protein skimmer
- ○ coral sand
- ○ marine salt
- ○ RO water
- ○ hydrometer
- ○ thermometer
- ○ live rock
- ○ phosphate remover
- ○ light tubes
- ○ light starter units

System type

The system used in this example tank is the Berlin method (see page 200), using live rock, a good-quality protein skimmer, and powerful lighting and water movement. If you are still nervous about not having the physical presence of an external filter, by all means add one (see page 36). It will make the system even more stable and provides a place to put carbon and a phosphate remover.

Live rock

Make sure that the live rock you purchase has been cured (see page 213). If you have seen it sitting in the shop for many weeks, it will be cured anyway, but one way to tell is to smell it. If it smells like fresh, inviting seafood, it is cured, but if it smells like decay, it is not cured.

To cure rock in the tank before adding any fish is easy, but you will need the skimmer to be on from day one and you may need to change the water several times, too. However, there is no financial benefit from buying rock uncured.

Also, when buying live rock, purchase it from a reputable source, as low-grade rock will have poor coralline algae coverage and may have spent a period after collection drying on the beach. It can also harbor bristleworm infestations, which are potentially harmful to some marine invertebrates, and may cause skin irritations in humans or bites if handled.

Phosphate remover

Phosphate-removing resins are recommended for all types of aquariums, but should be considered essential for the reef tank (see page 109). A tiny trace of phosphate in the water can turn a pristine reef into a green swamp, so add lots of it as soon as the tank is set up.

RO water

Like the phosphate remover, RO (reverse osmosis) water is considered essential for the modern reef aquarium (see page 84). Tap water has so many additives that are detrimental to reef tanks that you may as well start with pure

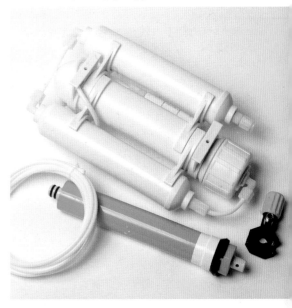

Below A reverse osmosis unit (or RO) is a worthwhile investment for providing quality purified water for the tank.

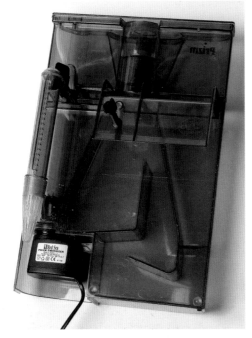

water. Water will need to be changed as regularly as if you were keeping freshwater fish (see page 170), so invest in an RO (reverse osmosis) unit if you are some distance away from a retailer that sells RO water in drums.

Protein skimmer

Buy the best skimmer that you can afford, and preferably one that has a good reputation (see page 206). In a Berlin system (see page 200), the skimmer is critical to the success of the livestock. You cannot overskim and reef tanks that are fitted with skimmers rated to skim twice the volume of the aquarium are standard. Keep the unit running 24 hours a day and clean it regularly. Make sure that the skimmer that you choose will actually fit the aquarium and hood that it is intended for. The tank used has no bracing bars and a luminaire light unit instead of a hood. This makes fitting the skimmer easy.

Left The protein skimmer will provide filtration and work with the live rock to clean the water.

Step-by-step guide to setting up a marine reef aquarium

Once you have assembled all the items on the shopping list on page 223, you are ready to begin setting up your reef aquarium. This kind of tank can be a complex and daunting prospect, but remember that the key to success is effective protein skimming, good lighting, and keeping levels of nutrients, such as nitrates and phosphates, as low as possible. Follow these steps to set up an effective and trouble-free reef aquarium.

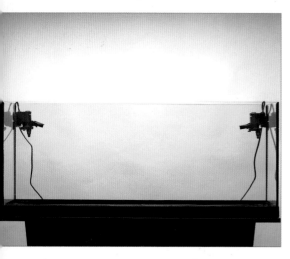

1. To provide adequate water flow in the reef tank, place power heads at opposite rear corners of the tank. Choose models that have a combined hourly output of ten times that of the total tank volume. Do not use the optional Venturi devices on the power heads (see page 42), because these can hinder coral growth.

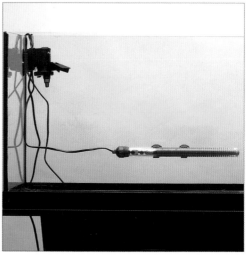

2. Place the heater/thermostat on the rear glass of the aquarium above the bottom but below the water line. The strong flow of water should adequately spread heat throughout the tank. Set the heater to 75°F (24°C).

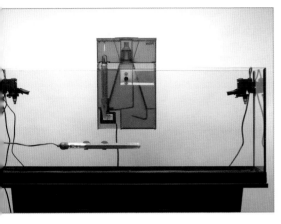

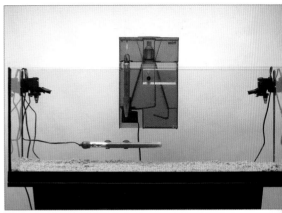

3. Fit a protein skimmer to the aquarium (see page 206). This model is a hang-on type of skimmer, which is designed to stretch over the top of the tank. When choosing a skimmer for the marine tank, choose a model that will suit larger aquariums than yours. Effective protein skimming will be an integral part of this reef tank's success, and you cannot overskim.

4. Place a thin layer of coral sand on the bottom of the tank. Deep layers of sand can hold nitrates and phosphates and so are not desirable for this type of system, where nutrients need to be kept to a minimum.

5. Add premixed saltwater to the tank that has preferably been made using RO (reverse osmosis) water (see pages 214–215). The key benefit of RO to the reef tank is that it is free of nitrates and phosphates, meaning less algal growth. Pour it into the tank over a dish so as not to disturb the sand. If using live sand (see page 213) do not add it to the tank until there is water in it.

6. One of the biggest problems for modern reef aquariums is overheating. Even a 1° rise in temperature can have devastating effects on a reef in the wild. The reason for heat rise in a reef tank is due to all the equipment and high-specification lighting that is used. Use an accurate thermometer and be prepared to use fans or cooling equipment during hot weather.

7. Test the salinity of the new water using a hydrometer (see page 215). The specific gravity should be 1.024 for corals and invertebrates to be happy. If the water is too salty, add more freshwater. If it is not salty enough, add more salt, but do this away from the main tank.

8. Once the tank water is stable in temperature and salinity, live rock can be added. Make sure that it has been cured (see page 213) otherwise it may cause tank maturation to take six weeks, and no fish can be added before the process is complete. If using cured rock, bacteria on and in the rock should help to mature the tank right away.

9. Phosphate has been found to be a major cause of nuisance algae in aquariums, and with the bright lights and high oxygen content and pH of marine tanks, nuisance algae can really take hold. Use an oversized amount of phosphate-removing resin (see page 109) and place it in the tank or in a compartment in the skimmer.

10. The bright light needed by the corals is provided in this case by special T5 lighting (see pages 208–9). These bulbs are fitted to a luminare, which holds four light tubes and reflectors. This model sits on the edge of the tank glass and eliminates the need for a hood. Water evaporation is greater when the aquarium is lit in this way, but light penetration is better.

11. After several weeks of water testing (see page 100), live corals can be added (see pages 244–49). Fish can either be present or can be added at the same time (see pages 228–41) or after the introduction of the first corals, but the key is that water quality must be consistently good for any fish and invertebrates (see pages 250–53) to be introduced.

Aftercare

The biggest problem for the new reefkeeper is nuisance algae. The combination of new live rock and bright lighting will cause an algae bloom in the first few weeks after setting up the tank. To help combat the problem, keep the lighting to a minimum until corals are added and continue to use plenty of phosphate-removing resin.

12. The setting up of the tank is now complete. Reef aquariums become more beautiful with time. As more corals and fish are added, the intricate picture of a flourishing coral reef is formed, and the tank will command the attention of aquarists and nonfishkeepers alike.

Marine fish profiles

Now that your marine aquarium is set up and maturing, it is time to choose the fish that will live there. The following fish profiles are designed to offer an at-a-glance visual reference, along with key information about their ease of keeping and suitability for the reef aquarium. All marine fish should be quarantined and acclimatized for a period before they are added to the main tank.

Fish size

The sizes quoted are average sizes for adults in captivity. Note that in an aquarium many marine fish never grow to the size that they would attain in the wild.

Tank size

The tank size quoted is a sensible minimum size for the adult species, but remember all species benefit from being in a large tank. With some species, such as tangs or surgeonfish (see pages 229–30) for example, you may need to double the tank size to prevent fights from breaking out among a group.

Ease of keeping

As has previously been explained, all marine fish species should be considered as sensitive, and so when a fish is described as easy, this would be equivalent to a moderate to difficult freshwater species. Optimum water quality must be maintained at all times, because no marine species will tolerate either ammonia or nitrite.

Reef friendly

The species that are listed as reef friendly are classified on the basis of personal experience as well as the experience of many other aquarists around the world. Marine fish can have quite different characteristics from one another, and sometimes a dwarf angelfish (*Centropyge* spp.) (see pages 231–32), for example, may bite a clam (*Tridacna* spp.) (see page 253), feather duster (*Sabella pavona*) (see page 252), or coral polyps (see pages 244–45), so should be added with caution.

Tip

When you purchase marine fish at the aquatic store, make sure that they are accepting the foods that they are offered. If they were caught in the wild, most of the fish will have spent only days in captivity and may be stressed and disoriented and reluctant to feed. Ask the retailer if you can observe the fish feeding. If they take foods with vigor and are otherwise healthy, then they will be OK to take home. If the fish are refusing to feed, ask the retailer if he will reserve the fish for you, and don't be tempted to take them home until they are feeding. Some species may take several weeks to acclimatize fully to life in captivity.

SURGEONFISH (Acanthuridae)

Powder Blue Tang *Acanthurus leucosternon*

Origin Indian Ocean

Fish size 8 inches (20 cm)

Tank size 48 inches (120 cm)

Ease of keeping Difficult

Reef friendly Yes

Comments The powder blue tang, like all tangs, is prone to marine whitespot (see page 180). It can be treated with a specific copper-based treatment, but this is not suitable for use in reef aquariums. For tangs kept in reef tanks, it is advisable to fit a UV sterilizer to the tank (see page 210). The powder blue tang is quite intolerant of other tangs and should be kept as the only tang in the tank. It is, however, a stunning-looking fish, which is reef safe.

Regal Tang *Paracanthurus hepatus*

Origin Indo-Pacific Ocean

Fish size 8 inches (20 cm)

Tank size 48 inches (120 cm)

Ease of keeping Moderate

Reef friendly Yes

Comments The regal tang is vividly colored, with a bright blue body and a yellow tail. It can get a little aggressive when larger and may pick on other fish. Fit a UV sterilizer to the tank (see page 210) to help prevent marine whitespot (see page 180), to which this fish is particularly prone. Regal tangs can be kept in groups when small. Feed with all types of algae and frozen foods (see pages 164–65).

Yellow Tang *Zebrasoma flavescens*

Origin Pacific Ocean

Fish size 6 inches (15 cm)

Tank size 48 inches (120 cm)

Ease of keeping Moderate

Reef friendly Yes

Comments This species makes an excellent addition to the fish-only (see pages 216–19) or reef aquarium (see pages 222–25), and they look effective when kept in groups in large aquariums. Their bright coloration and appearance have made them popular with aquarists, and they also graze on marine algae. This strong swimmer appreciates lots of water movement.

GOBIES (Gobiidae)

Neon Goby *Gobiosoma oceanops*

Origin East Atlantic Ocean

Fish size 2 inches (5 cm)

Tank size 36 inches (90 cm)

Ease of keeping Moderate

Reef friendly Yes

Comments Neon gobies are an excellent choice for reef aquariums that do not contain large fish (see page 222). Tank-bred fish are often available, which means that they are even hardier and they sometimes also act as cleaner fish. Keep them in groups with lots of live rock (see page 213).

Blue Cheek Goby *Valenciennea strigata*

Origin Indo-Pacific Ocean

Fish size 6 inches (15 cm)

Tank size 48 inches (120 cm)

Ease of keeping Moderate

Reef friendly Yes

Comments This species is a tireless substrate sifter, and fish can be kept in pairs. They will keep the bottom clean, but may cover lower lying rocks with sand. They tend to become rather thin over time, so feed regularly with a variety of frozen marine foods (see pages 164–65). Only add to mature aquariums that have an open area of sand.

ANGELFISH (Pomacanthidae)

Coral Beauty *Centropyge bispinosus*

Origin Indo-Pacific Ocean

Fish size 4 inches (10 cm)

Tank size 39 inches (100 cm)

Ease of keeping Moderate

Reef friendly Yes

Comments The coral beauty is one of the best behaved of the dwarf angelfish and is also one of the hardiest. It may on rare occasions nip at clams (see page 253), but it is on the whole reef safe. Keep as the only dwarf angel in the tank, or keep as a mated pair, although a pair is a rare find.

Flame Angelfish *Centropyge loriculus*

Origin Pacific Ocean

Fish size 4 inches (10 cm)

Tank size 39 inches (100) cm

Ease of keeping Moderate

Reef friendly Yes

Comments The flame angel is much sought after because of its coloration, and it can be rarely found and stocked as a mated pair. They are generally reef safe but may nip at clams (see page 253). Add to a mature tank with no other dwarf angelfish (these are angelfish that are less than 6 inches/15 cm long) and plenty of hiding places. A reef tank is the best place for them, because they will find food among the rockwork.

Emperor Angelfish *Pomacanthus imperator*

Origin Indo-Pacific Ocean

Fish size 12 inches (30 cm)

Tank size 60 inches (150 cm)

Ease of keeping Difficult

Reef friendly No

Comments A very impressive fish that commands a high price. The juvenile form of the emperor angelfish is quite different from the adult form. Many juveniles of large angelfish look similar, so make sure you are getting the right species. Keep in a large fish-only tank with a suitably sized skimmer (see pages 206–7) and feed a variety of frozen foods (see pages 164–65).

DAMSELFISH (Pomacentridae)

Common Clownfish *Amphiprion ocellaris*

Origin Pacific Ocean

Fish size 4 inches (10 cm)

Tank size 36 inches (90 cm)

Ease of keeping Easy

Reef friendly Yes

Comments The common clownfish is now being bred in captivity, making it even hardier and more suitable for aquarium life. Keep in pairs with or without a host anemone (see page 243) and offer a varied diet of frozen and dry foods (see pages 164–67). Keep only one species of clownfish in a tank, as they will fight.

Green Chromis *Chromis viridis*

Origin Indo-Pacific Ocean

Fish size 3 inches (7.5 cm)

Tank size 36 inches (90 cm)

Ease of keeping Easy

Reef friendly Yes

Comments This is the perfect marine fish; it is easy to keep, hardy, can be kept in groups, and is cheap and readily available. This species is popular in reef tanks, because they do not touch corals or invertebrates (see pages 242–53). Often recommended as the first fish for a new tank, these fish are highly suitable for any tank. Keep in groups of five or more.

Domino Damsel *Dascyllus trimaculatus*

Origin Indo-Pacific Ocean

Fish size 5 inches (13 cm)

Tank size 36 inches (90 cm)

Ease of keeping Easy

Reef friendly Yes

Comments The domino damsel has been recommended for new aquariums for a long time because of its hardiness, but it often gets too aggressive when it reaches adulthood, so it should be added last and combined with larger fish. Mature pairs will spawn in captivity.

Blue Damsel *Pomacentrus caeruleus*

Origin Indo-Pacific Ocean

Fish size 4 inches (10 cm)

Tank size 36 inches (90 cm)

Ease of keeping Easy

Reef friendly Yes

Comments This hardy fish is often recommended as the first fish for new tanks, but it can become a little territorial so is better added after a few other species have been in the tank for a while. They are inexpensive and readily available, and will accept a variety of foods, including flakes (see page 166).

Maroon Clownfish *Premnas biaculeatus*

Origin Widespread

Fish size 6 inches (15 cm)

Tank size 48 inches (120 cm)

Ease of keeping Moderate

Reef friendly Yes

Comments The maroon clownfish is one of the larger and more aggressive clownfish species. They are seen at their best in the aquarium when they are in partnership with an anemone (see page 243), as their commitment is total. There is a yellow-banded form, which is very appealing.

DOTTYBACKS (Pseudochromidae)

Royal Gramma *Gramma loreto*

Origin West Atlantic Ocean

Fish size 3 inches (7.5 cm)

Tank size 36 inches (90 cm)

Ease of keeping Moderate

Reef friendly Yes

Comments A fish with stunning coloration, the royal gramma is suitable for reef aquariums with plenty of places to hide. They stay hidden for much of the time but will always appear at feeding time. This species can be kept in groups, but rarely is, and may even spawn in captivity.

Orchid Dottyback *Pseudochromis fridmani*

Origin Red Sea

Fish size 3 inches (7.5 cm)

Tank size 36 inches (90 cm)

Ease of keeping Moderate

Reef friendly Yes

Comments This species is one of the most strikingly colored fish available, and it is well behaved, too. It does best in tanks with plenty of live rock (see page 213) and can be kept in groups in large tanks. Do not keep it with species that are similar looking, as it may chase them.

OTHER MARINE SPECIES

Copperband Butterflyfish *Chelmon rostratus*

Origin Indo-Pacific Ocean

Fish size 8 inches (20 cm)

Tank size 60 inches (150 cm)

Ease of keeping Difficult

Reef friendly No

Comments The copperband may nip at some corals so is not totally reef safe. Many specimens are difficult to feed, so make sure that it is feeding in the store before you buy one. The butterflyfishes are a beautiful group of marines, but they are all considered quite difficult to keep in captivity.

Porcupine Puffer *Diodon holocanthus*

Origin Tropical oceans

Fish size 12 inches (30 cm)

Tank size 60 inches (150 cm)

Ease of keeping Easy

Reef friendly No

Comments The porcupine puffer, a representative of the puffer fish group, has great character and will be well liked by its owner. At feeding time it will perform many antics to get attention, including spitting water and back swimming. They are generally hardy and should be kept either on their own or with other tough tank mates.

Firefish *Nemateleotris magnifica*

Origin Indo-Pacific Ocean

Fish size 3 inches (7.5 cm)

Tank size 36 inches (90 cm)

Ease of keeping Moderate

Reef friendly Yes

Comments The firefish is an excellent choice for a reef aquarium containing smaller fish. They are prone to jumping, so make sure that the aquarium is covered, especially after introduction. Its cousin, the purple firefish, is also particularly attractive and should be kept in a similar way. Provide plenty of retreats.

Flame Hawkfish *Neocirrhites armatus*

Origin West and South Pacific Ocean

Fish size 4 inches (10 cm)

Tank size 36 inches (90 cm)

Ease of keeping Moderate

Reef friendly No

Comments The flame hawkfish is often kept in reef aquariums (see pages 222–23) but is predatory of smaller mobile invertebrates, such as crabs, shrimp, and snails (see page 250). On the plus side, it does remain small, is brightly colored, and performs interesting antics.

Pajama Wrasse *Pseudocheilinus hexataenia*

Origin Indo-Pacific Ocean

Fish size 3 inches (7.5 cm)

Tank size 36 inches (90 cm)

Ease of keeping Easy

Reef friendly Yes

Comments This species is recommended for beginners, as it is hardy and can be kept in smaller tanks. It is good at ridding the tank of pest invertebrates that are introduced with live rock (see page 213). Keep in a tank with plenty of live rock to provide cover and do not combine with other wrasses.

Banggai Cardinalfish *Pterapogon kauderni*

Origin Indonesia

Fish size 3 inches (7.5 cm)

Tank size 36 inches (90 cm)

Ease of keeping Moderate

Reef friendly Yes

Comments The Banggai cardinalfish is a beautiful marine fish that does well in home aquariums and may even breed, with the male mouth-brooding the eggs and fry. The species is in danger of extinction in its natural habitat through overcollection, which is ironic considering its willingness to breed in captivity.

Volitans Lionfish *Pterois volitans*

Origin Indo-Pacific Ocean

Size 14 inches (35 cm)

Tank size 60 inches (150 cm)

Ease of keeping Moderate

Reef friendly No

Comments Lionfish have always been popular. They will eat small fish and shrimp, so could be kept in reef aquariums not containing them. They are hardy as long as they will take frozen dead foods (see pages 164–65). The only acceptable live foods to be offered should be river shrimp. The practice of feeding them goldfish is unacceptable.

Picasso Triggerfish *Rhinecanthus aculeatus*

Origin Indo-Pacific Ocean

Fish size 10 inches (25 cm)

Tank size 60 inches (150 cm)

Ease of keeping Moderate

Reef friendly No

Comments Triggerfish are bizarrely shaped creatures, which have evolved to crunch invertebrates. They should be kept in large tanks with tough tank mates and are best as the only triggerfish in the aquarium. Feed on a mixture of meaty foods, including cockles and mussels. The Picasso has stunning coloration and appeal.

Algae Blenny *Salarius fasciatus*

Origin Indo-Pacific Ocean

Fish size 5 inches (13 cm)

Tank size 48 inches (120 cm)

Ease of keeping Moderate

Reef friendly No

Comments The algae blenny has excellent character and can change shade to match its surroundings. These fish graze on marine algae and will become thin if there is not enough of it, so supplement their diet with flakes (see page 166), which they should readily take. Although safe with most invertebrates, they may nip at clams (see page 253) and some corals, so they are not totally reef safe.

Chalk Bass *Serranus tortugarum*

Origin West Atlantic Ocean

Fish size 3 inches (7.5 cm)

Tank size 36 inches (90 cm)

Ease of keeping Moderate

Reef friendly Yes

Comments The chalk bass is a good choice for the reef aquarium (see pages 222–23) because it is well behaved and undemanding. It can be kept in groups in larger tanks and should be fed on a diet that includes larger shrimp, such as mysis and krill. They tend to jump out of open-topped aquariums.

Mandarin *Synchiropus splendidus*

Origin Pacific Ocean

Fish size 3 inches (7.5 cm)

Tank size 36 inches (90 cm)

Ease of keeping Difficult

Reef friendly Yes

Comments This species is much loved by aquarists because of its strange shape and pattern, but they often waste away. For proper care, add to modern-style reef aquariums where live rock and live sand predominate (see page 213), encouraging lots of invertebrate life for food. Add to aquariums over six months old. Do not keep with sifting species such as gobies (see pages 230–31), because these will out-compete them for food.

Marine coral profiles

The allure of live corals is hard to describe, but their appeal is universal with aquarists and nonfishkeepers alike. The coloration and movement are simply spectacular, and aquarists are fortunate indeed to be able to keep and treasure something so beautiful. The corals described here represent a tiny proportion of those that occur in the wild, but they are the most commonly kept species and so should be readily available from aquatic retailers.

Size

Sizes stated are the averages that aquarium species will reach within two years. Bear in mind that coral colonies in the wild can grow to several yards or meters across and live for several hundred years.

Anemones

Anemones have been available for as long as there has been a marine hobby. Although similar in appearance to corals, they do behave differently, with the fundamental difference being that they can move around the aquarium. Moving is usually a result of there either being too much, or not enough, light and water movement in the aquarium. To remedy this, the anemone simply moves, usually at night. The problem with this is that its sting is more powerful than that of corals, and if it opens up and touches a coral in its new location, it can irritate it or even kill it.

Adequate water flow and bright lighting are recommended, along with a resident clownfish (*Amphiprion ocellaris*) (see page 233) to feed and clean it.

Soft corals

These should be the first corals attempted by the aquarist because they are tougher than hard corals and are generally less expensive.

Lighting and water flow

Use four or more T8 light tubes, two or more T5s or metal halide lighting (see pages 208–9), and offer them moderate to strong water flow (see individual profiles)—about ten times the tank volume per hour—via power heads (universal underwater pumps).

Hard corals

These are recommended only for the experienced aquarist but have been included in the profiles so that you will recognize them when selecting corals at a retailer. They are beautiful but currently represent the biggest challenge of all in the marine hobby.

Lighting and water flow

Hard coral species need even more lighting and water flow than soft corals, so provide them with four or more T5 light tubes with reflectors or metal halide lighting (see pages 208–9) and a strong water flow—10–20 times the tank volume per hour.

Tip

When you purchase corals at the aquatic store, make sure their tissues are healthy and that the polyps are fully extended. If growing on a small rock, a healthy coral should cover it when fully extended. If the coral is receding and patches of rock are exposed, the coral could be dying and the tissue could well be necrotic. Anemones should also be fully open and not climbing up the side of the tank trying to improve conditions for itself. Avoid very white anemones: Healthy anemones should be brown with florescent tips, meaning that their photosynthetic algae are present within them.

ANEMONES

Bubble Anemone *Heteractis* spp.

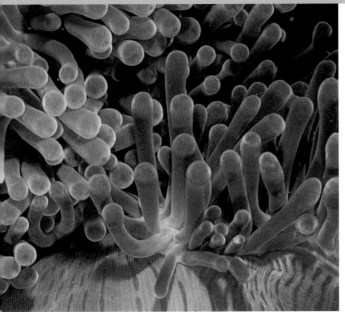

Size 18 inches (45 cm)

Ease of keeping Moderate

Lighting requirements Bright

Water flow Strong

Comments Bubble anemones are easier to keep than most anemones, and so they can be recommended for those keeping one for the first time. The bubble tips vary in size according to the lighting and water conditions it is being kept in and its maturity. They do better when kept with symbiotic clownfish (*Amphiprion ocellaris*) (see page 233) because they receive nourishment from their hosts.

Carpet Anemone *Stichodactyla* spp.

Size 18 inches (45 cm)

Ease of keeping Moderate

Lighting requirements Bright

Water flow Strong

Comments Carpet anemones are available in white, blue, and green. They are striking but may catch and eat fish, so either keep symbiotic species of clownfish (*Amphiprion ocellaris*) (see page 233) to feed it or offer it frozen food every now and again (sees page 164–65). They require bright lighting (ideally from a metal halide lamp; see page 208) and good water circulation. If they are unhappy, they will move and may sting neighboring corals.

SOFT CORALS

Star Polyps *Clavularia* spp.

Size 1 inch (2.5 cm)

Ease of keeping Moderate

Lighting requirements Bright

Water flow Moderate

Comments Star polyps are highly desirable because the bright green polyps are on a purple structure. This coral spreads rapidly if it is doing well and can be harvested and given or sold on to other aquarists. It appreciates planktonic foods.

Knobbly Mushroom *Discoma florida*

Size 3 inches (7.5 cm)

Ease of keeping Easy

Lighting requirements Moderate

Water flow Moderate

Comments Knobbly mushrooms or mushroom anemones are normally found for sale on live rock (see page 213) and are sold as "mushroom rock." They are easy to keep and actually do better when kept in lighting and water flow that are not too strong, so fluorescent lighting will be fine (see page 46). At feeding time, the mushrooms spread over the rock surface, and food particles will be caught on the rough surfaces.

Bush Coral *Nepthea* spp.

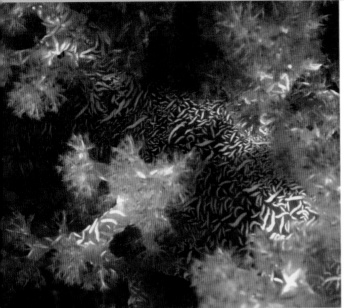

Size 18 inches (45 cm)

Ease of keeping Moderate

Lighting requirements Bright

Water flow Strong

Comments There are many types of bush coral available, and most do well in captivity. Growth can be fast when they are kept in adequate water flow and under bright light. They have no special requirements, but they do dislike being moved, because they weld themselves to rocks and may tear if prised away.

Yellow Polyp Colony *Parazoanthus axinellae*

Size 1 inch (2.5 cm)

Ease of keeping Moderate

Lighting requirements Moderate

Water flow Moderate

Comments This species is desirable because of its coloration, and it is not expensive. Some aquarists do well with it and others do not. Those that do succeed are almost certainly feeding it with a plankton solution. The polyps should be fully extended if a specimen is healthy.

Toadstool *Sarcophyton* spp.

Size 18 inches (45 cm)

Ease of keeping Easy

Lighting requirements Moderate

Water flow Moderate

Comments Toadstools are quite simple to keep and will tolerate a wide range of conditions. They can be grown under multiple fluorescent tubes, but will only get huge under halide lighting (see page 209). They prefer areas of good water flow, but if given too much turbulence, their large disks can be swept to the side.

Finger Coral *Sinularia* spp.

Size 12 inches (30 cm), depending on species

Ease of keeping Moderate

Lighting requirements Bright

Water flow Strong

Comments Finger corals can vary in shape, but the form usually seen resembles a hand with fingers. They generally do well in captivity and spread horizontally across the rocks. Like many of the soft corals, they will survive under moderate lighting and water current, but will show marked growth under strong lighting and water flow.

Clove *Xenia* spp.

Size 3 inches (7.5 cm)

Ease of keeping Moderate

Lighting requirements Bright

Water flow Moderate

Comments You can tell when a clove colony is doing well because the polyps will be open and the frilly extensions will be intact. It will also spread across the rocks quickly, providing a pleasing display. Colonies can be split by hand or with a knife.

Pulse Coral *Xenia* spp.

Size 6 inches (15 cm)

Ease of keeping Moderate

Lighting requirements Bright

Water flow Strong

Comments Pulse corals are very desirable, because the individual polyps pulse every few seconds independently of each other. If they are doing well, they spread, forming new colonies, which can be attached to upward-facing coral skeletons to take advantage of the more abundant food in the upper levels of the water.

Button Polyp *Zoanthus* spp.

Size 2 inches (5 cm)

Ease of keeping Moderate

Lighting requirements Moderate

Water flow Moderate

Comments Although the individual polyps are small, *Zoanthus* grow as colonies, and under optimum conditions they can spread over the rocks like a weed. They range in color but are generally brown with hints of other colors, such as purple, and can be seen closing around items of food that are swept past them at feeding time.

HARD CORALS

Sunflower or Flowerpot Coral *Goniopora stokesi*

Size 8 inches (20 cm)

Ease of keeping Difficult

Lighting requirements Bright

Water flow Moderate

Comments This readily available hard coral is very popular because of its stunning coloration and the way that it moves in the water flow, but it is difficult to keep and fails in all but the best marine aquariums. It will need to be fed on copious amounts of plankton, and its powerful sting will irritate any other corals that are situated near to it.

Bubble Coral *Plerogyra sinuosa*

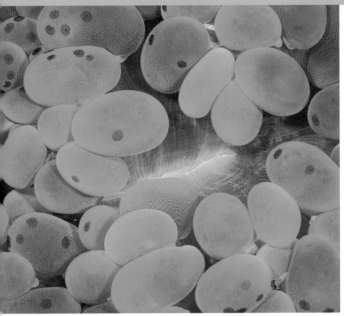

Size 6 inches (15 cm)

Ease of keeping Moderate

Lighting requirements Bright

Water flow Strong

Comments Not to be confused with the bubble anemone (*Heteractis* spp.) (see page 243), this species is one of the easier-to-keep hard corals, and its form and light coloration make it quite desirable. If it is growing well, it may split to form siblings, which can go on to form new colonies.

Open Brain Coral *Trachyphyllia* spp.

Size 8 inches (20 cm)

Ease of keeping Difficult

Lighting requirements Bright

Water flow Moderate

Comments The open brain coral is very attractive when open and comes in a variety of colors, some of which are almost fluorescent. It should ideally be placed on the substrate and not on the rockwork, as it is found naturally in beds of seagrass. It is a hard coral that is quite difficult to keep in good health.

Marine invertebrate profiles

There is a vast number and range of marine invertebrates, and many species can be kept alongside fish and corals in a reef aquarium. The group includes invertebrates that can move, such as crabs and shrimp, and those that cannot move, such as clams (see page 204). The invertebrates featured here are just a few of the most readily available, and most are suitable for beginners to marine reefkeeping. If you come across new species in an aquatic shop, always find out about their particular requirements and compatibility, because they may not be suitable for your setup.

Ease of keeping

Marine invertebrates range in difficulty from feather dusters (*Sabella pavona*) (see page 252) and hermit crabs (*Pylopagurus* spp.), which are as easy to keep as the easiest marine fish, through to challenging species that should not be attempted by beginners.

Feeding

Snails, crabs, and shrimp can find their own food, and their diets are not specialized, with all three getting by on uneaten fish food and morsels found on rocks. Feather dusters (*Sabella pavona*) (see page 252) rely on food being blown past them by the current, so place them in areas that receive moderate water flow. The clam featured, *Tridacna* spp. (see page 253), will also obtain food from light-feeding algae within its tissues and relies on you to place it in the best position—in an area of good water flow and strong lighting.

Acclimatizing

Invertebrates are sensitive to changes in salinity and water conditions, so you should acclimatize them very slowly after you have purchased them.

The addition of many different types of invertebrates can really make the reef aquarium come alive with movement and vibrant color on every part of the tank decoration. A fully stocked reef tank is a

Tip

When purchasing invertebrates at the aquatic store, there are several things to look for. Shrimp should have all their legs intact and should be colorful and active. They should also respond quickly to food being placed in the tank. Starfish should have all five legs and should not be exuding their stomach contents from underneath. Feather dusters should be fully extended and responsive to food particles being placed in the water. Finally, clams should be colorful, with the mantle filling the shell and overlapping the sides when fully open. Clams should also be placed under bright lighting in the store, and those that have not been for a period of time should be avoided.

mesmerizing sight and can be achieved by a beginner if it is carefully planned, set up, and maintained (see pages 222–23). Water quality and stability are the first essentials, followed by proper lighting and feeding.

Blue Starfish *Linckia laevigata*

Size 6 inches (15 cm)

Ease of keeping Difficult

Reef friendly Yes

Comments The blue starfish is incredibly striking but can be sensitive to changes in salinity levels and temperature. When purchasing, check underneath the creature to ensure that the stomach contents are not protruding, which can be a sign of health problems. A healthy starfish will make a stunning addition to the reef aquarium.

Cleaner Shrimp *Lysmata grabhami*

Size 3 inches (7.5 cm)

Ease of keeping Moderate

Reef friendly Yes

Comments The brightly colored cleaner shrimp lives up to its name and cleans fish to remove parasites. It can be kept in groups or singly, and females are often observed carrying eggs. They accept a wide variety of frozen foods (see pages 164–65) and are active in daytime.

Pincushion Urchin *Lytechinus variegatus*

Size 3 inches (7.5 cm)

Ease of keeping Easy

Reef friendly Yes

Comments Sea urchins make great scavengers and can help to keep the aquarium clean. The pincushion urchin has interesting coloration, and there is less risk to the owner from being impaled on the spines, because it is shorter than other species. It may, however, eat desirable coralline algae from rocks.

Feather Duster *Sabella pavona*

Size 6 inches (15 cm)

Ease of keeping Easy

Reef friendly Yes

Comments Feather dusters and other tube worms are filter feeders, and they are not dependent on bright light. They should be placed in the substrate or in gaps in rocks, and healthy specimens should be out all the time. Feather dusters are designed to emerge from their tubes, unravel their featherlike arms and catch food particles from the water. Do not combine with species that are likely to nip them, such as angelfish (see pages 231–32).

Boxing Shrimp *Stenopus hispidus*

Size 4 inches (10 cm)

Ease of keeping Moderate

Reef friendly No

Comments Boxing shrimp are common additions to reef aquariums, but they can become badly behaved over time. They can catch and eat smaller invertebrates and may evict hermit crabs from their shells and then eat them, leaving only the claws. They should be kept singly or in pairs.

Clam *Tridacna* spp.

Size 12 inches (30 cm)

Ease of keeping Difficult

Reef friendly Yes

Comments Clams are exquisite to look at, with the color of the mantle (the fleshy part between the two inner shells) ranging from rich turquoise to purple. They require the best lighting (from metal halides; see pages 208–9) and calcium supplements in the water to build their shells. They also need space around them to allow for growth. Do not combine with angelfish (see pages 231–32) or blennies (see page 240) because the clam may get nipped by them.

Index